Cycles of Influence

Cycles of Influence

fiction ❖ folktale ❖ theory

Stephen Benson

W

Wayne State University Press   Detroit

06 05 04 03 02   5 4 3 2 1

Library of Congress Cataloging-in-Publication Data

Benson, Stephen (Stephen Frank)
Cycles of influence : fiction, folktale, theory / Stephen Benson.
    p.   cm.
Includes bibliographical references and index
ISBN 0-8143-2949-7 (cloth : alk paper)
1. Literature and folklore.   2. Postmodernism (Literature)   3. Tales—History and
criticism.   4. Fiction—History and criticism.   I. Title.
GR41.3 .B46   2003
809'.9113—dc21   2002008513

ISBN 0-8143-2949-7 (cloth)

The paper used in this publication meets the minimum requirements of the
American National Standard for Information Sciences—Permanence
of Paper for Printed Library Materials, ANSI Z39.48–1984.

This book is done with the assistance of a fund established by Thelma Gray James
of Wayne State University for the publication of folklore and English studies.

FOR

Lucia & Patrick

Contents

Acknowledgments

I would like to thank Elizabeth Maslen and Cristina Bacchilega for their help at various stages during the writing of this project. My meeting with Cristina was serendipitous to say the least, but nonetheless inspiring for that. Arthur Evans has been a generous and friendly guide at the Press, not least in arranging for the manuscript to be read by two such supremely wise and thoughtful readers. Their attention to detail went beyond the call of duty. Michael and Deborah Benson enabled me to get started and, perhaps unbeknownst to them, saw to it that I persevered. The financial assistance of The British Academy was gratefully received.

Above all else, I would like to thank Lucia for just about everything; Patrick helped simply by being.

Introduction

In his influential study, *The Language of Modern Music*, Donald Mitchell compares and contrasts what are commonly considered to be the twin defining features of the music of European modernism: serialism, as formulated by Arnold Schönberg, and neo-classicism, as exemplified in a series of works by Igor Stravinsky. Both of these compositional strategies represent a break with particular musical practices and traditions, a new way, and yet both can, to varying degrees, be seen to have grown out of the music of the past, whether the immediate past of late Romanticism or the modernities of a recontextualized classicism and earlier. In passing, however, Mitchell nominates another compositional feature as a potential third characteristic, a third way, of musical modernism, one in which the paradox of the tradition of the new is most strikingly evident: the use of folk music, as exemplified in the works of Béla Bartók, in which the rhythms, structures, and melodic patterns of the folk musics of Eastern Europe act not only as source material but as formal model, a genuinely traditional route—and, particularly in Bartók's case, root—to innovation.[1]

I have chosen to introduce my study via Mitchell's suggestion of the importance of folk material in twentieth-century music because, as far as I am aware, no like claim has been made with regards to twentieth-century literature.[2] With the possible exception of Yeats, to make such a claim for European modernist literature would be untenable; for a significant range of European and American literature of the past fifty years, however, a case can be made, as the present volume aims to demonstrate. Partly as a result of the more explicit technicalities of the musical work, it is easier to chart the interaction between folk music and Western classical music than it is to quantify the influence of the folktale on literature (hence my recourse to music at several points). While the particular characteristics of verbal, as opposed to non-verbal, texts undoubtedly complicate the possibility of transposing Mitchell's suggestion, it nevertheless still allows for a comparable proposal of the folktale, in all its aspects, as a significant narrative model and source of material in both the literature and the narrative theory of the past fifty years.

To substantiate this proposal involves bringing together two sets of materials—literature/narrative theory and the folktale—and two disciplines—literary theory and folkloristics—which provide a range of methodologies for dealing with these materials. Any attempt to chart the influence of a form of folklore in a specific area is by definition interdisciplinary, involving a recognition not only of similarities and connections but also of differences, of the specificity of both the folkloric material and the established methodologies for interpreting this material. With regards to the relationship between folklore and literature, of which that between the folktale and literature is a part, the period since 1950 has been characterized by a gradually more detailed recognition, among both folklorists and literary critics, of the prerequisites necessary for the establishment of a properly formulated dialogue between the two disciplines and their respective materials. On the side of the literary critic, this must obviously involve a genuine understanding of the particular characteristics of any folklore genre, along with a basic grounding in the methodology of folkloristics; for the folklorist, the need for the interpretation, and not merely the identification, of folkloric material in the literary text—for a reading of the assimilation of folklore in literature in all its aspects—has been more broadly recognized. In sum, the undoubtedly necessary call has been for rigor in folkloristics and depth in literary analysis.[3]

My aim in the chapters that follow has been to consider as many as possible of the multiple contexts that the relationship between the folktale, literature, and narrative theory engages, as well as to point to the cyclical nature of the relationship in the particular period with which I'm concerned. As regards the folktale, specifically the European folktale on which I have largely concentrated, this has involved a consideration of the originally oral status of the narratives, together with the concomitant fact of their performance, the various routes via which tales pass into and out of written texts and the status of these texts in relation to oral traditions, the question of national traditions and the geographical passage of folktales, and the historical rise of folkloristics as an independent field of enquiry. I have attempted to include reference to the recognized classics of the written form of the European folktale, such as the cycles of Basile and Straparola, Charles Perrault's *Histoires ou contes du temps passé* (Stories or Tales of Past Times) and the Grimms' *Kinder- und Hausmärchen* (Children's and Household Tales), and to texts that have had a profound influence on European literature, most notably the *Arabian Nights* (Alf layla wa-layla).[4]

The contexts pertaining to the literature and narrative theory of the past five decades are equally manifold, beginning with narrative, that most fundamental point of connection with the folktale. The years since 1950 have seen the idea of the structuring action of narrative, in literature, historiography, and as a pervasive form of social discourse, become a prime focus for enquiry. Concomitantly, a significant range of the literature of the period can be characterized in terms of its self-conscious reassessment of narrative, and I am considering the possible role of the folktale in this reassessment. If structuralism and postmodernism have contributed to the theoretical and literary questioning of narrative, the question of gender has also acted as a central topic in recent literature and literary studies, just as contemporaneous studies in folklore have increasingly acknowledged the role of gender.

The five chapters which constitute this volume stand both as individual studies and as representative considerations of the various fields brought into play by the recontextualization of the folktale in recent literature and narrative theory. Each chapter is based on a specific interaction: between narratology and ideas of the folktale in the first two chapters; between the work of Italo Calvino and the folktale, specifically his *Italian Folktales* (Fiabe

Italiane), in chapter three; between selected fictions of John Barth and the *Arabian Nights* and between the work of Robert Coover and the related genre of the fairy tale in chapter four; and, in chapter five, between the "Bluebeard" fairy tale, its related tale types, and recent feminist retellings, specifically those by Angela Carter and Margaret Atwood. Given the nature of the material, the language and argument of the first two chapters are necessarily more abstract. Yet as will be apparent, it is precisely the figural repertoire utilized in the process of the abstraction of a structure and grammar of narrative that has fed back into many of the narrative fictions under consideration.

In order to read these individual dialogues on the terms laid out by the framework of the book as a whole, I have clearly separated any theoretical considerations within the respective chapters. In addition, because I attempt to survey a large area and to include within this survey a majority of the major texts, both of literature, the (written) folktale, and folkloristics, my individual readings tend at times toward the expository rather than the analytical. Yet, as I suggest, the practice of exposition is always tendentious, indeed can only be carried out in relation to a theoretical position. My primary aim has been to understand the nature of the relationship between two "texts" or sets of "texts," while being aware of the danger of considering the multivalent folktale as "text" and of the rather quaint nature of this preoccupation with sources. The idea of influence, such as that suggested in my title, has for some time now been less clear-cut than might once have been the case. The positivist cataloguing of sources, models, and antagonists has been complicated by conflicting ideas of intertextuality and, more recently, newly theorized and invigorated conceptions of historicism. While the former unpicks the boundaries between subject and object on which the idea of influence is predicated, the latter problematizes the notion of a distinct and static object which passively brings about a certain affect in that which it influences; as readers, we are now more sceptical of such subject-object relations. The subject always *constructs*, and is *constructed by*, the object, to various effect.[5]

The net result of such methodological shifts is that the idea of influence comes to function as an idea of ideas. To say that such-and-such a text or writer was influenced by the folktale is to say that the former constructed a particular conception of, a necessary fiction about, the latter. This generative idea will be discursively related to its moment, not least to the extent that it stands as another instance of the ongoing history of literature's— not to mention other disciplines'—engagement with the folktale. Hence the ideas of the folktale set forth in the work of Calvino are an idiosyncratic mix of structuralism, conceived as another generative fiction, and a postwar brand of Romanticism. In the case of structuralism, Calvino was working with a field which had itself conceived of the folktale in a quite particular manner, as a narrative store exemplary in its manifestation of difference in similarity. As I will suggest, the extrapolation of this idea beyond the confines of folk material—the possibility of a universal narrative grammar, for example—is flawed precisely because of the specificity of the material itself. Nevertheless, along with feminist engagements, both critical and celebratory, the structuralist paradigm stands as one of the defining twentieth-century conceptions of the folktale.

In part, this is as much to say that the present study is an example of a sort of localized interdisciplinary literary history, not teleological or summative, but rather anthological. One of the most enjoyable aspects of researching this area has been the time spent with the folkloric story cycle, that anthological narrative form which has been particularly influential in recent fiction, and at the risk of ending this introduction as I began—with another borrowing that involves a considerable contextual leap—it is in terms of such story cycles that the present volume is perhaps best considered. Framed by this introduction, the enclosed individual chapters each set out to tell their own story, in the process echoing and commenting on one another through reference to common material, setting up parallels between the use of particular tales or forms in different contexts and demonstrating the manifold potential implicit within the dialogue between folktale and literature. To varying degrees, the folkloric story cycle encodes an element of chance as regards the particular contents it includes; again, this is a theme I discuss in the ensuing chapters, but to accept these chapters as themselves produced by a series of chance encounters—both in terms of the dialogues they discuss and in terms of their inclusion here—is to acknowledge the open-ended nature of this area of enquiry. The story cycle is based on a series of potential connections, and it is some of the fertile connections that exist between the folktale and recent literature that I discuss. If the chapters that follow understand anything, it is what Wittgenstein referred to as an understanding that consists in seeing connections.

Chapter 1

Tales in Theory:
The Role of the Folktale in the
Development of Narratology

To begin in the twenty-first century a study of the roles played by the folktale in post-1950 literature and narrative theory by focusing on the development of theoretical models of narrative may seem perverse from the standpoint of both theory and fiction. In the case of theory, enquiry into the workings of narrative has moved away from, indeed critiqued, the search for deep structures and abstract, essential geometries, in favor of a pluralistic concern for desire itself in the productive interaction of narrative and psychoanalysis; for non-geometric conceptions of narrative space, including the possibilities of interactivity, in postmodernist theories; and for the specificities of context in feminist and postcolonial concerns for a pragmatics of narrative. In the case of fiction, the pole position granted to theory might seem a characteristically academic betrayal of a set of narratives, oral and literary, in which the implicit emphasis is on telling, on practice. The majority of the literary fictions I discuss share a common interest in tale-telling: in compact narratives that eschew both the descriptive fabric of the classic realist text and the modernist preoccupation with consciousness and fragmentation; in the construction of extended forms out of these discrete elements rather than via the holistic arch of the novel; in narratives that relegate the question of realism in favor of a self-contained, overtly fictional environment; and in the storyteller as self-confessed fabricator. However, if these features are to be seen to a significant extent as a result of the influence of the folktale, it is a folktale (as individual tale or genre) which has been filtered through the net of one or another mode of theory—a folktale which is already read—and it is thus not so perverse to begin by setting the tale within such a context.

While I return in later chapters to the continued role of the folktale in more recent theories of narrative, the specific field of theory which has had the most extensive recourse to the folktale is that of narratology, or narrative grammar, in particular the un-raveling of plot and the isolation of various types of constituent unit. What this chapter thus aims to describe is a series of formal-ist readings of the folktale, readings that have sought to produce a model for all folktales and for narrative, in abstract, itself. Having been historicized and deconstructed these readings may now ap-pear more provisional, more fictional than was once the case, and my own account is in part an analogous localizing of the scope of narrative grammar. Yet it is important to acknowledge that it is precisely such generative models which have in their turn gener-ated possibilities for the use of the folktale in narrative fiction.

The folktale is one of the materials out of which narratology grew and around which the following account of narratology is centered. Yet it has tended to be treated merely as a launching pad, a means to an end of a comprehensive abstract model of nar-rative. As far as materials are concerned, the structural linguistics of Saussure and the phonology of Jakobson and the Prague Lin-guistic Circle dominate as the source models for narrative gram-mar. The founding text in any account is undoubtedly Vladimir Propp's *Morphology of the Folktale* (Morfológija skázki), published in Russia in 1928 but little known elsewhere until its translation into English in 1958, thus placing it at the inception of the struc-turalist movement. Propp's working method and results became the starting point for a series of attempts to account for the struc-ture of narrative, and thus for narratology, arguably conceivable as a series of rewritings of this seminal text. As the *Morphology* is very much concerned with reworking nineteenth- and early twentieth-century models of the folktale, narratology itself can be seen as linked from its own inception to this particular type of narrative, a link that has become part of a distinctly twentieth-century attitude to the folktale in general.

In using the term "folktale" here I am following the definition given by William Bascom, according to whose conception of folkloric "prose narrative"—the "category of verbal art which includes myth, legends, and folktales"—the folktale is that category of "prose narratives which are regarded as fiction," as against those originally regarded as true (7–8).[1] Thus the folktale is held to be an originally oral, secular narrative which, in the case of those tales discussed here, has at some point been set down in written form, whether as part of an explicitly folkloric or literary text.[2] Most important in this context is the folktale's fundamental difference from literature as a written text, a difference that is constitutive of its suitability as material in the understanding of the formal aspect of narrative. Both Propp's "The Nature of Folklore" (1946) and Roman Jakobson and Petr Bogatyrëv's "On the Boundary between Studies of Folklore and Literature" (1934) stress this fact, pointing to "essential structural differences between these two forms of verbal creativity" (Jakobson and Bogatyrëv 91), and to the "most distinctive poetics" of the folktale, "peculiar to it and different from the poetics of literary works" (Propp 6).[3] Folktales have no acknowledged author—beyond the myth of an original source—but rather a series of narrators whose relationship to the tales is both intimate and detached; the folktale is "extra-individual," that is, it exists both within and beyond each individual and personalized telling. Any name that becomes attached to the written version of a tale—Charles Perrault, Andrew Lang, Italo Calvino—theoretically points to the transcriber of a pre-existent narrative, and any named source in a collection is again simply a representative narrator of a pre-existent narrative. (I will return in more detail to the various questions surrounding the status of written collections of folktales in relation to their oral sources.) A particular tale exists only in so far as it is told, acknowledged by some form of audience, a fact which highlights the originally communal existence of the folktale. Any tale which we, as readers, encounter will almost invariably have passed through various stages of transcription (Jakobson and Bogatyrëv, "On the Boundary" 91).

Despite the stability conferred by the passage into written and literary forms, folktales are profoundly unstable narratives. As there is no fixed text each telling can potentially add or subtract material, as can the passage to and from different communities and across national boundaries. What Propp refers to as "the changeability of folklore compared with the stability of literature" means that tales exist in a "constant flux," and the result, once traditions have been artificially frozen in written collections, is that multiple variations on similar themes and motifs can be detected and compared ("The Nature of Folklore" 8; modified literary versions can of course pass back into oral circulation). There is thus no hierarchy of versions or authoritative tellings, but rather what Calvino characterizes as "infinite variety and infinite repetition" (*Italian Folktales* xvii).[4]

As individual narratives, folktales are generally compact and condensed, repetitive, episodic, and formulaic. Their telescoped structure stems from the lack of extraneous material. The substance of any tale consists almost wholly of a chain of events with little pause for description or characterization, the latter resulting from its apsychological, or more specifically "preindividualistic," nature.[5] The classic exposition of the "phenomenology of folk narrative" is Max Lüthi's *The European Folktale: Form and Nature* (1947). Dealing with the tale as literary text, Lüthi distinguishes its "principal formal traits" (3): "one-dimensionality" (the lack of "a sense of any gap separating the everyday world from the world of the supernatural" [10–11]), "depthlessness" (the absence of "physical and psychological depth" [12]), and an "abstract" (24) or "diagrammatic" (36) style (including vivid and clearly defined characters and objects, formulas, and a "single sharply defined plot line" [34]). When faced with this use of repetition (events and tasks repeated three times, groups of three siblings) and formulae (openings, dénouements, character types), it is necessary to take into account our readerly vantage point: the unavoidable fact that we approach folk narrative traditions with a knowledge of the various forms of literary narrative, in particular the comparably thickly descriptive, densely psychological realism of the classic European novel. Thus Lüthi repeatedly stresses that the characteristics he identifies are not to be taken in a pejorative sense, but rather as indicative of the distinct form of the folktale, its stylistic consistency. Similarly, it is the particularities of the various (literary) vantage points offered by the twentieth century that have given rise to a set of readings of, and ideas about, the folktale, based on the pertinence of certain aspects of the material. These include the questioning of ideas of authorship, the work and the text, and theories of intertextuality, each of which find parallels in the traditions of the folktale.[6] The constituent tales of such traditions can be read with a high level of abstraction and are perhaps particularly conducive to theoretical appropriation, yet in terms of a modern (post-Renaissance) idea of fictional narrative, they are themselves remarkably abstract in character: apsychological, authorless, unstable yet formulaic.

The various characteristics of the folktale have given rise to a number of theories regarding how best to understand and record the narratives, and I am concerned here with tracing the extent to which twentieth-century narrative poetics developed out of, and continued, one interpretative strand of these theories. Narratology is commonly taken to be a methodological development of structural linguistics and phonology, and the narrative raw material that I am focusing on here also has a history of being read in terms of language; indeed, a strong historical thread links the three areas of folk narrative studies, contemporaneous language studies, and narrative theory. This results from the first of the aforementioned characteristics of the folktale: its authorless, originally communal status. As Propp comments (on folk material in general), "in its origin folklore should be likened not to literature but to language, which is invented by no one and which has neither an author nor authors. It arises everywhere and changes in a regular way, independently of people's will" ("The Nature of Folklore" 7); similarly, Jakobson repeatedly links folklore and language as products of a "collective creation" and thus comparable in certain essential respects ("On Russian Fairy Tales" 90). This link was first formulated in the early nineteenth century by Jacob Grimm, who recognized parallels between the study of the dissemination and origin of folklore and the newly developed theory of a common linguistic heritage among the family of Indo-European languages. The occurrence of similar tales in different locations could thus be explained by a common linguistic ancestry, and beginning with the second edition (1819) of the Grimms' *Kinder- und Hausmärchen*, this "comparative" approach became an integral element in the study of folk narratives, instigating the analysis of folklore as a scholarly discipline.[7] As linguistic theories have developed, so opinion on the status and dissemination of folktales has also shifted, in particular away from the over-arching, holistic approaches of the nineteenth century, which stressed the search for origins and the status of the tales as fractured remnants of older myths. This historicist approach to language and folklore was gradually replaced in the first half of the twentieth century by the linguistic theories of Saussure and Jakobson, in which the synchronic analysis of language is primary. Concurrently, the question of the origin and diffusion of folktales was relegated, as indicated in Jakobson and Bogatyrëv's statement on the "folklore work," made in 1929: "it is a skeleton of actual traditions which the implementers embellish with the tracery of individual creation, in much the same way as the producers of a verbal message (*la parole*, in the Saussurian sense) act with respect to the verbal code (*la langue*)" (91).

While the nineteenth-century approach to the folktale has now been, to varying degrees, discredited, it is nevertheless partly out of such theories that narratology developed. One of the by-products of the comparative approach was the growth in the collection and transcription of tales, facilitating a more detailed study of the interrelationship of traditions. Folktales are intrinsically unstable, furnishing perhaps the best example of the theory—fundamental to narratology—that the basic constituent elements of a narrative can be manifest in a number of different versions, and it was partly a desire to account for this instability that gave rise to catalogues of tales. The first of these, following on from the prototypical annotated and numbered tales of the Grimms' editions, was published by Antti Aarne as *The Types of the Folktale* (Verzeichnis der Märchentypen) in 1910 (enlarged and translated by Stith Thompson in 1928; revised, again by Thompson, in 1961). Aarne was a product of the Finnish "historical-geographical" school—exemplified in the work of his teacher Kaarle Krohn—which advocated the formulation of a classification system that would allow for the systematic and updateable cataloguing of multiple versions of any particular folk narrative. As his introduction states, at the time "there existed no system that arranged the various types to be found in the variegated multitude of folk-tales and united them into a well-ordered whole" (quoted in Thompson, *Folktale* 416). This index was primarily intended to be of practical usefulness in the cataloguing of tales from a single area. It consists of a list of numbered items split into three main groups—animal tales, folktales, and humorous tales—further differentiated within each group by subject matter. Each numbered item or tale type represents a complete narrative and it is this feature that marks the fundamental classificatory difference between Aarne's index and the other major twentieth-century folktale catalogue: the *Motif-Index of Folk-Literature*, compiled by Stith Thompson between 1932 and 1936 (following his translation into English and enlargement of the Aarne catalogue).

In the *Motif-Index*, Thompson sought to dismantle individual tales into constituent parts or motifs, an important but problematic step, as indicated in his cautious introductory definition of the motif as "[a]nything that goes to make up a traditional narrative. . . . When the term motif is employed, it is always in a very loose sense, and is made to include any of the elements of narrative structure" (*Motif-Index* 19).[8] The catalogue is divided thematically into twenty-three sections, commencing with "motifs having to do with creation and the nature of the world" and concluding with "several small classifications which hardly deserve a chapter each." Despite introductory circumspection, the scientistic nature of the enterprise is made explicit:

if an attempt is made to reduce the traditional narrative
material of the whole earth to order (as, for example, the
scientists have done with the worldwide phenomena of
biology) it must be by means of a classification of single
motifs—those details out of which full-fledged narratives
are composed. It is these simple elements which can form a
common basis for a systematic arrangement of the whole body
of traditional literature. (*Motif-Index* 10)

As with the Aarne index, stress is placed on the underlying objectivity of the catalogue, hence the recourse to positivist, Linnaean
principles as justification for the classificatory endeavor. While
the Finnish method works on the identification and labeling of
an entire narrative, metaphorically viewing the material from a
height, Thompson focuses on the constituents of the individual
tale, detached from their context and reassembled in ostensibly
self-apparent, natural groupings.

Both indexes thus construct order out of a seemingly endless
proliferation of material, from a point *outside* of or *above* the tales
themselves: literally, in the sense of an avowed objectivity, and
metaphorically, in terms of the relative distance maintained from
the structure of the narratives (relative to the extent that Thompson's methodology dismantles the structure of the individual tale).
In terms of a reading of the pivotal role played by these indexes,
the Aarne index in particular, in the development of a grammar
of narrative, this distance, together with the claims to a scientific
classificatory methodology, is crucial.[9] Indeed, adopting again the
metaphorical spatial model of structuralism it is possible to characterize the formation of narrative grammar as a gradual passage
down from a relative distance to a point *below* or *within* the structure of narrative itself. Faced with the simultaneous multiplicity and similarity exhibited within folktale traditions, the Aarne
index, as an extension of nineteenth-century methodologies, attempts simply to collate the material, working on the assumption
that one tale that appears to resemble another does so because
they are variants of some core subject matter or *theme*—a theme

which hence defines the tale type. No attempt is made to probe this paradox—as mentioned above, the index is above all a practical tool—or to speculate on what these differences and similarities imply; the analysis remains *external*.[10]

While Propp's *Morphology of the Folktale* is the founding text of narratology it also offers the possibility of a paradigm shift in the methodology of the folk narrative index, and Propp contextualizes his project as such in the opening chapter: noting, for example, the importance of the then recently published volumes of Johannes Bolte and Georg Polívka's extensively enlarged version of the annotations to the Grimms' tales, *Anmerkungen zu den "Kinder- und Hausmärchen" der Brüder Grimm*).[11] Propp makes the Linnaean aims of such an index explicit: the need for a "well-ordered classification, a unified terminology," as in "the physical and mathematical sciences" (4); again, the end result is to be the rigorous ordering of a mass of material, the discovery of patterns within "the labyrinth of the tale's multiformity" (xxv). Yet such order is not to be based on what he refers to elsewhere as "external similarity" ("Fairy Tale Transformations" 114)—the imposition of a classification "from without," as in the Aarne index—but rather on the "formal, structural features" of the tales themselves (6). Propp is attempting "an examination of the forms of the tale which will be as exact as the morphology of organic functions," and we can detect here the influence on this text of the formal method that had been advocated by a group of Russian critics in the years prior to the publication of the *Morphology*. Turning away from studies based on psychology, philosophy, and symbolism, the formal method aimed at the precise study of the literary text as an independent artifact. As Boris M. Èjxenbaum wrote in an essay published two years before Propp's text, the aim was to create "a special scientific discipline concerned with literature as a specific system of facts," involving "the investigation of the specific properties of literary material" (4).[12] Folklore played a role in the Formalist approach, partly because of the health of Russian folk traditions and partly because folkloric texts were ripe for readings which focused on the tales as tales rather than as the coded depiction of social or cultural realities (the critique of the latter approach was indicative of a critical school whose methods were markedly at odds with post-Revolutionary Marxism and which ultimately led to its suppression).[13] Thus, as has been noted, it was the historical, and not unproblematic, conjunction of the new methodologies of the Finnish school of folk narrative research with this short-lived Formalist movement that produced the *Morphology* (Pirkova-Jakobson, "Introduction to the First Edition" (1958), Propp, *Morphology* xx).

Propp's method is based on the isolation of the component parts of a tale and is thus closer to a motif index such as Thompson's in viewing the tale as a composite of smaller units. However, in terms of classificatory exactitude, the isolation of the motif as the constituent element is still too subjective and ill-defined. A motif index simply registers common material without attempting clearly to define the nature of this material or account for the similarities. Propp attempted a far more systematic dismantling of a set of narratives in order to isolate explicitly defined units and describe the relationship between them. Already, in the preface to the first volume of the first edition of the Grimms' tales (1812), reference is made to the "essence" of the European folk narrative, the "stable core" of elements that remain fixed despite changes in character and setting.[14] Propp himself cites the more contemporaneous work of Joseph Bédier (*Les Fabliaux*, 1893), who proposed a relationship between "elements," or constants, and variables within a particular tale tradition, and it is a refinement of this basic proposition that underlies Propp's methodology (13).

Using one hundred tales from the classic nineteenth-century Russian collection of A. N. Afanas'ev (first published between 1855 and 1864), Propp isolates an alternative, strictly defined set of invariables—"functions"—which occur, to varying degrees, in all the tales and which point to a structural rather than thematic unity underlying the surface multiformity. These thirty- one functions are actions of the characters in the tales, defined not in terms of who carries them out but by their position and role in the plot. The sequence of functions is fixed regardless of which particular group appears in any single tale and the individuality of each narrative stems from the variety of means, character, and setting that arrange themselves around this core plot pattern (a type of meta-narrative): "all functions fit into one consecutive story. The series of functions given . . . represents the morphological foundation of fairy tales in general" (25). Propp proceeds to demonstrate how these plot units can be grouped into "spheres of action," each of which is a set of functions carried out by one of seven generically defined character types; and finally, he defines the series of functions which constitute an identifiable basic plot or "move," demonstrating that the majority of his chosen folk narratives consist of a structure of interwoven "moves." Taken as a whole, then, it is the isolation of functions that Propp proposes as the potential basis for this revised folk narrative index: "[t]ales with identical functions can be considered as belonging to one type. On this foundation, an index of types can be created, based not upon theme features, which are somewhat vague and diffuse, but upon exact structural features" (22).

In order to avoid excessive paraphrase I have limited myself to this skeletal summary of Propp's work.[15] As will be apparent, the narrative materials that Propp uses are dismantled into abstractly defined structural units with a specific position in the schematized plot (Propp's Formalism can be seen in this decontextualization). Such practice marks a significant break with the predominantly historicist (diachronic) theories of the nineteenth century and can be situated, beyond the immediate Russian context, in terms of the shift towards synchronic analysis in the linguistics of Saussure, and in the fusion of Saussurian linguistics and Formalism in the work of the Prague Linguistic Circle. Indeed, the isolation of minimal distinctive and mutually defined units as the invariant elements of the tale as a self-contained system is strikingly similar to the methods of phonology developed by Roman Jakobson and N. S. Trubetzkoy in the 1930s (Liberman, in Propp, *Theory and History* xix–xxx). As I suggested above, the folktale is particularly conducive to being read in this Formalist manner, and Propp's methodology offers a persuasive model of its formal characteristics. The manifest similarity of plots, together with the ostensibly endless generation of narratives, are accounted for by the positing of a stable series of functions, a combination of which constitutes the structure of a particular tale and which are enacted in various ways by various characters; the instability of a particular tale or tradition can be thought of as the generation of limitless variety around limited structural foundations. Viewed literally, the schematic nature of the folktale is accounted for by Propp's classificatory narrative units, his functions—"interdiction," "struggle," "recognition"—the Formalist nature of which is made explicit: "[d]efinition of a function will most often be given in the form of a noun expressing an action. . . . [A]n action cannot be defined apart from its place in the course of narration" (21).

To adopt Propp's own metaphorical schema, the *Morphology* identifies internal, as opposed to external, similarity, a sequential structure that underpins the surface flow of the narrative. Rather than isolated content or thematic material, as in Aarne and Thompson, Propp isolates form (Jameson, *Prison-House* 64). Read in these terms we can relate Propp's schema to the Formalist distinction between plot (*sjuzet*) and story (*fabula*). In the folktale there is ostensibly little difference between plot and story, which accounts for the perceived one-dimensionality of folktales, and Propp's *Morphology* produces what Robert Scholes pertinently refers to as "a grammar and syntax for a certain kind of narrative" (67). The historical links between linguistics and the folktale are thus further developed. Not only are folktales analogous with language in terms of diffusion (the Grimms) or communal status (Jakobson and Bogatyrëv): they are individually constructed in the same manner as individual linguistic expressions, hence Propp's definition of a function as "a noun expressing an action."

As this interpolation suggests, in the wake of its translation into English in 1958 Propp's *Morphology* has been interpreted from two different but related perspectives, a result of its affiliations to both folkloristics and Russian Formalism. Firstly, as a critique of traditional folk narrative indexes, the model proposed in this study of Russian fairy tales has been used in the analysis of other tale traditions. At the forefront of this work has been the American folklorist Alan Dundes, whose 1964 study, *The Morphology of North American Indian Folktales*, was one of the first of its kind.[16] Secondly, Propp's findings have been read as marking the inception of a nascent grammar of narrative, a grammar applicable, by extension, beyond the scope of the folkloric raw material to the structure of narrative itself. It was as part of this second developmental strand that Propp's study was newly contextualized. I have referred (and return below) to the retrospectively identifiable similarities in methodology between the *Morphology* and the structural linguistics of Saussure and, in particular, the Prague Linguistic Circle. It was the latter that influenced the rise of structuralist theory in the late 1950s; coinciding with the translation and first extensive discovery of the *Morphology*, this text became a core work in the early formulation of a structuralist narrative theory. Two basic weaknesses exhibited by Propp's text have been central in the readings of the folktale that have followed, both of which are raised in Claude Lévi-Strauss's extended review article, "Structure and Form: Reflections on a Work by Vladimir Propp," written in 1960 (published simultaneously under the title "L'Analyse morphologique des contes russes"). This influential essay, which functioned as a stepping-stone for A. J. Greimas in his reshaping of Propp's schema, pivots on a critique of Propp's Formalism from a structuralist perspective—although Lévi- Strauss's reading of Formalism is rather cursory (characteristic of his eclectic mix of the general and the densely specific), as is his understanding of the tensions that exist between Propp's text and the tenets of the formal method.[17] Lévi-Strauss's central anthropological point is that while Propp acknowledges the possible roots of the folktale in myth—a distinctly un-Formalist aspect of the *Morphology*—he proceeds to treat the former as a separate entity, whereas for Lévi-Strauss the two types of traditional prose narrative "exploit a common substance": "[t]ales are miniature myths, where the same oppositions are transposed to a smaller scale" ("Structure and Form" 130). The thinly veiled narrative of origins suggested by Propp goes against Lévi-Strauss's argument that "a myth is made up of all its variants": his technique of using all extant versions of a myth in analysis, regardless of provenance or form, based on the belief that a myth resides in the story and not in the mode of conveyance.[18]

However, my object here is not to attempt a detailed account of Lévi-Strauss's structural anthropology but rather to extract the salient points of his critique from the contextual standpoint of the role played by the folktale as narrative model. Lévi-Strauss highlights the extent to which the end result of Propp's methodology is a view of the tale as a simple mathematical equation, a fact illustrated by Propp's use of letters and symbols to signify the various functions and their relative position within the formula; as Lévi-Strauss summarizes: "a fairy tale is nothing more than a narrative that puts into words a limited number of functions in a constant order of succession. The formal differences between several tales result from the choice, made by each, among the thirty-one functions available and the possible repetition of some of them" ("Structure and Form" 124). It is the nature of these functions that is at stake. On the one hand, Lévi-Strauss disagrees with Propp's distinction between form and content, or, more specifically, between constants and variables within the tales, a distinction he considers "inherent in Formalism." Propp's listing of a limited number of species within each function-type or genus is, for Lévi-Strauss, an unavoidable reintroduction of content in the guise of form: "[u]nless the content is surreptitiously reintroduced into the form, the latter is condemned to remain at such a level of abstraction that it neither signifies anything any longer nor has any heuristic meaning" ("Structure and Form" 132). From a structuralist perspective there is no distinction between form and content—"[there] is not something abstract on one side and something concrete on the other"—as both consist of the same material and are accessible to the same analytical methods. Read thus within this new historical context, what Propp has produced is a model in the form of a meta-tale, an answer to the problem of accounting for the characteristics of the folk narrative that tautologically takes the form of another narrative. As Fredric Jameson comments, Lévi-Strauss critiques Propp's schema for being "still too meaningful" and "not yet meaningful enough." On the one hand, the schema fails "to attain an adequate level of abstraction," demonstrated by its reliance on "storytelling categories" (the episodic linear movement of the narrative); the aim of this new type of index—scientifically to categorize and reduce particular groups of folk narratives and to extract structural essentials common to all—is thus not achieved, and the schema remains "not sufficiently distanced methodologically from the surface of the storytelling text." On the other hand, the schema is simultaneously too abstract in insisting on the irreducibility of this linear progression or formula; the formula is simply an abstract version of the narrative and not an explanation, "not a solution, but rather the problem itself." As Jameson summarizes: "both the insufficient formalization of the model (its anthropomorphic traces) and the irreversibility it attributes to its functions are different aspects of the same basic error, namely to have rewritten the primary narratives in terms of another narrative, rather than in terms of a synchronic system" (*Prison-House* 120–22). In attempting to move beyond this impasse, Lévi-Strauss proposes that selected functions in Propp's formula appear "assimilable to the same function, reappearing at different moments of the narrative, but after undergoing one or a number of transformations" (136). This proposal represents a fundamental break with Propp's methodology and marks the next pivotal shift in readings of the folktale. Despite initial contrasts with the folk narrative indexes of Aarne and Thompson, Propp's schema remains on a similarly external level, represented by the narrativized series of functions. Again, as with Propp, Lévi-Strauss suggests a deeper level at which this narrativity is merely the manifestation of underlying structures— a synchronic level that underpins the apparent diachrony of the tale, and at which "the order of chronological succession is reabsorbed into an atemporal matrix structure, the form of which is indeed constant" ("Structure and Form" 138). Ironically, when read in terms of the history of the folktale index, this synchronic level echoes Aarnes's original system, in the latter of which the narrativity of *each* tale is reduced to a single theme.[19]

The *tale* in the folktale is thus no longer a given but rather one element, reducible to the manifestation of "deeper" structural units. The problem thus shifts to the understanding of another species of unit than the "type," "motif," or "function" (at least as the latter is defined by Propp), and the manner of its combination in the form of a narrative. What becomes clear at this point is the extent to which analysis of the folktale in these terms has ramifications for an understanding of the functioning of all narratives, although the specificity of the folktale as narrative material—the central point I am attempting to stress here—raises problems for the application of any theoretical system beyond the confines of this source material.

The working through of the theoretical suggestions made by Lévi-Strauss has been carried out by A. J. Greimas, perhaps the most methodologically formidable of the structuralists. The folktale as a genre or subspecies of narrative, specifically Propp's chosen corpus of tales, represents what Greimas refers to as a "micro-universe," and as such exhibits the same structural characteristics that are common to the world as it is perceived by the human subject.[20] As a rigorous structuralist, Greimas's methodology is built around the tenets and methodology of structural linguistics, and his reading of the folktale, via Propp, provides the most striking example of the continuing historical link between the tales and linguistics. The fundamental assumption that underlies his work is the link between the isolated sentence—the subject of linguistics—and the group of sentences that make up a particular discourse, in this case the discourse of narrative. Greimas thus seeks to demonstrate how the structure of the sentence—a surface structure produced by transformations of a deep structure comprising a core of a predicate and a noun—is reproduced in narrative. As mentioned above, Propp's formula can be read in terms of the structure of language, in that it posits a string of functions or verbs acted out by generic subjects or nouns as the grammar of the tale, the abstract sentence from which an individual tale is constructed. The *Morphology* can thus be identified as one of the first studies to suggest the manner in which narrative, as a string of sentences, can be analyzed in terms of sentential linguistics.

Methodologically, Greimas uses the models of Saussure and, in particular, the phonology of the Prague Linguistic Circle: the isolation of simple elements that combine in hierarchical form to produce complexity; the differential definition of these elements in terms of distinctive features, with no positive term but rather a structure of "reciprocal presupposition" between two terms productive of signification (structure is thus semantic, a series of meaningful differences); and concentration on the isolated synchronic system as a structure of conjunctions (similarities) and disjunctions (differences). In his major work, *Structural Semantics: An Attempt at a Method* (Sémantique structurale: Recherche de méthode, 1966), he takes as his starting point Propp's "double definition of that narrative which is the folktale": a narrative with thirty-one functions arranged in an "obligatory sequential order," and, arranging these functions into "spheres of action," "a narrative with seven characters" (222). It is the latter that Greimas analyzes first, as a means of testing his model of actants. An actant is Greimas's term for a role in deep structure, hence anterior to the manifestation of characters or actors on the surface level of discourse (an actant thus "possess[es] a metalinguistic status in relation to the actors"). In terms of syntax, the actant is coupled with a predicate to form the core deep structure of a sentence, Greimas's actantial model being "borrowed" from "the syntactic structure of natural languages": "since 'natural' speech can neither augment the number of actants nor widen the syntactic comprehension of signification beyond the sentence, it must be the same inside every microuniverse" (199). As Greimas's methodology involves understanding meaning-effects in terms of meaningful conjunctions and disjunctions between elements, he structures the actantial categories of the sentence in terms of oppositions: "subject vs. object" and "sender vs. receiver" (152). To confirm these "linguistic extrapolations," Greimas turns to Propp's "dramatis personae," the "spheres of action" of his formula of functions. In terms of linguistics, these constitute actants that have been insufficiently formalized, and Greimas thus structures them in terms of the prototypical actantial model: for example, Propp's "hero" is the actantial "subject" and the "sought-for person" is the actantial "object."

However, drawing on Lévi-Strauss's critique of Propp's schema as, paradoxically, both insufficiently and excessively formalized, Greimas's second point is that the semantic dimension which is the product of organizing discrete elements into the structure of a binary opposition must be considered. The semantic invest-ment generated by the structuring of the syntactic categories sub-ject/hero and object/sought-for person is "desire," manifest in the archetypal narrative form of the quest (202–3). Ronald Schleifer provides a clear summary of this point: "[i]n actantial analysis the object of desire of an anthropomorphized subject is also conceived of as the syntactic object in a linguistic frame which posits the conjunction of subject and object as the narrative realization of signification" (104). This describes in abstract structural terms an archetypal folk narrative, variously manifested in the search of prince for princess or hero for prized possession.

The narrative form which remains unaltered in Propp's lin-ear sequence of functions thus becomes, in Greimas's account, the manifestation or transformation of an underlying structure of relations, following Lévi-Strauss's suggestion that "the order of chronological progression" that Propp presents as the underpin-ning of the folktale could be "reabsorbed into an atemporal matrix structure, the form of which is indeed constant" ("Structure and Form" 138). Greimas attempts to account for the fact that we are able to comprehend a given narrative both as a whole—as a num-bered entry in a folktale index—and as a diachronic sequence. He thus refers to the "drama" (spectacle) of narrative, the "paradig-matic interpretation" which is "the very condition of grasping the signification of the narrative as a whole" (236). It is worth quoting him at length on this point:

> everything is diachronic in the manifestation of signification
> except signification itself, conditioned by our aptitude to
> apprehend achronically, as wholes, very simple structures of
> signification. In other words, what allows us to apprehend
> a folktale . . . as having a meaning is the permanence
> throughout the narrative of a small number of categories

of signification. Any text, consequently, is at the same time permanence and diachrony. (*Structural Semantics* 171)

The dramatic relationship between two actants thus generates the events which constitute the syntagmatic chain of narrative that Propp implicitly conceived of as irreducible. The fact that these relationships are fixed within the limits of syntax accounts for the similarity that underlies the surface multiformity of the tale traditions.[21] Thus the question that has remained at the root of the study of folktales from its inception as a scholarly pursuit in the early years of the nineteenth century is once again answered in terms of linguistics.

Greimas proceeds to analyze Propp's functions, in syntactical terms his narrative predicates (verbs)—and thus the second component of the core deep structure of the sentence (the "propositional" element). In Greimas's reading, functions constitute the content of the actants in narrative and are necessary for the narrativization of the logical paradigmatic relations between actants. Just as Propp's spheres were structured, so the functions of his formula now undergo "reduction and structuration"—a process Greimas refers to as "homologation," based on the elementary structure implicit within binary oppositions. As Greimas acknowledges, Propp himself suggests the "coupling" of functions— "interdiction" with "violation," "struggle" with "victory"—resulting in a reduction of the original thirty-one to twenty (*Structural Semantics* 224–25). However, as these examples demonstrate, such a reduction is not a logical formulation but rather an extension of the linearity of Propp's schema, and Greimas thus suggests a "methodological justification that would make it operational": the latter term (violation) is linked to the former (interdiction or prohibition) by a relationship of implication; in terms of abstract logic, violation is also linked to the function that Greimas refers to as "mandate" by a relationship of opposition; and to complete the structuration process, the acceptance of the hero implies the aforementioned mandate, just as violation implies interdiction. This homologation is central to Greimas's methodology and is developed in subsequent work into what he terms "the elementary structure of signification": "a structure made up of four terms mutually interdefined by a network of precise relations that can be described as being the correlation between two schema" (*On Meaning* 68).[22] This is the now famous semiotic square, representing in abstract diagrammatic form what Ronald Schleifer refers to as "the logical possibilities of binary opposition" (28).

As with the structuring of Propp's "spheres of action," it is only possible to outline the basic procedures that Greimas follows, but in line with the elaboration of Lévi-Strauss's suggestion of a two-levelled narrative structure, the result is once again the uncovering of an achronic level *within* the narrative of Propp's formula—"a paradigmatic and achronic interpretation of the relations between functions" which, as already stated, is "the very condition of grasping the signification of the narrative as a whole" (235–36). It is not that Greimas magically causes linearity to disappear but rather that he seeks to explain how we are able to construct meaning out of the flow of narrative, and how narrative functions as an interaction between a paradigmatic and a syntagmatic dimension, "permanence and diachrony." Greimas concludes with a series of highly suggestive extrapolations on this basic duality (extrapolations which need to be read as the outcome of the detailed structuration process), pointing to the manner in which a fully worked out structural analysis of Propp's corpus of Russian tales can logically account for the existence within a single tale of contradictory elements, such as a challenge to, and affirmation of, an existing social order, between which the narrative form acts as "mediation." This suggestion has interesting ramifications for a view of the folktale as both conservative—a conservatism characteristic of the ritualized nature of all traditional cultural forms—and subversive, in terms of its function as a socially sanctioned expression of desire and dissatisfaction.[23] While Greimas speculates on the applicability of this essentially mediatory concept of narrative, it is rather the methodological insights that constitute his attempt to refine and extend Propp's *Morphology* in the form of a structural account of narrative as a species of discourse.

Greimas's structuralism can be compared with the work of Claude Bremond, the other major narrative theorist to have concentrated on Propp's *Morphology* and on the folktale as narrative model. While Bremond does not use the methodologies of structural linguistics, he nevertheless works to establish categories that explain levels of organization within the folk narrative. He seeks to extend and formalize the work of Propp by drawing "a map of the logical possibilities of narrative" ("The Logic of Narrative Possibilities"), and it is this stress on what Greimas refers to as "decisional logic" that characterizes Bremond's approach (*On Meaning* 63).[24] The core of his thesis, maintained across a number of essays, is refreshingly simple. Retaining Propp's function as "the basic unit, the narrative atom," he groups three functions together in the form of an "elementary sequence," corresponding to "the three obligatory phases of any process." Unlike Propp, Bremond allows for the possibility of choice in the path a narrative may take: the first function—the possibility of an action or event—can be enacted or remain unfulfilled, and similarly, if fulfilled, can succeed or fail to achieve its aim. Bremond thus encodes a degree of freedom from the point of view of narrator—the possibility of free choice within strict limits—and audience/reader—the experience of being in the midst of a narrative rather than at the knowing point of conclusion at which all is retrospectively made clear.[25] These "triads" combine to produce "complex sequences" by means of any combination of three possible configurations: "end-to-end succession," "enclave," and "coupling" ("The Logic of Narrative Possibilities" 388–89). In addition, as well as accounting for the experience of the temporal unfolding of a narrative, Bremond's schema acknowledges that "[e]ach agent is his own hero": there is no fixed, omniscient point of view from which all characters are defined, as there is in the work of Propp and Greimas, but rather the potential for a shifting focus dependent upon who is performing any particular function.

Taken together, these two elements of Bremond's account of the folktale—the logical possibilities that structure the narrative and the multiple definition of sequences of functions according to the undifferentiated viewpoint of each character involved—break with the strict linearity of Propp's schema, although not in the deconstructive manner of Greimas. Bremond envisages "the structure of the tale (and that of any story) as being composed, like a braid, of multiple superimposed elementary sequences, entwined, and bound together. Each event and action may fulfil simultaneously several functions in the story" ("Morphology of the French Folktale" 250). While the methodology is different, Bremond concurs with Greimas in his theoretical account of the simultaneous presence within a single tale of freedom and restraint—two versions of the structuralist notion of limited creative potential within the pre-existent and inflexible structure of language. In Bremond's version, the folktale, as narrative, is "both free and controlled at the same time: free (for the narrator must at every moment choose the continuation of his story) and controlled (for the narrator's only choice, after each option, is between the two discontinuous and contradictory terms of an alternative)" ("The Logic of Narrative Possibilities" 406). Additionally, both Greimas and Bremond provide generative theories. The former systematically charts the path from immanence to manifestation via the constraints of the structure of language, while the latter attempts "a logical reconstruction of the potentialities of story," illustrating the generation of plot via a series of choices and sequences.

Bremond has subsequently written "A Critique of the Motif," in which he returns to the indexes of Aarne and Thompson to point to fundamental flaws in methodology, a surprising subject given that the possible flaws in these indexes were critiqued in Propp's *Morphology*, which has in turn been reworked by Bremond himself ("A Critique of the Motif"). In one sense, this provides a neat symmetry to the trajectory of this area of research, as well as a justification for the folktale-centered account of narratology offered here. However, as the increasingly undifferentiated reference to narrative as opposed to folktale in the preceding account indicates, these theories have outgrown their (narrative) source material. The attempts to account for the similarity in diversity that characterizes the folktale have lead to the development of theories of structure, levels, and generative trajectories that are proposed as applicable to narrative per se, as both Greimas and Bremond attest. Thus, in Roland Barthes's contemporaneous summary article, "Introduction to the Structural Analysis of Narratives" (1966), we already see the systematic exposition of a theory of narrative that is, or attempts to be, universal. Barthes stresses the pivotal relationship between narratology and linguistics, in terms of subject matter and hence methodology: the narrative analyst "finds himself in more of less the same situation as Saussure confronted by the heterogeneity of language [*langage*] and seeking to extract a principle of classification and a central focus for description from the apparent confusion of the individual messages" (*Image Music Text* 80). Yet is this not precisely the problem that confronted the folklorists of the nineteenth and early twentieth century with regard to their own field: the Grimms, Aarne, Thompson, and Propp? The problem is indeed the same, but the original narrative material that played as important a role as structural linguistics—indeed has been inseparably tied to the shifting theories of language—has been subsumed in the process of understanding its nature.

Greimas himself suggests potential problems resulting from "the fact that interest has shifted from oral to written literature," and the question thus becomes whether narrative grammar can *successfully* outgrow, in applicability, its source material (*On Meaning* 107). Such problems stem from the aforementioned apsychological nature of the folktale: the fact that characters in the tales tend to fit neatly into types or actantial categories and that events can thus be read unproblematically in terms of the trajectory of a clearly differentiated actant. The abstract schematization of the folktale may transfer to similarly formulaic narratives such as Boccaccio's *Decameron*, or to popular generic fiction, certain genres of which are, like the *Decameron*, heavily influenced by the folktale (a subject covered in my final chapter); yet it is far less successfully mapped onto a nineteenth-century European novel, not to mention a modernist text.[26] In a similar vein, Jameson argues that while Greimas (following Lévi-Strauss) succeeds in achieving "a real advance toward the deanthropomorphization of the study of narrative," he still conceives of narrative in terms of abstract roles. Just as the folktale fails to adhere to our notion of authorship, so the characters within the tales are fundamentally at odds with our modern conception of the narrative subject. They are "preindividualistic," issuing from "a social world in which the psychological subject has not yet been constituted as such." Thus Greimas's actantial categories are in a sense simply not applicable: "they result from projecting later categories of the individual subject anachronistically back onto narrative forms which precede the subject's emergence" (Jameson, *Political Unconscious* 123–24).

The potentially universal scope of a grammatical narrative structure is thus questioned (in Jameson's reading, historicized) in terms of the very specificity of the original narrative material. This has resulted in three related developments. First, a shift in more recent literary studies away from narrative grammar (in linguistic terms, the "propositional" element of sentence structure) in favor of the discourse level of the narrative: the "modality" element, the "how" as opposed to the "what." Second, there has been a reassessment of the two-leveled model on which narratology is built: the underlying notion that a particular basic story can be told in a number of different versions, a notion obviously underpinning Aarne's folk narrative index. Narratology is built on this search for similarities, in the process of which the manifold differences between, for example, the Walt Disney account of a folktale and its seventeenth-century predecessor are potentially silenced. Finally, the stress on universal applicability has masked the role of gender, sexuality, and cultural specificity in both the source narratives and the resultant categories of narratology. In each of these last two examples the theoretical objectivity of narratology has been troubled and problematized by a reaffirmation of context, of historical and cultural specificity.[27]

In the following chapters I return in more detail to these developments, in order to demonstrate the continued influence of the folktale as both model and object of study—the different aspects of the folktale and its history that are pertinent to particular developments in narrative theory. However, as will become apparent, the insights of narratology are not denied in more recent theory but rather adapted to a more pragmatic approach. This attests to the fact that the readings of the folktale that gave rise to narratology have left an indelible mark on our conception of this source material. Putting aside individual methodological disputes, the Formalist and structuralist analyses undeniably capture the inherent formalism of the tales themselves, a formalism which is tacitly recognized in the various folk narrative indexes. Thus, as I remarked at the beginning of this chapter, the folktale that appears in the narrative fiction of the past fifty years bears the mark of the theoretical recognition and account of this aspect of the tales. However, the possibility I want to consider before turning to these fictions is the extent to which we can locate a recognition of this formalist aspect in the literary history of the folk narrative tradition itself: not a formalism that is discovered by modern theory but that is already being manipulated, exhibiting an understanding of the abstract, structural aspect of the narratives that significantly predates twentieth-century insights.

Chapter 2

THEORY IN TALES: CYCLES, LEVELS, AND FRAMES

This story should be written down.
—THE ARABIAN NIGHTS

The structural dissection of the folktale detailed in the preceding chapter relies wholly on the written presence of the tales, indeed would be literally impossible without the permanence conferred by writing. The comparison of multiple versions of a particular tale type and the dismantling of individual narratives into constituent units can in retrospect be seen as a direct result of the systematic transcription of popular oral narratives instigated by the Grimm brothers in the early nineteenth century—thus Propp uses Afanas'ev and Bremond uses the French collections of Paul Delarue and Marie-Louise Tenèze. Yet while the tales used in the theorizing of a narrative grammar were taken from, and dependent upon, written sources, these sources grew out of the shift in the nineteenth-century away from literary folktale collections— the French interest in literary fairy tales that began in the late seventeenth-century and the earlier cycles of Straparola, Basile, and Boccaccio—towards the accurate transcription and collation of oral narratives, published as collections of ostensibly authentic, unadorned, and unconnected (that is, not arranged as a cycle) folktales. While the authenticity of such collections has long since been questioned, along with the notion of authenticity itself in relation to the transcribed folktale—subjects to which I return in my final chapter—there is one particular sense in which these national collections of tales are less faithful to their sources, less authentic, than the overtly literary cycles of medieval and

Renaissance Europe, or the earlier and profoundly influential cycles of India and the Near/Middle East. While a collection such
as the Grimms' *Kinder- und Hausmärchen* presents a realistically
unconnected repertory of extant tales, the ontological shift from
the oral to the literary is signaled clearly in the decontextualized
status of the narratives. An oral tale does not exist unless it is being
told—it "exists only potentially" (Jakobson and Bogatyrëv 91)—
and in this sense *cycles* of folktales are closer to the performative
nature of the material in framing the string of narratives with a
teller or tellers and a dramatic situation, whether it be the gathering of an exiled group, as in Giovanni Francesco Straparola's *Le
Piacevoli Notti* (The Pleasant Nights; 1550–1553); a group in flight
from disease, as in Giovanni Boccaccio's *Decameron* (ca. 1351);
or the elaborate narrative frames of Giambattista Basile's *Il Pentamerone* (1634–1636) and the *Arabian Nights*. Similarly, while
the unifying framework of a cycle is a literary device, the resultant
texts clearly demonstrate the interconnections that characterize
folktale traditions, with motifs and characters recurring within the
cycle. If the text of a collection does in practice attest to this fact,
the cycle actively demonstrates both the repetition of material
by a single narrator and the communal knowledge of tale types
shared by groups of tellers.

It is to these cycles that I now turn in order to provide a companion piece to the preceding chapter. While there I sketched the
path from collections of folktales, via the catalogues and indexes
of Aarne and Thompson, to the formulation of models of narrative structure, here I illustrate the manner in which the folktale
cycle, a form which preceded the shift to academic folk narrative studies—and which provided important access to earlier material for the new discipline—*manipulates* narrative in a manner
which anticipates the basic procedures and conceptions of structuralist narrative poetics. The purpose is thus to counter the primacy of theory suggested in the previous chapter, as well as further
to suggest the ties with the folktale of the combinative, generative model of narrative. The main exhibit in what follows will be
the *Arabian Nights* (Alf layla wa-layla); I will also be drawing on

Somadeva's eleventh-century Sanskrit *Ocean of Streams of Story* (Kathasaritsagara, originally in verse), and Giambattista Basile's *Il Pentamerone*. These are fascinating texts in their own right, and they also serve to indicate the formal scope of the folkloric cycle. The historical and geographical range of these cycles is obviously vast and while I have attempted to respect their historical and contextual specificity, the hybrid nature of the texts—the eclectic use of pre-existent material—is at least a partial justification for such a grouping. In addition, the two non-European cycles are bound up with both the histories of colonialism and orientalism and with the European folk tradition: for example, the first acknowledged version of the *Arabian Nights* to be published in Europe was Antoine Galland's extensively adapted French translation, the first volume of which (1704) instigated what has come to be referred to as the second phase of the literary fairy tale vogue in Paris, giving rise to a host of exotic fictions, based around a set of ideas of the Middle East and variously influencing this major flowering of the European literary fairy tale.

The dominant presence that links the English-language versions of these three cycles is that of the English scholar N. M. Penzer. Using Benedetto Croce's modern Italian version, Penzer translated, edited, and annotated *Il Pentamerone* in 1932, and also edited a new edition of C. H. Tawney's late nineteenth-century translation of Somadeva in a ten-volume, privately printed edition between 1924 and 1928. The latter, a genuine textual marvel in its scope and detail, rivals Richard Burton's notorious translation of the *Arabian Nights* (1885–1886), although successfully avoiding its rabid orientalist fantasies. Burton haphazardly translated *Il Pentamerone* (1893) at a time when, as Penzer comments, "[h]is mind was still saturated with the *Thousand Nights and a Night*." And Penzer tells us in his Terminal Essay to *The Ocean of Story* that his idea for a new edition of Tawney's translation came to him while he was at work on a biography of Burton himself, as if the ghost of Burton "was offering me the chance of giving to the public the Indian counterpart of his own great *Arabian Nights*."[1] Penzer's enormous enthusiasm, together with his more enlightened and informed approach, is one of the delights of these cycles, and if he is now viewed as representative of a dying breed of gentleman scholars—albeit one fully aware of the work of Aarne and Thompson—it is equally true that his holistic approach to the study of the folktale and folklore is faithful to the interweaving streams of tradition that characterize the material. If generative models of narrative seem, in spite of themselves, to offer an explanation of the abstract aspect of the folktale, the same could be said, albeit in a more overtly metaphorical sense, of the encyclopedic and classificatory zeal of a folklorist such as Penzer—all charts, notes, appendices, and heady erudition.

The folk narrative cycles I refer to here are, in their various ways, liminal texts, situated on the fertile boundary between the oral and the literary. As mentioned above, while the standard collections of folktales are ostensibly authentic but implicitly literary, the various cycles of unashamedly literary tales are structured, both implicitly and explicitly, around a staged orality: they mimic orality by staging the event of their narration, thus initiating a series of narratives which have narrative as their subject: to quote what is in fact the title proper of *Il Pentamerone*, they present *The Tale of Tales* (Lo cunto de li cunti). Indeed, cycles such as *The Ocean of Streams of Story* revel in the multiplicity of narrative and the possibility of uniting tales within tales, while the *Arabian Nights* is built out of equations of character with story, generating strings of narrative from the successive entry of characters into the expanding space of the frame. While they variously enact orality, they are also completely reliant on the written text to provide the permanence and interconnections that characterize the form of the cycle. Similarly, the device of the delayed conclusion and the subsequent play on curiosity have structural consequences that are specific to the written word, and the precisely divisioned narrative feasts offered by *Il Pentamerone* and *Piacevoli Notti* are a product of, and dependent upon, literary form.

Despite the manipulation of structure and basic dramatic situation, the orality of the folkloric cycle is not primarily a self-conscious device, a metafiction *avant la lettre*, but rather a sign of historical provenance. As Walter J. Ong comments, there is a "heavy residue of primary orality" in European medieval literature, and the influence of an oral environment can still be detected in the cycles of Straparola and Basile (as well as in the *Arabian Nights*, the textual history of which I sketch below). Such cycles depict the act of narration, complete with situation, narrator, and audience; as well as providing an aid for group or public performance, their episodic nature is characteristic of an "additive rather than subordinative" form of expression, and the manipulation of pre-existent material is certainly indicative of oral and orally influenced narrative.[2] Similarly, the framing of tales within a setting that provides a specific teller or tellers is reflective of the shift, in European culture, towards the more widespread production and ownership of manuscripts and, from the mid-fifteenth century, printed texts. Ong comments that "[e]arly writing provides the reader with conspicuous helps for situating himself imaginatively. . . . Boccaccio and Chaucer will provide the reader with fictional groups of men and women telling stories to one another, that is, a 'frame story,' so that the reader can pretend to be one of the listening company" (103).[3] While the frame is thus a mark of residual orality, it also allows for the imposition of a degree of coherence on a collection of disparate tales—tales possibly from multiple sources or traditions and of different generic types. This element of multiplicity, of the miscellaneous, is again broadly characteristic of oral culture—of the "additive" and "redundant" or "copious"—which encourages "fluency, fulsomeness, volubility" (Ong 39–41; tales written primarily for public reading rely on frequent summaries and repetitive formulas, techniques particularly evident in the *Arabian Nights*); as Katharine S. Gittes comments, regarding the anthological aspect of European cycles: "[t]he frame narrative's structure . . . makes it an ideal genre for oral delivery (as well as written) because the frame narrative leans away from internal cohesiveness" (147).[4]

The folkloric story cycle is, by definition, compiled from traditional material, as Stith Thompson attests: "[t]he great written collections of stories characteristic of India, the Near East, the

classical world, and Medieval Europe are almost entirely traditional. They copy and recopy" (*Folktale* 4). In the Greeting Straparola added to the 1555 edition of his cycle (originally published
in 1551 and 1553), he unashamedly acknowledges his sources: "to
tell the truth, they [the tales] be not mine. . . . But I have faith-
fully set them down according to the manner and fashion in which
they were told me by a company of ten fair ladies gathered together
for recreation" (Vol. I, xiv).[5] The recourse to extant material, the
venerableness of which is attested by the fact of its retelling, is
most extravagantly displayed in Somadeva's *The Ocean of Streams
of Story*, which well-nigh literally attempts to encompass all types
of tale and thus live up to its wonderfully resonant title.[6] In pursuit
of this aim, it includes within its voluminous pages the entire earlier cycles of the *Panchatantra* and *Vetalpanchavimsati* (25 Tales of
a Vampire, some of which were very freely translated by Richard
Burton, as *Vikram and the Vampire*, in 1870), as well as numerous other pre-existent narratives. In addition, Somadeva recounts
that his cycle is actually taken from a much larger collection by
another author—a text that has never been located—the history
of which he gives in the first book. Characteristic of Indian and
Middle Eastern folk narrative cycles is the "openness" of the texts,
the process by which tales that coalesce to form a given group are
often subsequently detached in various forms, as if the seeming
permanence of the cycle is really only a momentary pause in the
random passage of tales. *The Ocean of Streams of Story* is thus now
remembered largely for the fact that it contains a version of the
Panchatantra, a cycle of morally instructive narratives which, in
its numerous recensions, has been widely influential in both the
West and the Middle East, under various titles: *Kalilah and Dimnah, Fables of Bidpay, Lights of Canopus*.[7]

The *Arabian Nights* is the only one of the three cycles not to
have a designated author—although if the modern conception of
author is anachronistic when applied to the folktale, it is at least
problematic in relation to the explicitly "authored" folkloric story
cycle.[8] Not only are the texts that make up the various versions
of the cycle the product of traditional oral and written material

from throughout the Near/Middle East and India; tales have also
been added, subtracted, rewritten, and translated throughout the
cycle's history. It is tempting to revel in this multiplicity, especially
within the context of a discussion of the structural complexity of
the story cycle; to appropriate this fluid, anonymous text as the
paradigmatic narrative machine, presciently demonstrating key
formal aspects of the folktale. Such a reading would treat the numerous hands that have touched the *Nights* on equal terms: in
David Pinault's words, as "successors in a long tradition of reciters
and professional storytellers," furthering "the creative interaction
of the manuscript-redactor with the narrative tradition" (250–
51).[9] To an extent, an ahistorical, decontextualized approach is
unavoidable in a predominantly formalist reading, but it is important, not least within the broader framework of this study, to be
aware of the complex textual history that lies behind the cycle.
While there is no definite fixed text of the *Nights*, and while the
plurality suggested by its textual history is to an extent implicit in
the nature and form of the work itself—traditional material compiled within a flexible frame—I prefer to follow Sandra Naddaff
in seeing the history of the texts less as a free play of communal
composition than an encapsulation of "the difficult metamorphosis from oral to written text and . . . of the forced translation from
East to West" (4). Since the first volume of Antoine Galland's
translation appeared (1704)—even earlier if we presume a degree
of oral diffusion—the *Nights* has been enormously popular and
influential in the West, not least as the source of a set of representations of the East.[10] Prior to his work on the *Nights*, Galland
had assisted in the compilation and publication of Barthélemy
d'Herbelot's seminal *Bibliothèque orientale* (1697), and a list of the
Nights' subsequent translators includes two significant figures in
the West's discursive fixing of the East: Edward Lane, whose translation was published between 1838 and 1841, and Richard Burton, whose massively annotated ten-volume translation, together
with an additional six volumes of supplementary tales, was published between 1885 and 1888.[11] As Robert Irwin points out, the
search for origins that characterized nineteenth-century folklore

studies was contemporaneous with the high tide of scholarly Orientalism, and the *Nights* is caught within the historical context of the history of the European folktale, both as literary adaptation, following the rise of the orientally influenced literary fairy tale in France in the wake of Galland's translation, and as academic discipline (42–43).

In what follows I have used what have been identified as the "core" tales of the *Nights*. Galland's translation was based in part on what has since been recognized as the earliest surviving "complete" version, originating from fourteenth-century Syria and containing two-hundred-and-eighty-two nights. However, he also supplemented his text with a number of additions and interpolations, thus initiating a tendency to use the cycle as a frame within which to place any number of narratives, prompted at least in part by a desire to fulfil the promise of the title. The most famous of the *Nights'* offspring—"Sindbad the Sailor" (separately published by Galland three years prior to the first volume of his *Nights*), "Aladdin and the Enchanted Lamp," and "Ali Baba"—were all added as part of Galland's creative editorial endeavor.[12] In 1984, Muhsin Mahdi published an edition of the *Nights* that was the result of an attempt to extract a core set of tales common to all later editions, based on the Syrian manuscript and free of the emendations of generations of editors and translators. The tales contained in this attempted ur-text are linked by a set of shared themes and motifs and by the structure of the embedded tale which the frame inaugurates. This core cycle is the most interesting from the point of view of narrative form, but it is also used here as a small attempt to inject a sense of historical specificity into what has become an excessively Westernized legend.[13]

The basic structural device of the folkloric story cycle is of course the frame tale: the narrative (or narratives) which encloses within itself the body of the cycle. Its function in relation to this body of tales is manifold. It acts as the narrative base on which is constructed the set of internal tales, a base which, in the case of the three cycles I refer to above, is systematically returned to at the introduction and conclusion to each successive tale (or each night, in the case of the *Nights*). This repeated touching of base is largely formulaic, most obviously in the daily ritual of exchange between the sisters Shahrazad and Dinarzad, and, to varying degrees, in the final return to the frame that acts as the conclusion in each cycle. The formulaic nature of this dénouement is evident in *The Ocean of Streams of Story*, whose main frame-narrative characteristically concludes three books prior to the end of the text; in the *Nights*, the traditional conclusion of which is apocryphal; and less so in *Il Pentamerone*, where the folktale frame is properly worked out in the final episode. Cycles are not a means to an end but an end in themselves and, at least in the *Nights*, the framing device is lost among the copious details of the multiple internal plots. The frame imposes a loose order on what it encloses and, to the extent that this order is only possible in a written text, could be said to literarify the internal tales. However, as was suggested earlier, it also provides the context or setting for the narrations that follow, thus introducing a cycle of pseudo-oral narratives, whether told by a single character or an assembled group. In the case of the *Nights* and *The Ocean of Streams of Story* this frame structure is carried over into the cycle itself. The bulk of the core *Nights*—the aforementioned ur-text—have in common the use of a framed narrative structure and thus echo the form of the cycle as a whole, as well as that of the main frame-tale itself, which consists of three separate narratives.[14] The difference between the main frame and the respective internal frames in the *Nights* is that the latter are periodically developed as full narratives in themselves, thus presenting structurally tight internal blocks. As well as sharing the theme of narration as a means of avoiding death, these internal cycles are supreme examples of the embedding of tales and of the techniques of negotiation between narrative levels.

The proliferation of tales is indicative of a numerical preoccupation variously evident in each of the cycles, from the deliberate suggestion of infinity in the alternative title of the *Nights*—*The Thousand and One Nights*—to the fixed numbers of *Il Pentamerone*: five days, ten tales a day, fifty tales in total (compare the five books or sections of the *Panchatantra*).[15] *The Ocean of Streams of Story* is constructed from one hundred twenty-four tarangas—"waves" or "billows" in Penzer's translation—but has been known in the West, following the first European (German) translation in 1839, in the form of eighteen lambakas—"surges" or "swells." In contrast to such organicism, Penzer adds clarity by signalling the appearance of the Main Story whenever it recurs, and by designating each story by a number, plus a letter for each sub-story and a repeat of the number for each sub-sub-story—a pseudo-structuralist formula (Penzer, in Somadeva, *The Ocean of Story*, vol. I, xxxi and xxxviii). There is an obvious tension in the Eastern cycles between the mathematics of proliferating narrative and the mutability of the material included (or excluded), a tension brought under more rigid control in the European cycles (although as I suggest below, the strings of narrative that go to make up any cycle are always prone to disorder as a result of the incongruous juxtaposition of pre-existent material). While the *Nights* is in many ways the paradigmatic cycle—anonymous text, anonymous tales, present in multiple versions—Basile's *Il Pentamerone* is the most textually secure and as such provides a model of the numerical precision of the European cycle: a fixed text consisting of fifty separate folktales told over five days, introduced by a frame tale and with an eclogue at the end of the first four sittings.[16] In the appendix to his edition of *Il Pentamerone*, Penzer comments on the fact that the Eastern framed cycles tend to be more structurally elaborate than later Western texts such as the *Decameron*; more recently, Gittes, studying the origins of Chaucer's formal devices, makes a strong case for the East, in particular the Arabic Near East, as the place of origin for the "loose structure and . . . general flexibility" of the framed cycle (2).[17] She bases her argument on the characteristics of medieval Arabic arithmetic and algebra, and takes the more structurally rigid European cycles, especially the *Decameron*, as evidence of the contesting influence of the more precise and formal Greek geometry. It is certainly true that the Eastern cycles are structurally more elaborate, and that the Middle Ages in Europe was a time during which Eastern collections were particularly influential, giving rise to a number of translations and adaptations (most notably Petrus Alfonsi's twelfth-century *Disciplina Clericalis*), as well as "original" texts using similar structures (along with the *Decameron* and *The Canterbury Tales*, these include Giovanni Sercambi's early fifteenth-century *Novelle*, John Gower's *Confessio Amantis* [ca. 1390] and, contemporaneous with Straparola, Marguerite de Navarre's *Heptaméron* [1559]).[18]

Yet this variously expressed numerical preoccupation, together with the analogous themes of game and play, is a central element in the somewhat abstract nature of folk narrative cycles in general, a form of playing with narrative as a material for construction that parallels the apsychological characters and formulaic plot structures that are intrinsic to twentieth-century views of the folktale itself. Such indigenous formalism is summarized by H. B. Hinckley in relation to the *Decameron*: "Boccaccio is preoccupied with other considerations than the character of his storytellers, with considerations that may be classed as mathematical and structural; with mass, variety, proportion, symmetry and rhythm" (78).[19] Approached in this manner, the links with the structural grammar of narrative first formulated by Propp become apparent. We can see these cycles as self-contained, interconnected, self-generating narrative systems, offering fertile parallels with the generative and combinative theories summarized in the previous chapter. In one sense, this foreshadowing can be explained by considering the subject matter of the tales themselves. While within the safe confines of this chapter the tale cycles can be seen to enact a manipulation of the formal properties of the folktale as narrative, the narrators of the *Nights* and *Il Pentamerone* in particular tell exemplary narratives for the more immediately pressing reason of being threatened with (*Nights*), or by threatening (*Il Pentamerone*), death. In the latter, the usurping slave threatens to murder her unborn baby if her curiosity is not appeased, while in the former there is the repeated motif of tale-telling as a means to circumvent the death of the narrator or another character. In "The Merchant and the Demon," the elderly men who pass by as the demon prepares to murder his captive propose that the former give up a third of the merchant if the tale told by each proves to be more strange and

amazing than the events that have led the merchant and the demon to this point (in effect, if their tales turn out to be better than
the framing tale), and in "The Story of the Hunchback," the four
men condemned by the king of China offer, in exchange for their
lives, to tell tales more amazing than that which has landed them
at death's door. Of necessity, these must be exemplary narratives
and, as I hope to demonstrate in what follows, their exemplarity, as defined and valued in the *text* itself, lies precisely in those
features which structuralist models of narrative grammar take as
paradigmatic of *narrative* itself. Once again, there is the possibility
that such models, variously rooted as we have seen in the folktale,
offer as universal examples features which are better conceived as
abstract expressions of structural features of the *folktale*, as written
text, itself.

It is the workings of combination and generation, as fundamental to the notion of narrative grammar and its appropriation
of the basic methodological procedures, and metaphorical tropes,
of structural linguistics, that I want to demonstrate at work in
the *Nights*. Taking the sentence as the material of narrative, the
findings of these linguistic schools are extrapolated in narratology
beyond the level of the sentence to that of the combination of
sentences that form the discourse of narrative. This discourse is
perceived as a hierarchical structure with the narrative itself as the
surface manifestation of a series of levels of increasing complexity.
Diagrammatically, the basic movement is from the simple to the
complex, via the combination of a limited number of distinctive
units, and the narrative form is thus produced via a process of generation: from deep structure to surface manifestation. As we have
seen with the work of Lévi-Strauss and Greimas, while the linear chain of combination—the syntagmatic axis—is irreducible
in Propp's schema, structuralism focuses on the process by which
this chain is generated out of a deeper set of paradigmatic relations
between units, thus producing a structural model rather than a
skeletal formula. Combination—the combinatory principle—and
generation—the generative principle—are thus part of the same
process.

In one obvious sense the folk narrative cycle is a combinatory mechanism: a text built out of single narratives which, through the combination of these relatively simple units, exhibits enormous complexity. It provides a concrete demonstration of the passage from simplicity to complexity and of the coexistence of syntagmatic and paradigmatic dimensions. The internal chain of narratives is constantly in flux, while the frame provides fixed points of connection throughout the cycle, thus allowing it to be perceived as a unified whole. Indeed, the folktale tradition itself, as approached via the indexes of Aarne and Thompson, is a *combinatoire*: a mechanism that describes and enables the generation of stories. In the case of the Aarne index, the basic unit is the "tale type," defined by a particular event or series of events. Once a type has been labeled—for example, the forbidden-room or "Bluebeard" type (Aarne-Thompson type 312)—all extant versions can be recorded as such, building up a catalogue of all the narratives that can be, and have been, generated out of the core material. Similarly, in the Thompson index the units are a tale's motifs, defined as the elements or building blocks from which a whole narrative is constructed. Thus, in structuralist terms the motif is the minimal distinctive unit: in the case of the "Bluebeard" tale type, the forbidden chamber is identified as a distinct motif (C611), potentially capable of appearing in any number of independent narratives. This type of index therefore illustrates even more explicitly the combinatory principle, in that it contains within itself a huge number of potential stories, imminent but unrealized. As Fredric Jameson comments, "[a] full-scale demonstration of the narrational *combinatoire* or story-generating mechanism" is limited (in abstract, ahistorical terms) only by "the total number of permutations and combinations inherently possible in the model in question" (*Prison-House* 127–28). In practice, a relatively small number of narratives are, or have been, realized, a fact characteristic of the conservative nature of traditional material: in Saussurian terms, "folklore is set specifically toward *langue*, while literature is set toward *parole*" (Bogatyrëv and Jakobson 39).

In his foreword to the eighth volume of *The Ocean of Streams of*

Story, W. R. Halliday recognizes the combination of units as the basic structural feature of the folk narrative, yet warns against the comparison of isolated motifs:

> My main contention is that a story may be regarded as a kind of composite pattern of coloured bricks. Individual bricks considered by themselves are almost worthless for our particular purpose of tracing the history of the design. The whole point is the relation of the bricks to each other, and in our analysis the smallest effective unit must be an integral piece of the pattern. (in Somadeva, *The Ocean of Story*, vol. VIII, xvi)

This is an important point—note the stress on the "relation" of units, a key principle of structuralist analysis and central to the critique of the methodology of the indexes of Aarne and Thompson. However, Halliday is obviously concerned more with the history of the tales than with the theoretical implications of approaches to the cataloguing of the folktale. What folk narrative cycles demonstrate is the circulation of motifs and a basic combinatory mechanism. For example, in the *Nights* we find the recurrence of the motif of storytelling as a bargaining tool, a means of avoiding death or punishment; indeed, the whole cycle can be seen to be generated out of this motif, illustrating its use as a unit of construction in various combinations. In *Il Pentamerone* we can identify the use of a particular motif by different narrators in different contexts. Penzer notes that the tale of "The Dove," told as the seventh tale on the second day, is made up of "a jumble of numerous motifs we have already noticed in previous tales": for example, the motif of a curse cast by an old woman precipitates the main bulk of the action in the frame tale; the "ladder of hair" occurs in the first tale of the second day, while the familiar motif of tasks set for a character to perform occurs on several occasions throughout the cycle.[20] Any number of these recurrences can be listed and it could be argued that the tales generate one another precisely through the cross-combination of such motifs.[21]

Cycles illustrate the combination of narrative units at several levels.[22] Within individual tales, the basic unit is undoubtedly what amounts to a motif; while there is a certain degree of concurrence between the motif and the Proppian "function"—"understood as an act of character, defined from the point of view of its significance for the course of the action" (*Morphology* 21)—I am more concerned here with the formal functioning of the cycles in particular rather than what we can now read, in the wake of the structuralist model, as their modus operandi.[23] Motifs or functions combine to form a single narrative, and in the more complex cycles—the *Nights* and *The Ocean of Streams of Story*—single narratives are combined to form internal cycles, the next level in the hierarchy of cyclical construction. The bulk of the core tales of the *Nights* consists of five such internal cycles—"The Story of the Merchant and the Demon," "The Story of the Fisherman and the Demon," "The Story of the Porter and the Three Ladies," "The Story of the Three Apples," and "The Story of the Hunchback"—together with the frame tale, itself a combination of three narratives. The "Hunchback" cycle consists of eleven tales-within-tales, one told by each character, followed by a series of stories told by a character within the last of these internal tales. "The Fisherman and the Demon," a cycle consisting of four internally narrated tales, demonstrates the yoking together of two separate narrative blocks. The first concerns the characters of the title, each of whom tell individual tales, concluding with a repentant demon and a rewarded fisherman. The second block is initiated by the colored fish caught by the fisherman, but largely concerns a king and his journey to uncover the mystery of these fish.[24] Ferial Jabouri Ghazoul remarks that "the entire narrative has the structure of two overlapping circles where the common surface or link is that of the fish episode," and these "overlapping circles" or blocks—defined by Ghazoul as "textual unit[s] . . . that can (potentially) make narrative sense autonomously"—are analogous with what Propp identifies as a "move" (140 and 37).[25] In the section of his *Morphology* devoted to "The Ways in Which Stories are Combined," Propp defines a "move" as the combination of basic functions that make up a single, complete tale, proceeding with "villainy" or some form of "lack" and resulting in "marriage" or another function of dénouement (*Morphology* 92–95). The majority of Propp's canon is found subsequently to exhibit a combination of two or more moves, leading to the formation of the next level of organization in the Proppian schema. Ghazoul refers to this process in the *Nights* as "co-ordination," one of the organizational modes in the collection's internal cycles, "where different narrative blocks combine and overlap to construct a narrative whole" (140). David Pinault makes a similar point by comparing these units of narrative with the mode of construction used in oral recitation: the use of pre-existent formula and phrases that are arranged rather than invented by the performers. In the various constructions of the *Nights*, "the given redactor often borrowed Arabic tales freely from other already existent and completely different story-cycles. . . . [T]hese stories comprised the redactor's building blocks, which he frequently fitted . . . into the structure of his narrative edifice" (32).[26] The nature of the material itself is thus directly implicated in the foreshadowing of narrative grammar, just as the structure of the framed cycle was to a significant extent the result of specific historical circumstances (the influence of an oral culture and the desire to reproduce the dramatic aspect of oral narration).

The next level is obviously the internal cycle itself, which functions as a unit in the construction of the full cycle—a unit which, as can be seen by the inclusion of the *Panchatantra* in *The Ocean of Streams of Story* and the Sindbad cycle in some recensions of the *Nights,* is freely and often confusingly inserted to supplement the size and inclusiveness of the whole. Yet the cycle is nevertheless following the internal principles of combination throughout, building a hierarchical structure that proceeds from motif to tale, tale to block or "move," block to internal cycle and internal cycle to "complete" cycle.

In the core group of *Nights* the internal tales are often metaphorically generated by a character in the enframing tale; indeed, the entire cycle is generated out of the motif of storytelling as a means of avoiding death. Shahrazad uses the curiosity aroused by narrative to prevent the proposed ending of her own life-story, and the tales she tells repeatedly reflect on her own situation and strategy. In "The Merchant and the Demon," three old men offer their life-stories in return for a third of the condemned merchant; in "The Porter and the Three Ladies," the overwhelming curiosity of the assembled male guests at the ladies' house leads to the three dervishes narrating their life-stories to save their heads; and in "The Story of the Hunchback," the condemned characters relate a series of narratives in an attempt to move the king to forgiveness. These are the "narrative-men" referred to by Todorov in an influential essay dealing with the "a-psychological" narratives of cycles such as the _Nights_: as he writes, in these cycles "a character is a potential story that is the story of his life. Every new character signifies a new plot. We are in the realm of narrative-men" ("Narrative Men," _The Poetics of Prose_ 70).[27]

"The Story of the Hunchback" is perhaps the most revealing of the internal cycles in this respect, as well for the fact that it vividly illustrates the combination of a limited number of motifs in the construction of several tales. The exposition sets out the basic premise: a hunchback appears to choke to death while eating with a tailor and his wife; they dump the body in the house of a Jewish physician, who—believing he is the cause of the death—passes it on to a Muslim, who in turn leaves the corpse with a Christian tradesman. As he is about to be hanged, the Christian is saved by a sudden onset of honesty on the part of the Muslim, who in turn is saved by the Jew, who is himself eventually saved by the tailor. To prove their guilt each presents a mini-narration of the events, which completes the exposition and provides a perfectly symmetrical form: a winding up and then down, beginning with Shahrazad's narration of the relay of the hunchback's body and concluding with each character narrating his own role, in reverse order. A coda provides a third and final version of events, this time relayed from the chief of police to the king, who is devastated to hear of the death of his favorite clown and subsequently orders that the tale be recorded: " 'Have you ever heard anything more amazing than the adventure of the hunchback?'" This tag acts as the link with the development section, beginning with the offer of a more impressive story from the Christian; as this fails to amaze the king, the Muslim steward steps forward and offers his narrative in return for the lives of the condemned, if it should duly impress; he fails, as does the Jewish physician, and it is only with the tale told by the actual culprit, the tailor, that the four are pardoned. However, this convoluted summary tells only half the story. The individual tales told by each character turn out to be frames for the life-stories of one of the characters in each of the tales. These are genuine "narrative-men," in that their appearance signals a potential story, literally in the first three cases, as all of the men are marked by a physical defect—a missing right hand or a missing thumb—which is subsequently explained in their narratives (a motif which obviously connects with the figure of the hunchback himself, the original cause of the narrative activity). Each is in fact a variation on a core set of motifs: punishment inflicted as a result of love (hence the physical defect), and the exchange of money and food as part of the ritual of courtship. As each of the first three tales told by the accused fails to impress the king, the burden falls, as it should, on the first character of the cycle, the tailor. His tale must be the most impressive, the most persuasive, and it proves itself in characteristic fashion. While it begins in the same manner as its predecessors, with a young man explaining his physical defect to the narrator, it goes on to introduce a second internal teller, the wonderfully garrulous barber, who, after a series of events, tells the individual tales of his six brothers, each of whom—to continue the repetition of motifs—is characterized by a physical defect. In the dénouement of the cycle, the barber leapfrogs narrative levels to intervene in the action of the frame tale, revealing the hunchback to be only temporarily unconscious and proving that the whole cycle is either, as Mia Gerhardt says, "about nothing," or a graphic illustration of the restorative power of narrative that acts as a central concern throughout the *Nights* (415).

I provide this detailed summary not only as testament to what is a marvelous set of tales but as an illustration of the extent to which narratives are constructed and manipulated in almost clinical fashion in the *Nights*. The "Hunchback" cycle demonstrates the combination of two levels of units. The motif, a small number of which are combined to form a series of variations, and the tale itself, eleven of which make up the full cycle, split into three groups: the recurring frame, the tales told by the four culprits, and the six fraternal tales told by the barber. In a variation of the frame tale of Shahrayar and Shahrazad, storytelling is enacted as oral performance, offered in return for a spared or saved life; while these acts are judged in terms of content, what ultimately impresses is the narrative craft, the ability to manipulate levels of tales-within-tales. Thus the abstract is allied with the concrete, and form with content, a characteristic of the orally influenced cycle.

The "Hunchback" cycle is structured along the lines of mirror symmetry: the first character we meet is the last character to narrate. It is the tailor, as the putative villain, who needs to tell the most impressive tale, and it is the tailor, as final narrator, upon whom the other innocent characters rely. His tale must be the most persuasive, the most convincing; it must be an exemplary narrative. Yet its exemplarity does not lie in its content, which continues, like the preceding tales of the cycle, to be formed from a core group of motifs: physical deformity inflicted during complicated courtship. The tailor's tale is differentiated from the others by its form, a more complicated version of that of the earlier tales. Where the latter are embedded biographies, introducing a character who proceeds to tell his story, the tailor's tale contains a double embedding: the first internal narrator introduces a second, the barber, who then tells six individual biographies. Rather than a tale-within-a-frame, as in the preceding three biographies, we have six tales-within-a-tale-within-a-frame. This is the distinguishing aspect of the tailor's tale and its exemplary status is rewarded by the king's pardon. Furthermore, if this tale persuades through its structural complexity we must remember that it is itself already embedded: within the frame of the "Hunchback" cycle, within the overall frame of Shahrazad's narrative, and within the text that contains all of these, referred to in the Foreword. The barber's tales are thus located on the sixth narrative level. The subject of each of the preceding five levels is the narrative which it both contextualizes and, literally, tells: the enframed tale. More than any other cycle, the *Nights* is about narrative itself, and this central theme is embodied in the form of the frame, and enframed, tale. To think of the cycle in terms of levels involves perceiving it whole—that is, seeing the tale of the the third brother of the barber as primarily a constituent part of the single narrative that is the *Nights*. Within this single unit—the ultimate narrative block in the hierarchy of the cycle—the frame tale, as well as ordering and unifying what follows, is the initial generator of the internal tales, which in turn proceed to act as narrative generators themselves.

It is possible to conceive of the frame as a single sentence that generates the string of sentences that comprise the *Nights*—generates both in literal terms, by providing the impetus for a stream of narratives, and metaphorically, by providing the motif of narrative bargaining. The fact that the frame is (apocryphally) concluded at the end of the cycle sanctions this view, and it could equally be applied, for example, to *Il Pentamerone* (albeit in a simplified form). It should be stressed that the cycle itself functions as if the frame were a sentence, with the addition of varying numbers of internal tales as a series of clauses. As Todorov has illustrated, clauses are often indicated by the presence of a character—a narrative-man—and we can thereby locate a further anticipation of narrative grammar. Narratology is founded on the structural congruence between sentence and narrative, and Todorov links the technique of narrative embedding with the subordinate clauses of a sentence: "[t]he formal structure of embedding coincides . . . with that of a syntactic form, a particular case of subordination, which in fact modern linguistics calls *embedding*" (*Poetics of Prose* 70). These clauses, or embedded tales, were formulated by Gérard Genette in his discussion of "levels," where he attempts systematically to account for the various "insides" and "outsides" of narrative: as he comments, while it is more constructive to avoid thinking about these various levels in terms of hierarchy, we can nevertheless imagine them as a series of "hyper"-levels, "resting on" one another, as do the floors of a building (*Narrative Discourse* 212–67; *Narrative Discourse Revisited* 84–95).[28] Alternatively, we can view the process of embedding in terms of what Bremond refers to as a series of "enclaves": "when a process, in order to attain its goal, must include another which acts as a means for the first; the latter can in turn include a third, etc." ("The Logic of Narrative Possibilities" 388–89).

Whichever terminology we choose, there is no doubt that the *Nights* provides a string of such tales-within-tales and thus tales about tales. Narratives are explicitly constructed out of blocks or units through a process of combination and generation: combining simple units to build a complex whole, generating narratives out of frames that in turn act as generative units themselves. The whole cycle acts as a sort of narrative mechanism—a "marvellous story-machine," in Todorov's words—a true *combinatoire* which charts the generative possibilities embodied in the situation of the frame tale: the relationship between Shahrayar and Shahrazad.[29] We can even draw an analogy between this generative couple and the Greimasian "spectacle," the dramatic relationship between actants that he posits as underlying, in deep structure, the surface manifestation of narrative, and which allows for the comprehension of narrative as a meaningful whole as well as a linear chain of events.

While it is thus possible to see the cycle as a prototype for the conception of narrative grammar offered by the structualist model, the technique of embedding which forms the structural basis of the *Nights* has additional implications that lie outside the ordered realms of such a grammar. Other than those at the highest level, each of the narratives in the cycle is preceded by the story of its own creation, and in turn acts as the story of the embedded narrative it frames. Jorge Luis Borges refers to a probably counterfeit tale, in an edition of the *Nights*, in which Shahrazad narrates the story of the *Nights* itself—her own story, with the implication that the cycle encloses itself in an infinite spiral of increasingly vertiginous narrative complexity. Borges uses this example to illustrate the ontological aspect of the embedded structure: the fact that if all narratives are framed by realities that turn out to be themselves framed, we must ask at what point the fictional ceases: "these inversions suggest that if the characters in a story can be readers or spectators, then we, their readers or spectators, can be fictitious" ("Partial Enchantments" 45–46).[30] This notion is analogous with the suggestion of the infinite in the alternative title of the cycle, *The Thousand and One Nights*: as Borges comments, "[t]o say a thousand nights is to say infinite, countless nights, endless nights. To say a thousand and one nights is to add one to infinity," a suggestion which is also evident in the equally fertile *Ocean of Streams of Story* ("The Thousand and One Nights" 45).[31] Each title implies an infinite source of narrative, a narrative for all seasons, and as I have demonstrated in the case of the former, narrative is both a means of attaining identity and the primary currency. I could equally have focused on the proliferation of narrative as moral illustration, where a formulaic phrase in the *Nights*, such as "he who considers not the world, the world is not his friend," sparks off or generates a narrative exemplum, with a seemingly endless number of applicable tales for any one formulaic tag.[32]

The multiplicity and suggestion of endlessness are, as it were, the reverse side, the other, of the preoccupation with the mathematical exhibited in the *Nights*. The ordered combination of, and generation out of, various forms of unit is, as the titles referred to above suggest, potentially limitless. Just as Stith Thompson's motif index holds the seeds of any number of narratives, so the *Nights* exhibits the infinite generative possibilities of a single dramatic relationship, a single motif. The text can be, and has been, supplemented, and indeed many have suggested that to do so is to remain true to the encyclopedic thrust of the work; the ending of each narrative is the beginning of another, or rather each narrative contains within itself the subject, literally and metaphorically, of another. While we can chart the path of its construction, the resultant text is positively, not pejoratively, chaotic in its multiplicity: as Ghazoul concludes, it is a truly polyphonic work, in the Bakhtinian sense, in that the string of narrative voices, although framed and contained, can speak independently, can be added and subtracted and thus brought into contact with other voices (153).[33] Perhaps it is the tension between frame and enframed, between open and closed structures, that is the key to the work; or perhaps it is Calvino's suggestion, made with reference to Italian folktales, that is most apposite: "[n]o doubt the moral function of the tale, in the popular conception, is to be sought not in the subject matter but in the very nature of the folktale, in the mere fact of telling and listening" (*Italian Folktales* xxx). Every teller is in turn a listener in the *Nights*, as is to be expected from a text that grew out of oral storytelling, and it is in the representation of the commonplace act of narration, including the telling of tales about tales, that this paradigm of the framed story cycle self-consciously manipulates what later came to be proposed as the structural properties of narrative.

Chapter 3

THE IDEA OF THE FOLKTALE IN ITALO CALVINO[1]

The various interactions of structuralist narrative theory and the folktale that have been described in the preceding two chapters form perhaps the dominant context within which late twentieth-century interactions in the realm of narrative fiction need to be viewed, and it is with this in mind that I have placed theory before fiction. If, in the readings that follow, narratology is not explicitly referred to in any detail, this is precisely because it functions as such a ubiquitous influence in certain types of experimental narrative fiction; to read such fiction in terms suggested by narratology can seem tautological. Just as I have sought to demonstrate one of the histories of this branch of narrative theory, in terms of its appropriation of the folktale as source material, so I now turn to the folktale as a model in narrative fiction. The resulting triangle of connections linking tale, fiction, and theory is obviously central to this study and is implicit throughout. Indeed, the primary role given to the folktale in Italo Calvino's fictions is illustrative of the continuing presence of the material that gave rise to structuralist models of narrative, to the extent that these fictions demonstrate the influence of both models (folktale and narratology). Yet the tale is the primary focus.[2]

Calvino provides a smooth passage between the realms of theory and fiction. His later works are rooted in the intellectual milieu of 1970s Paris, where he was resident from 1967 to 1980, and his biography includes acquaintance with a number of the major figures in French letters of this period. This is common knowledge and I prefer to open this chapter by juxtaposing two disparate moments from his writing career. During his time in Paris, Calvino became a member of the Oulipo group, the "Ouvroir de littérature potentielle" ("Workshop of potential literature"), cofounded in 1960 by Raymond Queneau and François Le Lionnais and devoted to the exploration of the potentials of self-imposed artificial constraint in literature. In 1956, seventeen years prior to his enrollment in Oulipo, Calvino had published a selection of two hundred *Italian Folktales* (Fiabe Italiane), the extensively annotated result of a prolonged study of the Italian tale tradition, creatively reinvented by the editor. This bringing together of literary author and national folk narrative tradition would appear to be well-nigh unique in postwar European culture and for this reason alone Calvino can be placed alongside Propp as a seminal figure in this interdisciplinary field. The juxtaposition of these two events provides a clear example of the parallel strains in Calvino's writing—experiment and tradition—and is indicative of both his oeuvre and the work of the other writers included in these pages. To supplement this introductory snapshot, as well as to reintroduce the theme of music (which will be particularly prominent in what follows), I want to include a compatriot and near-exact contemporary of Calvino's, the composer Luciano Berio. Calvino wrote the libretto for two of Berio's operas: *Un re in ascolto* (A King Listening) in 1984 and *La vera storia* (The True Story) in 1982, the latter of which draws extensively on the processes of oral storytelling.[3] Berio provides a clear parallel with Calvino in that the works of his early career include direct settings of folk material, most noticeably the *Folk Songs* of 1964, which can be placed alongside his other experimental scores. Indeed, the two strands are often inseparable—see Berio's *Coro* (Chorus, 1976) and *Voci* (Voices, 1984), for example—and within the context of both Calvino's and Berio's work as a whole, each facet interpretatively reflects upon the other. With reference to literature and literary studies, Calvino commented on these seemingly incongruous elements in an essay written in 1970:

Dwelling on what is happening today in the most specialized
literary laboratories, we find two contradictory things. On the
one hand the novel . . . has, as its very first rule, not to rely on
a story (or a world) outside its own pages. . . . On the other
hand there is a move toward studies and analyses of what is
(or was) the traditional narrative in all its forms. Never before
has this human act of telling a story, always operative at all
stages of a civilization, been so often analyzed, dismantled,
and reassembled. . . . One might even say that storytelling is
at one and the same time reaching the nadir of its eclipse in
creative texts and the zenith of critical and analytical interest
in it. ("The Novel as Spectacle," *The Literature Machine*
193–94)

While this accurately describes certain fictional experiments of
the time, in particular those of the nouveau roman, it is far less applicable to Calvino himself, whose experimentalism tends towards
the discreet. Indeed, this quiet experimentalism is perhaps what
distinguishes him as, to quote Cynthia Ozick, "an authentic postmodernist" rather than a late modernist, and it was the continuing and multiple influence of his *Italian Folktales* that filtered,
in very particular ways, the tendency to experiment (350).[4] As
with Berio, the lure of folk material lay in part in its historical
and social provenance, and while Calvino's fictions exhibit an
ongoing engagement with popular forms—from the deceptively
plain *Marcovaldo or The Seasons in the City* (Marcovaldo ovuero
Le stagioni in città, 1963) to the interpolated genre pieces of *If on
a Winter's Night a Traveller* (Se una notte d'inverno un viaggiatore,
1979)—it is the folktale that acts as the most influential model of
a popular narrative type, an example of the realignment of different strata of culture in postmodernist fiction (a process to which I
will return). As such, I will attempt to survey the various aspects
of Calvino's engagement with the folktale, certain of which also
occur in the work of the contemporaneous writers I have chosen to read in the following chapters. The implicit positioning of
Calvino as paradigmatic in this respect is intentional.

The temptation in such a reading is to see the folktale in general, and *Italian Folktales* in particular, as the underlying model out of which the majority of Calvino's fictions are generated, much as it is possible to detect Venice lurking behind the multitude of cities described in *Invisible Cities* (Le città invisibili, 1972). The collection of tales forms by far the most substantial single text in Calvino's oeuvre, rivalled only by his comparable resetting of another monument of Italian narrative heritage, Ludovico Ariosto's *Orlando Furioso* (Orlando furioso di Ludovico Ariosto raccontato di Italo Calvino, 1970). His interest in this narrative tradition also forms the basis for a pivotal essay written, fittingly perhaps, in several different versions—most extensively as "Cybernetics and Ghosts" (1967)—and which provides a detailed introduction to a number of recurring concerns, as we shall see.[5] Nevertheless, to focus on the folktale, however various its influence, is unavoidably detrimental to other areas of interest. Calvino himself disliked what he considered to be reductive formulaic overviews. In the preface he added in 1964 to his first work, *The Path to the Nest of the Spiders* (Il sentiero dei nidi di ragno, 1947), he writes exasperatingly of "[h]ow easy it is, when you talk of literature, even in the midst of the most serious, factual discussion, to shift unaware to inventing stories" (viii). Yet by making the tendentious nature of my reading explicit—by not shifting unawares—I hope to cast this partiality in the form rather of a fertile restriction, in the Oulipian sense: a self-imposed constraint that is potentially productive of readings that would be lost to the eye of a less overtly biased interpreter. In an essay on Northrop Frye, Calvino concludes by comparing the system of literature with that of libraries, within which "each work is different from what it would be in isolation or in another library," and it is precisely the differences that result from the presence of *Italian Folktales* in Calvino's library that form the subject of this chapter ("Literature as a Projection of Desire," *The Literature Machine* 60).

Italian Folktales : Text and Contexts

The 1950s witnessed the publication of a number of important volumes of folktales, part of a renewed interest in national traditions that followed in the wake of World War II. These included Waldemar Liungman's three-volume collection of Swedish tales (1949–1952), the first (posthumous) volume of Paul Delarue's *Le conte populaire français* (1957) and Karl Haiding's Austrian collection (1953).[6] At the time of publication of Calvino's volume (1956), Italy had no recognized standard national collection of folktales, obviously in part a result of its relatively recent formation as a unified nation-state—the production of national collections being intimately bound up with nineteenth-century conceptions of national culture. There was, however, a disparate body of largely nineteenth-century, linguistically heterogeneous regional collections, together with one of the richest traditions of literary reworkings of folk material—"richer than all the others," according to the Grimm brothers in 1812, and including Boccaccio's *Decameron* (ca. 1351), Straparola's *Piacevoli Notti* (1550–1553), and Basile's *Il Pentamerone* (1634–1636).[7] In addition, the fusion of the tale with the medieval chivalrous epic was especially prominent in Italy, most notably in the aforementioned *Orlando Furioso* (1532).

Italian Folktales can in part be seen as a product of the redevelopment of Italian culture in the years following the end of the war. Influenced by experiences in the Resistance (Calvino himself spent time towards the end of the war as a member of a partisan group based in the mountains of his Ligurian home) and by the aftermath of both Fascist government and German occupation, there was an acknowledged need in the new Republic for some form of cultural renaissance—felt to be all the more pressing in a country unified for less than a hundred years and still displaying prominent rifts along geographical, class, and linguistic lines. The writings of Antonio Gramsci (one of the founders of the Italian Communist Party in 1921, imprisoned by Mussolini in 1928

until shortly before his death in 1937) were particularly influential in the left-wing/Communist intellectual environment of postwar Italy, and his conception of "national-popular" culture can be
seen, at least in retrospect, as emblematic of a range of postwar
cultural endeavors, most notably in literature and film. The notion of a "national-popular" culture recurs throughout Gramsci's
Prison Notebooks (Quaderni del carcere), which began to be published by Einaudi in 1947, the year Calvino joined its editorial
staff. As important as the formulation of what this culture might
comprise were the historical reasons for its lack: the perceived
absence in Italy, up to that point, of a shared sense of a popular
culture. Together with the distinct gap between various regional
literatures and cosmopolitan cultures, the lack of a body of Italian
children's literature, and the ongoing question of the constitution of a national language, Gramsci highlighted what he saw as
the absence in Italy's cultural history of an "Italian Romanticism,"
conceived as "a special relationship or bond between intellectu-
als and the people, the nation" (205). The fraught question of the
existence or otherwise of Italian Romanticism is too extensive
to be raised here, although if some form of nationalism is taken
to be a central strand of the construct of Romanticism, it would
be difficult to agree entirely with Gramsci's diagnosis.[8] Yet at the
risk of simplification, it is true that, in the decades preceding uni-
fication, it was rather canonical culture which fed into popular
culture than vice versa, most obviously in the case of opera and
the Risorgimento. Thus what Gramsci is referring to is a particular
mode of Romanticism. He cites the fusion of the "national" and
the "popular" that was one of the dominant strands of German
Romanticism, and while he remains vague as to specific figures,
we can here see the Grimms, together with Achim von Arnim
and Clemens Brentano, as representative of this endeavor: the
attempt to define, fix, and authenticate a national heritage, and
thus a national narrative temperament, through the collection
and transcription of popular folk material, subsequently filtered
into folk-influenced prose or poetry.[9] Due to this lack, the cosmopolitan writer and the intellectual are perceived as distanced

from the bulk of the population, with the resultant absence of a "national-popular literature." Whatever the merits of such an analysis there is no doubt that in Germany the Romantic movement stimulated the transcription and study of the folktale, and, in return, the folktale served as a model of "authentic" cultural production (a relationship reflected in the literary tales of Ludwig Tieck and E. T. A. Hoffmann, for example). While at the time of Gramsci's influence, the Grimms' reputation had been sullied by their association with the construction of a German Nazi ideology, they still provided a model for the resuscitation of, and advocacy on behalf of, a narrative heritage, a history which Gramsci saw as crucial in the formation of a new popular culture in Italy: "[t]he past does not live in the present, it is not an essential part of the present; in the history of our national culture there is no continuity or unity. . . . The past, literature included, is not an element of life, only a bookish and scholastic culture" (253).[10] This is the framework within which we can situate Calvino's own remarks, in the introduction to *Italian Folktales*, regarding the historical absence of an Italian Romantic movement, which he sees as partly responsible for the lack of an Italian equivalent to the Grimms' tales and, concomitantly, for the fact that "[t]he folktale as a genre . . . never had the romantic vogue among Italian writers and poets that it had enjoyed in the rest of Europe" (xv–xvi).

This is not to suggest that Calvino was following the dictates of Gramsci, but rather to trace the discursive resonance of the production of such a text at such a time, and of Calvino's choice of the Grimms' *Kinder- und Hausmärchen* as model. The explicit link here with Romanticism and the folktale is indicative. Just as Calvino's reading of the folktale—expressed in the text and apparatus of *Italian Folktales* and in his subsequent writings on the subject—is, to a degree, structualist in orientation, so it is also post-Romantic, mindful of Romanticism's strong interpretative appropriation of aspects of the folktale. Indeed, at least as far as literature is concerned, the folktale as read by these two opposing systems of thought—Romanticism and structuralism—is the folktale with which I am concerned throughout this study: the product of a set of historically contingent interpretations, various aspects of which have fed into, and been critiqued and transformed within, folktale-influenced fictions of recent years. In the case of Romanticism, my treatment of *Italian Folktales* as text reflects Calvino's own self-consciousness with regard to the ideologies of nineteenth-century folklorism and the constructedness of texts such as the Grimms'. The particular ontological nature of the tales (their written status and arrangement), the active role of the editor, the interpretative status of the apparatus, and the relation between commentary and tale: each of these is now brought to the fore rather than marginalized, or silenced, in favor of the presentation, as narrative heritage, of the national spirit.

Not only does the number of tales in Calvino's collection correspond with that in the final edition of the Grimms', he also uses their text and method as a "justification . . . for the hybrid nature of my work," to the extent that they "added their own personal touches to the tales," "translating a major part from German dialects . . . integrating the variants, recasting the story . . . touching up expressions and images, giving stylistic unity to the discordant voices" (xix). As we shall see in chapter five, this is certainly a post-Romantic reading of the Grimms' method, for the latter of whom such editorial touching was more a case of idealization than active participation. The hybridity of the tales lies in Calvino's explicit intervention in a series of narrative traditions, the fact that they are taken not from the source—however prevalent that elusive source may have been in the Italy of the early 1950s—but from written collections recast in a subtly modified modern idiom, "a language never too colloquial, yet colorful and as derivative as possible of dialect" (xix). As it appears in *Italian Folktales*, each tale is usually the distillation of a number of variants, although many draw heavily on what Calvino identifies as the most representative example, that which is most "rooted in its native heath," and the tales are thus active retellings, following the practice if not the purpose of what we now know to have been the Grimms' method. The value of the tale "consists in what is woven and rewoven into it. I too have thought of myself as a link in the anonymous

chain without end by which folktales are handed down" (xxi).[11]
As these editorial remarks suggests, the Romanticism in Calvino's
post-Romantic project is generally more modified than dismissed.

Turning to the text of *Italian Folktales* with this in mind, it is
noticeable that Calvino explicitly arranges the tales in terms of
region, beginning close to the French border in his own area of
Liguria and then passing systematically through Lombardy, the
Veneto, Trentino, Tuscany, Rome, Campania, to conclude with
the island tales of Sicily, Sardinia, and Corsica. The tales are
drawn predominantly from individual regional collections and
there is an attempt to preserve local characteristics, with the main
source indicated for each entry, thus maintaining an historically
apposite sense of discrete identities within a provisional national
whole. A reading of the full text can thus pick out the repeated
images of underground canals in the Venetian tales, for example,
or of the sea in those from the Italian Riviera, as well as develop
a gradual sense of what might constitute a specifically Italian aesthetic, which Calvino locates in the singular logic of the folktale and in the tendency towards benign images of a nature suffused with the fantastic, as opposed to the darker aesthetic of the
German tradition (xxix–xxx). The desire for the identification in
folklore of a national stylistic trait is, once again, a manifestation
of European Romanticism and nationalism. As Carl Dahlhaus
comments, with reference to the designation of particular musical
features as essential national characterstics, "the national aspect
of music is not a property attached to a musical creation from its
origins but one which emerges in a historical process" (*Nineteenth-
Century Music* 38–39). Certainly, the explicit regionalism of the
constituent tales of *Italian Folktales* is a sign both of the political realities within which such tales developed and of the essentially regional, as opposed to national, basis of such narrative traditions. In line with the post-Romantic ideology of the text, Calvino
draws attention to the fictional nature of the ties between tale
and place, the processes of transformation involved. Nevertheless, given the historical context of the collection we can identify
the first potential, the first generative idea, in Calvino's reading:

a recognition of the status of each tale within a tradition and the sense of continuity maintained by active intervention within the generic conventions of that tradition. Again, given the context of the collection this recognition of the historical specificity of his chosen corpus of tales can be seen as the ideological aspect of Calvino's actions as editor, translator, and narrator, an aspect never explicitly acknowledged but which informs in particular his early experiments with the tale in new fictions, as will be seen. Part of this potential ideology grows specifically out of an awareness of narrative traditions rooted in the everyday, in local surroundings and local activities. As mentioned above, this can be the canals of "The Crab Prince" and "The Dead Man's Palace," or the Turkish presence in "The Science of Laziness" and "Fair Brow," the folk-loric realism of descriptions of dirtiness in "The Devil's Breeches," or the numerous references to the harsh reality of peasant life in "Out of the World." Concrete details form the environment from which the magical elements in the narratives spring, and rarely does a tale lack such marks of empirical contexts. A magic which "has its grounds in one's actual experience" is repeatedly stressed by Calvino, who prefers to see the depiction of fantastic wish-fulfilment or malign forces as a direct extension or expression of real fears and desires: "the force of reality which bursts forth into fantasy" (xxxii). The similarities here with the utopian Marxist conception of the fairy tale evident in the writings of Jack Zipes is indicative of the political climate within which Calvino was working.

Such grounded fantasy forms the second potential in Calvino's reading, the expression of a desire to intervene in the historical shift of the tales towards an exclusively youthful audience, and to stem the resultant simplification and bowdlerization (processes to which I return in chapter five).[12] This potential can be further de-fined by the reliance of the fantasy element on an arresting image which functions as the organizational device, or pivot, in the nar-rative, most vividly apparent in the remarkable "Buffalo Head," in which the unearthed and living head functions as surrogate mother, helper, and moral focus for a tale which nonetheless works by dint of the paganistic strangeness of its central image. The collection opens with the image of a self-assembling man whose construction and dismantling follow the arc of the narrative ("Dauntless Little John"), and other tales include the less fantastic devices of a hollow silver goose as big as a man or the closely related hollow bronze horse ("Money Can Do Everything"; "Pome and Peel"); "The Cloven Youth," like the giant in the first tale, is structured around the image of an incomplete body, while the wonderfully cunning tale of "The Wife Who Lived on Wind" uses the device of a character who "fans herself, and thus fans away her appetite." Such images are irreducibly singular, retaining an otherness that belies interpretative frameworks, and it is the primacy of an image that is rooted in, and by, the commonplace that is assimilated and developed in Calvino's own fictions.[13]

The third discovery made by Calvino in the process of researching *Italian Folktales* is one instinctively felt during any extended reading of a group of such narratives. Faced with the sheer magnitude of material contained in the many sources, he writes of "a leap in the dark," into "ocean depths"; most disturbing is the sense of facing "an almost formless element" seemingly at odds with any imposition of order. Once immersed, however, the internal workings become apparent: "infinite variety and infinite repetition," an indigenous order functioning at each level of the roughly fifty narrative types identified. The result is a collection in which, more self-consciously than in other national collections, motifs echo repeatedly from tale to tale, both in terms of the usual generic groupings—three siblings, proliferation of events in sets of three, gifted youngest child—and on the level of individual functions carried out by a limited variety of methods. The uncanny image of the buffalo head is thus repeated with variation in the form of the "Invisible Grandfather," and the unravelling of a story using the device of an overheard retelling is achieved by the subtly varied means of a talking lantern, lamp, and knife ("Wormwood," "The Count's Sister," "The Dead Man's Palace"). Within individual tales Calvino repeatedly draws attention to "near-geometrical logic and linearity," often structured around the aforementioned

central image and nearly always comprising groups of three: the
Italian "Frog Prince" variant passes effortlessly from the traditional set of three sons and three wives through a trio of tests,
pausing at each point with a singular image ("The Prince Who
Married a Frog"), while "The Love of Three Pomegranates"—
identified by Calvino, following Thompson, as of probable Italian
origin—is structured not only in terms of triads but also as a cycle
of transformations grouped around the core images of blood and
water, red and white (for Calvino, "a series of metaphors strung
into a tale" [xxviii]).[14]

This is familiar territory given a knowledge of folk narrative indexes, to which Calvino alludes in passing, and of Propp, at least
some of whose work had been translated into Italian by the 1940s.
Nevertheless, Calvino makes repeated reference to these aspects
of the tales, at times annotating them in the manner of a set of experimental fictions. If this suggests the possible influence of early
structuralist texts, the allusions to variety, repetition, logic, and
above all geometry, can equally be read as an instance of the extent
to which the categories of structualist narrative grammar can serve
to articulate, in metaphorical terms, the surface effect of reading
such tales. As with the two other generative potentials suggested
above, Calvino's post-Romanticism identifies something specifically Italian in these features, despite his stated awareness of the
European tale as a generic form and of the interrelation of national
traditions. Yet given the retrospective insights provided by subsequent events—in this case, his association with the Oulipo group
and its focus on the potential of restrictive models—we can spot
a distinct inclination in this direction. The notion of "potentials"
which has ordered my reading of specific aspects of *Italian Folktales*
is obviously adapted from the methodology of the Oulipo group,
although to make such a comparatively loose analogy is markedly
at odds with the avowed mathematical precision of much of the
group's output. Placing these two areas together—within the same
library—is potentially productive of a more fruitful reading of
Calvino's fictional texts than one dictated simply by the frame-

work of twentieth-century (folk)narrative studies. The common link is the twin notion of invention within convention: the inventive potential of convention. Calvino detects the implicitly formulaic construction of narratives within the folktale tradition, a process that can be compared with the Oulipians' various attempts to codify as formulae a range of artificially imposed constraints, the potentials contained within which remain immanent.[15]

The group's first manifesto, written by cofounder François Le Lionnais in 1962, highlights the "two principal tendencies, oriented respectively toward Analysis and Synthesis." The former is defined as the investigation of "works from the past in order to find possibilities that often exceed those their authors had anticipated," while the latter is "a question of developing new possibilities unknown to our predecessors" (Le Lionnais 27). Read within the context of Calvino's oeuvre, we can see the complete text of *Italian Folktales* as a product of both analysis and synthesis, to the extent that the tale tradition is both rediscovered—"we belonged to a tradition," as Oulipian Jean Lescure writes (36)—and the formerly unrealized results of this transposition constitute a new synthesis or range of potentials: an historically contingent ideological reading, a highly visual conception of fantasy grounded in a form of realism, and the tradition of a narrative mode based on the variation and repetition of limited units.

While undoubtedly a critical imposition, the importance of such an organizing principle is that it helps to conceptualize the forms in which the tale manifests itself in Calvino's fictions. Calvino does not rewrite specific tales in the manner of the various feminist revisions I discuss in my final chapter. Only occasionally does he use specific folkloric motifs in an easily identifiable intertextuality, and he rarely signals any influence with referential titles or parodic hints.[16] In the essay-lecture project which was left unfinished at the time of his death in 1985, he returns to the folktale in the section dedicated to "Quickness." It is worth quoting at length, not least for the self-awareness Calvino displays with regard to *Italian Folktales* as post-Romanticist in orientation:

> If during a certain period of my career as a writer I was
> attracted by folktales and fairy tales, this was not the result of
> loyalty to an ethnic tradition . . . nor the result of nostalgia
> for things I read as a child. . . . It was rather because of my
> interest in style and structure, in the economy, rhythm,
> and hard logic with which they are told. In working on my
> transcription of Italian folktales as recorded by scholars of the
> last century, I found most enjoyment when the original text
> was extremely laconic. This I tried to convey, respecting the
> conciseness and at the same time trying to obtain the greatest
> possible narrative force. ("Quickness," *Six Memos* 35–36)[17]

What Calvino draws attention to are predominantly abstract elements: rhythm, logic, structure; they are ideas—albeit ideas redolent of a particular intellectual climate—and it is this notion of
the idea of the folktale that I wish to place alongside that of the
generative potential as a means of reading Calvino's own reading
of the tradition.[18]

While this concept has been suggested by other interpreters,
I approach it here via the example of music—an approach sanctioned by Calvino's aforementioned association with Berio—in
particular the music of the pre-eminent composer of the twentieth
century to have been involved with and extensively influenced by
folk music, Béla Bartók.[19] The relations between the influence of
folk music on Western art music and of folktales on literature are
manifold and would constitute a separate study, yet some aspects
are particularly pertinent to Calvino, most revealingly the ways
in which folk music can be used in composition, which tend to be
more easily quantifiable (and have been far more extensively discussed) than in the analogous appropriation of the folktale in literature. Bartók's defining essays on this subject clarify the three possibilities: firstly, the taking over of an existing folk melody with the
addition of a new accompaniment, ranging from a piece in which
"the accompaniment, introductory, and concluding phrases are of
secondary importance" to one where "the melody only serves as a
'motto' while that which is built around it is of real importance";

secondly, works in which "the composer does not make use of a real peasant melody but invents his own"; and thirdly, works in which there is no direct melodic link, real or invented, but rather new music "pervaded by the atmosphere of peasant music" ("The Influence of Peasant Music on Modern Music" (1931), *Béla Bartók Essays* 341–44).[20] The equivalent of these categories in literature would be the various forms of contemporary retellings of folk narratives—the contemporary treatment acting as the variously pitched accompaniment, in the musical sense, to the reciprocally transformed traditional material—and new works of fiction modelled in some way on aspects of, ideas of, the folktale.

Bartók's compositions, taken as a whole, exhibit all of these procedures—indeed his musical development can be charted according to the manner in which the influence of folk music is evident at any particular point—while Calvino's work tends largely towards the latter categories: towards the idea of the material rather than the material itself. The formative early years in the careers of both writer and composer involved direct exposure to folk traditions, with Bartók collecting music in the field and Calvino working to produce *Italian Folktales*, although only Bartók went on to maintain a close link with this material at first hand, as he worked to produce important studies and editions of Eastern European folk music.[21] The subsequent influence of this early exposure is obviously varied and there is a danger of over-simplification, particularly in the case of Calvino's more sporadic and diffuse use of folk material. Yet it is broadly true to say that the elements of the folk traditions seep more deeply into the texture of the writing or composing over time, as demonstrated by Calvino's intermittent return to the folktale in his essay writing. Bartók made a point of the fact that none of his original works used pre-existent material, but within these works the potentials of his chosen regions of folk music are rigorously expanded, in explorations of specific rhythmic patterns, melodic intervals, and tempi. Similarly, I have isolated analogous folktale-related ideas and potentials pertinent to Calvino and it is in the Bartók literature that these are best articulated. Accounting for this process of osmosis involves reference

to material "assimilated and transcended," "transformed," "trans-
muted," and "refracted."[22] The first two of these adjectives are
taken from the writings of Pierre Boulez, a contemporary and acquaintance of Calvino in Paris. Jean-Jacques Nattiez comments
that Boulez's relationship with the past in his compositions, and
with Bartók in his role as conductor, is another instance of the
preference for abstract idea over actual material: "[h]e never turns
to the past to borrow actual stylistic ideas, but rather to learn about
principles—not the manifest style but the idea on which that style
is based" (17–18). Similarly, Berio has spoken of his relationship
with folk material as categorically not based on authenticity: "it
is not my intention to preserve the authenticity of a folk song.
My transcriptions are analyses of folk songs"; "I do not quote folk
melodies but I do use certain folk techniques and procedures" (Berio 148 and 150).[23] Certainly, Boulez in particular goes one step
further than Calvino along the path of distillation and abstraction, but again these examples borrowed from analogous work in
music help to clarify the processes of assimilation and refraction.

Nevertheless, it would be disingenuous to limit my argument
to an imposed set of categories, and just as there are a number of
pieces by Bartók which invent relatively simple folklike melodies
(the most straightforward example of his second method for the
compositional use of folk music), so in Calvino there are clearly
identifiable ways in which texts relate to the folktale on a similarly
empirical level. Calvino is above all a writer of tales—*racconti*—
and this alone can be interpreted as a turning away from a dominant European tradition of novelistic writing based on the extended realist narrative and its attendant psychologically complex
characterization. The narrator of his story cycle, *If on a Winter's
Night a Traveller*, comments that "[l]ong novels written today are
perhaps a contradiction: the dimension of time has been shat-
tered, we cannot love or think except in fragments of time" (8).
Paradoxically, one alternative narrative model potentially suitable for articulating a sense of contemporaneity is the folktale in
its various written manifestations: a short, apsychological narrative collected as part of a cycle or anthology. Calvino's early career

consists mainly of a series of tale projects, collected and reorganized in 1958 as *I racconti*, and variously published in English as, for example, *Adam, One Afternoon* and *Marcovaldo*.[24] The first of these is a series of largely unconnected tales, while the latter uses the form of a collection built around a theme, idea, and character, and thus stands as a variant on the story cycle that figures so prominently in Italy's narrative heritage. Calvino went on to write variations on this structure in the cosmicomical stories, *Invisible Cities*, and *The Castle of Crossed Destinies*. The works that are manifestly not influenced by the folktale, indeed which are not identifiable as narratives in any sense—those equally Calvinoesque pieces of phenomenology that focus on the detailed unravelling of precise moments of time and on a description of the workings of a mind faced with the randomness of external stimuli—even these texts are presented in anthological form, as short pieces grouped in a collection (in particular, the early selection, partly from *I racconti*, *Difficult Loves* [Gli amori difficili, published separately in 1970], and Calvino's final completed text, *Mr Palomar* [Palomar, 1983]).

If this practice demonstrates a turning away from the form of the novel, Calvino's characters are similarly unnovelistic. From the early tales, through the trilogy *Our Ancestors* (with the possible exception of Cosimo, *The Baron in the Trees* [Il barone rampante, first published in 1957]), to *Cosmicomics* (Le cosmicomiche, 1965) and *Invisible Cities*, the multifarious characters are on the whole little more than figures: to borrow terms from Lüthi's phenomenology of the folktale, they tend towards the "depthless," the "abstract." Reflecting the conceptual influence of structuralism, they enact roles in the manner of the actants described by Greimas (Subject/Object; Helper/Opponent), a fact highlighted by the repeated structuring of characters in binaries, as is the case in the folktale: from the literal binary of the good and bad Medardo in *The Cloven Viscount* (Il visconte dimezzato, first published in 1952) to the conceptual binaries of Marco Polo and Kublai Khan in *Invisible Cities*, and the Reader and non-reader (Irnerio) in *If on a Winter's Night a Traveller*.[25] This effacement, or rejection, of "personality" is also carried through to Calvino, who casts himself very much in the role of the anonymous tale-teller drawing on a store of past materials rather than the author striving for the subjective expression of originality. Again, while this of course reflects contemporaneous critiques and historicizations of the author and the author function, it might equally be viewed as a self-conscious turning towards the idea of the narrator as artisan, the tribal storyteller who serves as the emblem of "Cybernetics and Ghosts" and whose role Calvino assumes in retelling his set of Italian folktales.

First Idea: Tradition and Ideology

The first of the generative potentials is what I have termed the ideological aspect of the continuation of a tradition: the idea of writerly engagement or commitment as embodied in the use of a particular form or model. Such an idea can be compared with the feminist revision of the fairy tale which I consider in chapter five. In each case it is the historical specificity of the model or canon of narratives in question that is influential, the perceived social and cultural provenance of the tales, as much as their content or form. As with Bartók's use of folk materials within the freighted framework of post-Romantic European art music—a practice which has led to his problematic status within normative histories of such music—there is an element of cultural leveling involved in the choice of the folktale as source material, an implicit rearrangement and relativizing of cultural hierarchies. For Angela Carter and Margaret Atwood the rediscovery of forgotten or silenced aspects of the genre is thus on a par with new readings of canonical interpretations, and with retellings. Such interactions are obviously strongly contingent on historical circumstances and this is especially evident in the case of Calvino's engagement with the folktale.

I referred earlier to the influence of Gramsci's writings on intellectual debates in the new Italian republic. For Calvino, the postwar years were a time of overt commitment, a direct result of his, and his family's, experiences of occupation and partisan resistance in their region of Northern Italy, and he has written of his attempts in subsequent years "to grasp the meaning of the terrible traumas I had lived through, especially the German occupation" (Weaver 29).[26] In 1947 he joined both the staff of the Turin-based publishers Einaudi and the Communist Party, remaining a member of the latter until 1957 when, in the wake of Kruschev's acknowledgment of the realities of Stalinist rule and immediately subsequent to the invasion of Hungary in 1956, Calvino formed part of a significant exodus—estimated at up to 400,000 members—from what was generally perceived to be an Italian Communist Party in thrall to the Soviet Union.[27] He wrote in many different guises during this period, including articles for the Communist daily paper *L'Unità*, and from 1959 to 1967 he coedited and contributed to the journal *Il menabò di letteratura*, with Elio Vittorini, establishing a link with journalism that was retained throughout his career. These articles deal with the effects of industrial change, both on the individual and on culture, in particular the political and environmental effects of the "economic miracle" of the late 1950s and the 1960s, and roughly coincide with what in retrospect stand as Calvino's most explicitly political works: *A Plunge into Real Estate* (La speculazione edilizia, 1957), *Smog* (La nuvola di smog, originally published in *I racconti*, 1958) and, a little later, *The Watcher* (La giornata d'uno scrutatore, 1963).[28] Together with his first novel, *The Path to the Nest of the Spiders* (1947), these works can be read alongside the contemporaneous neorealist cinema of Vittorio De Sica (and his scriptwriter Cesare Zavattini), Luchino Visconti, and Roberto Rossellini, as much for their similarities—an often austere concentration on postwar material conditions—as their differences.

It was in the metropolitan centres of Turin, Milan, and Rome, under the influence of Cesare Pavese (who wrote a prescient review of Calvino's first novel) and especially Vittorini, that Calvino engaged with contemporary debates concerning the role of the writer in the new Republic—a Republic potentially more unified (by anti-Fascism) in the immediate postwar years than at

any other time in its short history as a nation-state. Such debates
included the need to sustain the energies generated by the unifying struggle against Fascism and for these to be channeled into
a new aesthetic that spoke to and represented a broad range of
the population, including what he was to call the various "Italys
previously unknown to literature": the need for engagement, civic
responsibility, and education. Calvino aired these issues in a number of essays written throughout the period. One of the themes
repeatedly examined is the need both for new forms of writing and
for the classics of Italian literature to gain a wider readership.[29]
Calvino undertook the related project of a new and representative volume of Italian tales for Einaudi in the mid-1950s, and
as such it can be placed alongside his recasting of Ariosto's *Orlando Furioso*, episodes of which were linked with modern prose,
written by Calvino, for a national radio broadcast in 1968 (subsequently published in 1970).[30] In keeping with the early popularity
of *Italian Folktales* among young readers and in Italian schools—
demonstrated, according to Gore Vidal, by the schoolchildren
present at Calvino's funeral in 1985—two of his earlier works
soon became school texts: an illustrated edition of *The Baron in
the Trees* was published by Einaudi two years after its first general
publication, in its "Libri per ragazzi" series, and in 1965 it appeared
in an abridged and expurgated version, annotated and introduced
by the Calvino-anagram Tonio Cavilla.[31] *Marcovaldo*, perhaps
the most overtly childlike of Calvino's fictions, also appeared in
the illustrated Einaudi series in 1963, and subsequently in several
school editions.

This urge to popularize—or, indirectly, to create a national children's literature, the lack of which Gramsci felt to be significant—
is embodied most clearly in the shared heritage of the folktale
tradition, a tradition which Calvino introduces in *Italian Folktales*
as a record of the struggles of real people, passed on through the
anonymous but active participation of the narrator. He first encountered this form of narrative—communal, memorial—while
engaged with the Garibaldi Brigades in the Ligurian hills, and it
informs several early tales depicting brief incidents in the lives of

partisans and peasants. In the 1964 preface that he wrote for a reprint of his first novel—a tentative, questioning retrospective view that demonstrates the problems faced by Calvino in amply doing justice to the complexity of both the partisan experience and the immediate postwar environment—we can detect the influence of his exposure to a tradition of storytelling as a means of understanding the links between historical context and fictional narrative. Calvino writes of "a book born anonymously from the general atmosphere of a period," the sense of manifold possibilities felt in the early days after the war: "[w]e were face to face, equals, filled with stories to tell; each had his own; each had lived an irregular, dramatic, adventurous life." Hence the general "rage to narrate" that linked this community "in a varicoloured universe of stories":

> so anyone who started writing then found himself handling
> the same material as the nameless oral narrator. The stories
> we had personally enacted or had witnessed mingled with
> those we had already heard as tales, with a voice, an accent,
> a mimed expression. During the partisan war, stories just
> experienced were transformed and transfigured into tales told
> around the fire at night. . . . Some of my stories, some pages of
> this novel originated in that new-born oral tradition, in those
> events, in that language. (*Path to the Nest of the Spiders* v–vi)

This is carefully pitched and demonstrates the extent to which the idea of oral narration, and particularly of the oral narrator, a figure who recurs throughout Calvino's fictions, was a concern even prior to the folktale project (hence influencing Calvino's conception of the latter). If this idea was later used as a means of experimenting with narrational forms and processes, it serves here as an element in the casting of literature as a shared, active, and potentially unifying cultural presence. The novel itself—detailing the exploits of the mischievous orphan Pin, who, after stealing a gun from a German soldier, becomes involved with a mountain partisan unit of no distinction—refers to various groups of storytellers: the locals from whom Pin picks up scurrilous fables (7); the "storytellers at fairs" from whom, speculates Pin, originated the "wild hunting song" he sings (79); and the legendary partisan Red Wolf, the subject of tales himself, who narrates his exploits with the group "following the story breathlessly" (126–27). Calvino depicts the circulation of tales and the easy flow between fact and fiction, the creation of a "new-born oral tradition." Similar groups occur elsewhere, such as the families of workers whom Cosimo encounters in the forests in *The Baron in the Trees*, and on whose tales told round the evening fire he eavesdrops (*Our Ancestors* 136–37); and in "The Dinosaurs" (*Cosmicomics*), Qfwfq, the one remaining dinosaur, listens nervously to "stories of the dinosaurs, legends handed down from generation to generation," ritually told by "the New Ones" (100).

The popularizing of a tradition or the building of a new, genuinely popular culture, the appeal to children and the representation of peasant life, the stress on the links between teller and audience and the idea of a shared store of both popular and literary material: each of these can be seen as generated out of the idea of the folktale as an alternative narrative form, suitable for the embodiment of a shift away from prewar divisions and prewar literary modes and for sustaining the impetus and values of the unifying opposition to Fascism. The stress is on the group, the community, whether in the shared heritage of *Italian Folktales*—a national heritage that nevertheless acknowledges regional diversity and the hybridity of tradition—or the shared experiences of partisan resistance. Yet in this first period of Calvino's career the tale also serves as a rough guide to individual morality, an exemplum, specifically in the form of the emblematic hero or heroine facing a hostile environment. In his 1955 essay "The Marrow of the Lion" (Il midollo del leone), conceived while at work on material for the tale collection, he explicitly links a belief in literature as "an active presence in history, in literature as an education," with the fable or folktale: "what interests us [contemporary writers] above everything else are the tests that man passes through and the way he overcomes them," as depicted in "the most remote fables: the child abandoned in the woods or the knight who must overcome ferocious beasts and spells."[32] In the Italy of the 1950s this is the worker facing the necessary shift from a rural to an industrial society brought about by the postwar economic boom, and demonstrated in the migration of millions of Italians from the country to the city and from the South to the North, the committed individual facing up to the legacy of the war and of the Mussolini years, and, indeed, the writer attempting to maintain the postwar impetus for change and renewal. If this sounds slightly overstated today, it should be remembered that such issues were very much part of the intellectual climate of the time, as demonstrated repeatedly in Calvino's essays—essays which differ markedly from those written from the mid-sixties onwards and which highlight the seriousness with which the question of the relation between writer and society was viewed.

The quest-and-test structure of the majority of folktales serves as an example of heroic perseverance in the face of multifarious obstacles, including inequality. The triumph of the unassuming peasant is a recurring theme in *Italian Folktales*, perhaps most paradigmatically in the form of either the fearless confrontation—the self-explanatory "Dauntless Little John"; the perennial peasant cunning, a means of frustrating the more learned ways of the world, as seen in the wonderfully crafty devices of "The Peasant Astrologer," Gàmbara, "who was no astrologer, but a peasant and therefore cunning"; or in the equally wily means of the impoverished cobbler, "Tabagnino the Hunchback," "as crafty as the Devil himself." The equivalent figures in Calvino's contemporaneous fictions are the folkloric Pin and Marcovaldo, both of whom face a hostile environment, whether an adult world or a modern city confusingly at odds with rural codes. Despite their differences, both characters view their environment through the eyes of tradition. As a defence against his incomprehension and fear, Pin repeatedly reads events in terms of fairy tales: thus a partisan couple become "a gnome and his wife living alone in the middle of the wood," with Pin "their adopted son" who talks to the fairies. The pivotal moment in the boy's initiation is his witnessing of the killing of the partisan unit's mascot, Babeuf the hawk, after a dimly perceived sexual encounter (the familiar rites-of-passage themes of sex and death), and it is indicative of Pin's anomalous imagination that while burying the hawk he daydreams that it is still alive and that he could "follow it as they do in fairy stories, walking over mountains and plains until he reached an enchanted village in which all the inhabitants were good" (120). I discuss the roles of Pin and Marcovaldo in more detail with reference to the second set of ideas, but the fact that Pin's imagination is at least partly defensive, a means of avoiding the world, is indicative of Calvino's unsentimental attitude to the folktale in these works. He takes the conventional device of a central character facing a challenge but rejects the traditional benign conclusion. The exemplum lies in the act of facing the obstacle, of engaging with the environment, rather than in the generic triumph of luck, cunning, beauty, or virtue. While he functions as the modern equivalent of the "dauntless Johns" of the folktales, Marcovaldo is repeatedly unsuccessful in his attempts to make the city in his own pastoral image, and the formal and thematic parallels serve to foreground the denial of the traditional folktale dénouement.

Yet the fact that the above constitutes merely a partial reading of the interaction between tale and new fiction in these texts is indicative of the multiple potentials the tale and the tale tradition held for Calvino. His subsequent development was away from overtly political literature, as carefully demonstrated in the preface later added to his first novel. While this shift in emphasis was partly brought on by what many saw as the failure to build on the ideals of the Resistance and a gradual disillusionment with Communism, it can also be related closely to a growing interest in the fantastic elements of the folktale and other forms of fantasy fiction, which sat awkwardly with what was generally thought to constitute a literature of engagement (some form of socialist or critical realism)—as demonstrated in the negative reaction in Communist circles to Calvino's first major shift in this direction, *The Cloven Viscount* of 1952. That a folkloric form of magic is present in the first novel (noted at the time by Cesare Pavese) is evidence of a pre-existent bias towards a different mode of writing, retrospectively detectable in the most engaged texts, whether it be the far from unambiguous Kafkaesque environments of *The Argentine Ant* (La formica argentina, 1952) and *Smog*, or the startling passing reference to Little Red Riding Hood in the bleak tale of *The Watcher* (70), novellas which distantly echo the pitting of individual against environment evident in the more folkloric works.

Second Idea: Singular Fantasies

It is important to note that these texts, the nearest Calvino came to the neorealist style of the time, adopt an always questioning, disturbing attitude to political commitment and never lapse into overt eulogy or critique. They question the notion of political engagement itself and it is these questions that Calvino sought to answer in his own work by turning towards a more autonomous literature. Within the context of the interpretative framework I am using, we can identify the second potential of the folktale—the idea of fantasy—as a means of attaining the critical separateness from literature as political commentary that Calvino sought. As demonstrated in Calvino's reading of the folktale tradition, this potential involves a highly visual form of fantasy, built around singular images and framed by the everyday, thus suggesting two points of connection with the ideological potentials I have discussed. Firstly, the idea of an historical tradition is maintained in a fantasy environment often rooted in a specific period, despite the blurring of the boundaries between the two realms; secondly, the primacy of the image as the elusive center of the narrative is a means of allowing literature to retain a distance from critical or political appropriation, an otherness apparent in the dystopias of the aforementioned novellas. (I am still referring here to the works of the fifties and sixties. The simultaneous writing of two types of fiction, one predominantly realist, one predominantly fantastical, but with elements of each in both, is indicative of the bias in Calvino's writing mentioned earlier. While the fantasy element develops in the later works, it is less grounded and thus the categories imposed here are less applicable.)

Italian Folktales is artfully structured to demonstrate the regional voices that constitute the putative commonality of a collective folk narrative heritage. It tends to be out of the distinctive features of a particular area that the fantasy element develops and Calvino opts when possible for the most vivid variant in order to highlight this local flavor. Similarly, his early folkloric fictions are distinctly localized and located, certainly compared with the abstract settings of his later work, and this is most noticeable in the representation of the mountainous countryside that stretched behind his family's home in San Remo on the Italian Riviera, as it existed before the intervention of postwar building projects (the disastrous environmental effects of which are repeatedly bemoaned). This environment provides Calvino with a real-life parallel to the forest-and-sea settings of the Italian tales, and thus continues the interaction between landscape and narrative that he reads as intrinsic to the folktale. The autobiographical exercise "The Road to San Giovanni" (La strada di san Giovanni, written in 1962 but unpublished until 1990), carefully describes the Ligurian landscape of the author's childhood, where the peasant communities still populated the forested hills and through which he often walked with his father. The latter appears in retrospect to the metropolitan son as a true "woodsman," a "hunter," walking for miles "without ever leaving the woods, forcing open the path before him, that secret path that only he knew and that went across all the woods there were" (The Road to San Giovanni 8–9). We can detect echoes here of the continuous path of trees that maintains Cosimo in The Baron in the Trees, and Pin's unique secret knowledge of the path to the nest of the spiders. This first novel, together with the partisan tales from this period, are steeped in the woodland environment. Calvino writes of turning away from the coastal town of San Remo towards the surrounding countryside: "I ventured along the muletracks over the sedge-covered hills, up to where the woods begin, pines first, then chestnuts, and so I had gone from the sea . . . to the tortuous valleys of the Ligurian

Pre-Alps" (*Path to the Nest of the Spiders* viii–ix). Hence the often idyllic descriptions of the partisan unit's camp in the forest and Pin's dreamy wanderings, depicting "the fusion of landscape with people" that Calvino retrospectively, and perhaps nostalgically, believed to have been embodied within the Resistance as he experienced it.

What Calvino takes from his exposure to the Italian tale, however, is the potential for using this setting as the necessary grounding for elements of fantasy: a vivid environment, such as the folkloric Ligurian hills, in which the mystery and enchantment of a folktale represent merely a burgeoning or magnification of existing geographical features. This is noticeable in *The Baron in the Trees*, in which there are no specific magical elements but rather a realistic depiction of a system of inhabitable trees stretching throughout the area and across the border into France—much the same as that imagined in the above quotation from "The Road to San Giovanni," and which Calvino describes in the introduction to the trilogy which includes this text as "a kind of apotheosis of vegetation." In *The Path to the Nest of the Spiders*, Pin climbs a cherry tree when he is hungry, a fleeting image tinged with the boy's fantastical interpretation. He wonders if the tree has grown there by magic, and evoking memories of folkloric motifs, imagines his spat-out cherry stones as a path to be followed either by Fascists or his lost companion, Red Wolf (47). Developing this image a little further, we have the scene in which the Baron Cosimo, surrounded by cherry trees, senses them as anthropomorphically alive: "cherry trees talk"; "[h]e was on the lowest boughs, and felt all the cherries above weighing down on him . . . as if, in fact, he were on a tree with eyes instead of cherries" (*Our Ancestors* 103–4). Of course, the trees are populated by a gang of Pin-like fruit thieves, but the fleeting image is nonetheless magical—more so because of its transitoriness—and demonstrates the blurring of boundaries between real and imagined.

Calvino's theme of nature as fantasy, or of nature as the link between empirical reality and the fantastic, figures repeatedly in his early works. In *The Cloven Viscount*, the first text of his eventual trilogy, the central image of a man split into good and bad halves carries over into the animal world: the bad Medardo leaves a trail of halved nature in his wake: pears, melons, frogs, mushrooms, while the good Medardo repairs the wings of birds broken by his other with bandages, splints, and wax. The narrative plays with the liminal, locating the reader on the borderline between two worlds, and it thus appears logical within this "fantastically natural" locality that, in reaction to the final duel between the two halves of the Viscount, nature turns against itself in the form of self-consuming worms and self-destructive magpies. This is fantasy as anthropomorphism, a technique rooted in the folktale, where malign forces appear in human form and animals assume the role of helpers. In Ovidian acts of transformation, Calvino repeatedly blurs the boundaries between animal and human, on the one hand including animals in the human drama of *The Cloven Viscount* and on the other describing humans in animal terms, as in the depiction of Cosimo as cat, lizard, owl, bat, swallow, or in the enigmatic animalesque players in the fleeting meeting "seen in the Canteen" (*Adam, One Afternoon*). Calvino was himself described by Pavese as "squirrel of the pen," for his ability to treat the seemingly weighty subject of the Resistance with a lightness of touch, and just as Pavese identified the source of this in the use of the folk or fairy tale as model, so Calvino's anthropomorphism is a case of allowing the style or idea of the tale to permeate his narratives. This shift from technique to principle is tacitly referred to in his description of the original tribal storytellers: "[e]very animal, every object, every relationship took on beneficial or malign powers that came to be called magical powers but should, rather, have been called narrative powers, potentialities contained in the word, in its ability to link itself to other words on the plane of discourse" ("Cybernetics and Ghosts," *Literature Machine* 5). Charged with excessive anthropomorphism in the later collection of *Cosmicomics*, Calvino replied that it is "an absolutely basic literary procedure . . . linked to one of primitive man's earliest explanations of the world: animism," proceeding to link this motif in his work with his lack of interest in the novelistic

modes of psychological verisimilitude and introspection ("Two Interviews on Science and Literature," *Literature Machine* 33–34).
This is a prime example of the dialectic of the traditional and
the experimental, resulting in a historicist conception of innovation: in this case, the deployment, at a particular juncture, of
traditional material and forms (always already read). In Calvino
the seemingly incongruous mix of the anthropomorphic and the
apsychological can be read as the assimilation of specific folktale
potentials, employed in the construction of new narratives.

The idea of nature as a bridge between the real and the imaginary, and as a means of rooting the imaginary, also figures in
the urban environment of Marcovaldo, whose tales develop the
theme of the incongruous rural outlook suggested in the character of Pin. The fact that Calvino uses the folkloric Marcovaldo as,
in part, an elegiac critique of the inefficacy of the pastoral tradition in contemporary Italy, as well as a symbol of what is lost in
the inexorable rush to modernization, illustrates the complexity
of his assimilation of the folktale. Again, the analogy with music
is telling: whereas composers such as Bartók's compatriot Kodály
or the English Vaughan Williams treat the archaisms of folk music
as relatively unproblematic within the context of their new compositions, Bartók actively, and dialectically, uses the past to shape
the new, and vice versa.[33] Hence the role of folk music in his work
as, in part, an alternative, both to the tonal system of the Western classical tradition and to Schönberg's serialism, conceived as
the sole authentic route out of the harmonic impasse of late Romanticism. It is the synthesis pursued by Bartók and Calvino that
makes their use of folk material a genuine intervention in a tradition rather than a set of elaborate, even nostalgic borrowings
which ignore the anachronisms that separate the traditional from
the contemporary.

Marcovaldo is the last of Calvino's natureboys and girls, characters who populate his early landscapes and whose childlike view-
points generate the fantasy in the narratives. While this could
be a case of simple, unproblematized transplantation, Calvino
sets them either in enigmatic snapshot narratives, devoid of the

moral certainties of the folktale (as in the early short stories), or in historically precise periods in which the contemporaneity of the writing provides the distancing effect (as in the trilogy, which becomes more metafictional with each novella). Pin is the first of these figures and his folkloric credentials are impeccable: an orphan—"the little boy of Long Alley"—with one sister, who works as a cobbler's apprentice and whose name suggests that other folktale-influenced character from Italian literature, Carlo Collodi's Pinocchio.[34] I have referred above to the manner in which Pin's imagination injects his environment with a magical element, an anthropomorphic presence, symbolized in the nest of the spiders itself, "his own kingdom in the river bed," where "he can weave strange spells, become a king, a god." This untrammeled imagination working in tandem with nature is similarly evident in the figure of Liberoso in "Adam, One Afternoon," characterized in the tale as an extension of the animal kingdom whose inhabitants he offers as gifts to Maria-nunziata, and which ultimately cross the ontological boundary between animal and human to invade the man-made sanctuary of her kitchen. There is also Pamela, the clever goat-girl in *The Cloven Viscount*, whose communality with nature is suggested by her ability to converse with her animal friends and to read the signs left for her by the bad Medardo. Pamela is very much the descendant of the wise women that populate *Italian Folktales*: the eponymous Wise Catherine or the brilliantly inventive Mariuzza in "The Three Chicory Gatherers." Each of these characters is closely bound up with their natural environment—literally in the case of another, the Baron Cosimo—and the passage into the fantastic occurs in the narrative as a result of a lack of the blinkering effect of the modern adult world, just as the magic in *Italian Folktales* is often an expression of natural forces in tune with those who work and live with the land: what Calvino refers to as "the force of reality which bursts forth into fantasy" (*Italian Folktales* xxxii).

Marcovaldo is a natureboy out of place and grown up, an unskilled laborer brought down from the hills and into the city; a

Don Quixote faced with a new industrial landscape and, concomitantly, with increasingly conspicuous consumerism.[35] Yet nature still serves as the predominant bridge into a world imbued with magic, and while Marcovaldo possesses "an eye ill-suited to city life," he is attuned to the remnants of nature in the city, never missing "a leaf yellowing on a branch" or "a fig-peel squashed on the sidewalk" (*Marcovaldo* 1). His discoveries make the world seem "suddenly generous with hidden riches," and it is these riches that constitute the quiet fantasy of the tales, exactly analogous with those that fuel Pin's daydreams. Snow falling on the city appears to him as "a friend" and he lives for a morning in his own world of remade snow paths, houses, and cars, finally becoming a snowman himself before blowing the whole new world away with a mighty sneeze; a bout of fog encountered as Marcovaldo leaves the man-made fantasy world of the cinema leads to a series of escapades in a parallel world "capable of containing all continents and colors," and in a delicious twist lands him on a plane bound for Bombay, after beginning the evening watching a film set in the forests of India; and alone in the city in the holiday month of August, he sees "a whole different world: streets like the floors of valleys, or dry river-beds, houses like blocks of steep mountains, or the walls of a cliff" (98). The most revealing moment in this context occurs in "The Forest on the Superhighway," in which Marcovaldo the urban huntsman sets out to find wood to burn for his poverty-stricken family; yet it is his son, Michelino, spurred on by his reading of fairy tales, who discovers what he takes for a forest in the form of billboards at the side of a road. The primary locus of the writer's childhood and of the folktale itself is seen in a misread symbol of consumerism, and Calvino creates a neat web of connections between the real and the imagined, between a son who misreads his environment as a result of his reading of tales and a father who accepts this discovery because of his propensity to see in the city what are presumably echoes of childhood.

These wonderfully subtle tales have been collectively read as an elegy for traditional ways, a representation of the impossibility of successfully implanting a rural naiveté in the metropolis.[36] Marcovaldo causes, and gets himself into, trouble through his actions; he remains poor, disenchanted, stoically immune to immersion in city life. He is the last of this type of character in Calvino's fiction and marks a shift away from settings grounded in a recognizable rural landscape. Yet this shift is not towards the new realities of a mass consumer society, despite hints to this effect in the final tales of *Marcovaldo*. In the trilogy we can detect a developing awareness of, and interest in, the mechanics of storytelling, first in the figure of Cosimo, whose inveterate oral narrations are passed down as text by his brother, and then in the metafictional interventions of Sister Theodora/Bradamante in *The Non-Existent Knight* (Il cavaliere inesistente, first published in 1959). It is as if the implications of using an oral form in written texts begin to generate a more experimental approach, just as the alternative tonal system of folk music(s) can disrupt the Western art music context within which it is implanted.

Thus another way of conceiving of the representation of nature in *Marcovaldo* is that it is made to function in purely formal terms: nature plus city, the two materials which figure synecdochically in the majority of the tales, results in a discontinuity, a misapprehension, and it is this disjunction which forms the narrative itself. For all their childlike appeal, and for all that we can read them contextually as the expression of the rise and wane of two distinct ways of life, they appear (within the library of Calvino's oeuvre) as miniature formal experiments in which the influence of the tale is further refracted through the irreversibly self-conscious lens of the written narrative. As well as using a writer-narrator, Calvino hints at this direction, in the early works, with passing reference to the written nature of his orally influenced texts. In *Marcovaldo*, the city lost in snow appears to have been "replaced by a white sheet of paper," and the final tale ends enigmatically with Marcovaldo back in the forest, watching a wolf on the trail of a hare; suddenly the hare disappears, leaving an expanse of snow "white as this page." The forest of the imagination thus becomes the forest created by the writer, as if the self-consciously invented environment is the only one in which such a mythical world can still signify, the only route by which the pre-novelistic can meaningfully function without recourse to the security of nostalgia. In "The Road to San Giovanni," written in 1962, Calvino compares his father's urge "to scramble up through woods and wilderness" with his own "to plunge into a labyrinth of walls and printed paper," and this passage from the literal to the purely fictional, via the realist fantasies of the early nature works, takes us to the abstractly uprooted forests of *The Castle of Crossed Destinies* (*The Road to San Giovanni* 17); to the fertile "storyspace" suggested in *If on a Winter's Night a Traveller*, conceived as "a forest that extends in all directions and is so thick that it doesn't allow light to pass" (105–6); and ultimately to Mr. Palomar's lawn, "an artificial object, composed from natural objects, namely grasses," whose purpose is "to represent nature" in the form of "the substitution of the nature proper to the area with a nature in itself natural but artificial for this area" (26).[37]

The forest, one of the paradigmatic folktale topoi, becomes a space within the text rather than the sign of an essentially mimetic narrative, a Calvinoesque interpretative variation on the traditional function of the folktale forest as a locus for unexpected encounters and transformations; the route of the path from peasant hut to royal palace that embodies the idea of an enclosed world with its own internal logic, and which is thus analogous with the self-contained environment of the text. Yet while the idea of fantasy as exemplified by the folktale provides a stepping stone away from the strictures of the polemical narrative, as was demonstrated above, it also provides a means of initiating experiments with the tale form, via another aspect of the tradition: the limpid, vivid image. All of Calvino's early texts contain a distinguishing visual image, as do many of his canon of folktales ("Buffalo Head" and "The Canary Prince," to choose just two examples). In at least two works he appears actually to borrow images from these Italian tales: from the "The Cloven Youth" and "The Three Dogs" in *The Cloven Viscount*, and from "Invisible Grandfather" in *The Non-Existent Knight*. More commonly, however, he composes an original image which functions as the unifying center of the text:

the title image of *The Path to the Nest of the Spiders*, which acts as a leitmotif throughout the novel, or the environments constructed from snow, fog, cats, and soap-bubbles in *Marcovaldo*.

These singular images provide the focus, literally and metaphorically, for the narratives, around which events are arranged, and it is this idea of a single structural or ordering device that is developed in later texts such as *Invisible Cities* and *The Castle of Crossed Destinies*. In the introduction to the trilogy, Calvino comments that the common thread linking the three novellas consists of the fact that "they have a very simple, very obvious image or situation as their point of departure," an image that is developed "according to its own logic," extending around it "a network of meanings" (*Our Ancestors* ix). The idea of the logic of the folktale is one of the aspects stressed by Calvino—I referred earlier to his singling out of "style and structure," "rhythm," and "hard logic"—and it is the logic of the conspicuous visual image that he returns to again and again, nearly always in relation to the fantastic. In an essay on fantasy written in 1969, he stresses "the order of things" produced by "an extraordinary event," the result of "a different logic based on objects and connections other than those of everyday life" ("Definitions of Territories: Fantasy," *The Literature Machine* 72–73). In *Six Memos for the Next Millennium* he writes again of viewing the world "with a different logic," of the image "charged with meaning" and "implicit potentialities" as the primary source of a story which is "the union of a spontaneous logic of images" (7, 89, and 90). The sharply defined and singular image in the folktale is a sign of the historical provenance of these narratives in primarily oral cultures, in which, as Ong has written, thought and expression are "situational" rather than "abstract," with frames of reference remaining "close to the living human lifeworld" (49). What we see in Calvino's narratives is the assimilation of this mode of thinking with images as both a means of organization and a source of polemically enigmatic singularity. The image retains an otherness and hence an autonomy beyond the reach of interpretative appropriation.

Third Idea: A "Geometry of Story-Telling"

Again, it is the generative *idea* of the singular image that is assimilated in the resultant fictions, just as it is the idea of fantasy or of a narrative model with a particular social and cultural significance. Calvino views this idea of the image in the narrative not purely, but certainly partly, in formal terms, and it coincides with both his discovery of the abstract, structural potential of the folktale tradition and with a growing interest in the mathematical precision of scientific discourse as another alternative narrative model, one equally rooted in the Italian tradition of Galileo. The structural logic of the image is part of the idea of form suggested by immersion in the "submarine world" of the folktale: infinite variety and infinite repetition, a geometrically precise proliferation of narratives based on a restrictive form in the style of that explored by the Oulipo group. Writing about the mode of narration embodied in the oral tradition, he thus refers to a "geometry of story-telling" ("Notes Towards a Definition of the Narrative Form as a Combinative Process" 93), which appears to have been formative in the early stages of what became a "fondness for geometrical forms, for symmetries, for numerical series, for all that is combinatory, for numerical proportions" (*Six Memos* 68). While the gradual shift from a mimetic to an abstract landscape reflects the influence on the material of the folktale of a specific literary context, this formal aspect sees the influence working in reverse and is a salient reminder of the always historically determined means by which one tradition is read by another.

The first and perhaps most pervasive sign of this influence can be seen in the use of variation and formula, both of which are absolutely fundamental procedures in Calvino's fictions, and here again the comparison with Bartók and folk music is helpful. Variational forms are ubiquitous in Bartók's original compositions, a propensity rooted in his close study of specific folk music traditions: "[a]n inclination to variation, an aspiration related to the ever-changing, shaping nature of folk music that creates some-

thing new from what it finds, and derives its creative force precisely from leaving nothing untouched" (Szabolcsi 19–20).[38] That
both Bartók and Calvino should locate this aspect in the two genres of folk composition demonstrates again the two-way influence
between the modern and the traditional, and the historically determined routes by which the latter can appear strikingly contemporary. This is not folk music or the folktale as the font of
wistful simplicity but rather as a potentially innovative model of
compositional technique.

The corollary of the variational principle is the formula,
whether as theme and variations, in which the formula is both the
theme and the principle itself, or in terms of conventions of theme
or structure which occur repeatedly within a narrative. As with
the image, the use of formulae has its roots in primary oral cultures.
It was Milman Parry's work on Homer in the 1920s and 1930s that
first proved—to the extent that definite proof is possible—what
had until then been only speculatively suggested: that the *Iliad* and
the *Odyssey* were constructed using formulae, at the level of both
epithet and description, and of theme. They were the expression
of an oral method of composition in which to narrate was to use
flexible pre-existent materials to best effect: to sing a tradition.[39]
The folktale, as an originally oral narrative, exhibits both of the
aforementioned modes of variational form, most overtly when
sectioned off into a national collection such as *Italian Folktales*.[40]
The tale as a unit can be variously conceived, whether as an over-
arching structure which either re-establishes a disrupted status quo
or establishes a new order (as is suggested by Greimas in *Structural
Semantics*, at the end of his structuration of Propp's schema); or,
more locally, as a core set of relations: girl, boy, helper, opponent,
marriage, and so on to whatever level of specificity. In terms of formulaic schemes, the tales are built up, on both a deep and surface
level, from a set of pre-existent units which can be read as formulaic narrative bricks or thematic knots, the individual occurrences
of which are variations on the theoretical potential embodied in
the tradition itself. As Calvino discovered—prompted in part,
no doubt, by readings of Propp—the folktale tradition can be

conceived as a system (*langue*) comprising individual instances (*parole*), and given his later fictions and essays, along with his membership of Oulipo, we can perhaps imagine how startling the discovery of such a non-theoretical system must have been. Once again, we have an instance of a reading of the folktale reflective in part of structuralist geometries—hierarchies of narrative level, generative combinations, and formulae—that are themselves the product of generalized theoretical extrapolations of the folktale's perceived formal properties. On the one hand, Calvnio's creative use of this conceptual framework can be seen implicitly to be of a piece with post-structuralist critiques of structuralism's figural repertoire. Yet as the above references to Bartók and Berio suggest, such a framework has been seen repeatedly throughout the twentieth century as intrinsic to the folktale and folk music. Rather than read the resultant fictions as structuralist in orientation, my argument here is for a recognition of the folktale itself, or rather a set of ideas of the folktale, as primary model.

As early as *The Baron in the Trees*, Calvino interpolates the variational tendency of oral narration, at this stage simply in Biagio's repeated reference to the fact that the account of events he is presenting is only one of the versions told by his brother Cosimo, who increasingly fuses fact and fiction with respect to his adventures. However, it is in the later fictions, roughly from *Marcovaldo* onwards, that the principle of variation figures as the basic generative device. *Marcovaldo* itself exhibits this in a nascent, less overt form, as was suggested earlier with reference to the combinatory nature of the text. As presented in the final version, it appears to echo the Italian framed novelle tradition, following its subtitle—*The Seasons in the City*—in comprising four groups of five tales, one for each season in each section. While not rigidly distinct, the tales of each season share a common theme: a seemingly benign nature that turns out to be harmful in spring, an imaginative misreading of the city in winter, and so on. However, the collection also appears as a prototype of the formulaic model used in Calvino's next work, *Cosmicomics*. The majority of the short narratives commence with a general opening paragraph, followed by an illustration of the theme in the life of Marcovaldo which tends to undercut the optimism of the introduction with a turn towards bathos. This introduction-tale structure, a miniature theme and variation or general formula and individual expression, occurs more explicitly in *Cosmicomics*, in which each narrative is prefaced by an italicized extract from an unattributed scientific text, stating a general principle. This forms the ostensibly objective, factual formula which generates the gossipy relation of events from the infinitely varied life of Qfwfq. Similarly, *Invisible Cities* consists of nine sections, each framed with an italicized passage focusing on the relationship between Marco Polo and Kublai Khan. The individual "tale" is the description of a city and the cities are divided between eleven themes, each of which occurs five times in what can best be described as a self-proliferating curve. The formula is the mathematical model and the theme is the city, with the resultant text a set of theme and variations.[41]

The *Castle of Crossed Destinies* concentrates on the formulaic aspect, using two packs of tarot cards as the materials which generate the tales; again, the tales can be seen as variations—on the cards and of each other—as a single card can figure differently in several tales according to the pattern of appearance. *If on a Winter's Night a Traveller* uses the formula of a recurring main story intercut with a series of first chapters from texts read in this main story, although again the variational or formulaic aspect is thematic as well as structural. The author himself has written of the fact that early critics of the novel failed to spot the deliberate formulaic use of a core set of relations in the extracts, which thus form variations on an unstated theme. Furthermore, the twentieth publication of the Bibliothèque Oulipienne was a text by Calvino, in the form of a series of Greimasian semiotic squares, demonstrating the precise triangular structure of the twelve chapters of the main story itself.[42] Finally, there is *Mr Palomar*, in which the influence of the folktale extends simply to the idea of the numerically structured cycle, and to the proliferation of triads: three sections, each split into three internal sections, the latter of which in turn consist of three parts. Each of these parts is an exploration of varying degrees of three modes of experience: descriptive (centered on an object); narrative (a mixture of self and object); and meditative (centered on the self). The collection thus moves systematically through the various stages, from an attempt at pure description to pure meditation.

This chronological description of the structures of Calvino's later works is necessary simply to highlight the abstract, formal aspects of the texts. Few contemporary authors, other than his fellow Oulipians (most obviously Raymond Queneau and Georges Perec), have used structure in such an overtly mathematical fashion, and this has lead to the plethora of critical unravellings which follow the path of structuralist narratology. While this influence is pervasive, Calvino nearly always appears to be mindful of the roots of narratology in the folktale tradition, prompted no doubt by his immersion in that environment at an early stage—his experience of the principles of narrative grammar as unformulated practice—and it is this that makes him an emblematic figure here. What characterizes the influence of the tale during this period of Calvino's work is an abstract idea. Nowhere is the use of this concept for understanding such influences more appropriate.

While I referred earlier to his depiction of the communal nature of traditional narration, what is apparent in these later texts is a simultaneous interest in the opposite ends of the chronology of traditional narrative itself: pre-verbal communication and literary representation. While both can be interpreted in terms of narratology this would be to miss the continuity, the rootedness of what can appear solely as experimentalism. I similarly referred earlier to Calvino's interest in the tribal storyteller, as exhibited in the essay "Cybernetics and Ghosts," which begins with a thumbnail sketch of the first signs of narration: a combination of proto-phonetic sounds as a means to express the variety of daily life. In *Invisible Cities* the community of teller and audience is reduced to narrator and listener, in the form of Marco Polo and Kublai Khan. When the former first arrives he is unable to communicate via a common language and so turns instead to "gestures, leaps, cries of wonder and of horror, animal barkings or hootings," or alternatively to objects as a means of expression (20). His accounts are thus pantomimes which the Khan must interpret, never knowing if the interpretation matches the intent. Yet once they can communicate with words they both find themselves reverting to the original gestures, as both more precise and evocative, and the result is an exploration of narrative means and narrative slippage, from the manifold implications of silence to the chessboard as a replacement for words (a common structuralist analogy). Calvino explores communication as a process of creative (mis)interpretation and the narrator as bricoleur, the latter of which is intrinsic to the folktale's restrictive repertoire. Again, in *The Castle of Crossed Destinies* the travelers are struck dumb after their passage through the forest and, before the intervention of the tarot as a means of expression, resort to "gestures, grimaces, all of us like monkeys" (50). Narrative may be primordial but we do not necessarily perceive a narrative as intended. The tales in this cycle are the writer's interpretation of what he sees, often openly uncertain, and the process mimics the transcription of tales from oral sources, albeit at one further remove on either side: the narrators are forced to act as preverbal bricoleurs and the interpreter is armed with an explicitly contemporary understanding of narrative.

To interpret these signs of ostensibly primitive narration as an integral part of the influence of the folktale would be specious, yet it forms the complement to another recurring element in these texts: the influence of the written form of the tale, the end of a developmental process which began with the gestures and grimaces of unselfconscious communication. The idea of the folktale in Calvino's later texts is predominantly that of the tale in its written form, the form in which he encountered the tradition and which is the primary, if not sole means of access for Western readers. What Calvino explores in the later works are the potentials of the written tale as it appears in the literary cycle which, in the texts of Basile, Straparola, and Boccaccio, forms such a prominent part of Italy's narrative heritage: the internal cycle of narratives and the unifying frame tale, both of which can be read as structural formula and generative device, and which extend the processes of variation and formula evident within the tales themselves.[43]

In one of several essays devoted to *Orlando Furioso*, Calvino comments on Ariosto's method of composition, involving continual updating and expanding between editions, together with the possibility of a sequel. While Calvino views this "process of expanding from the inside, making episodes proliferate from other episodes, creating new symmetries and new contrasts" as intrinsic to *Orlando Furioso* itself, it also describes his own method of composition, particularly in the earlier works ("The Structure of *Orlando Furioso*," *Literature Machine* 163). Several of the individual tales in *Difficult Loves* and *Marcovaldo* originally appeared in *I racconti*, and were only later collected into individual volumes. In the case of *Marcovaldo*, what appears as a carefully conceived structure was actually imposed at a later date, and this process of collection over time, moving towards a structurally compact text, is characteristic of Calvino's propensity for anthological collections of short narratives, grouped or unified in some way to appear as a single text, most strikingly in the aforementioned 1958 collection *I racconti*. Charting the various paths leading to and from the fifty-two narratives which constitute *I racconti*, Franco Ricci sees a trend in Calvino's career towards the reworking and reassembling of earlier material: "[l]ike the primitive 'bricoleur' Calvino seemed content with the material of his closed, yet ever expanding, universe," and he refers to the compilation of *Italian Folktales* as an influence on the contemporaneous construction of *I racconti* itself (*Difficult Games* 16).

The various methods of organization in these early texts are also experiments with what is generally considered to be the more open structure of the Indian or Middle Eastern story cycle, examples of which tend to expand according to whatever narrative material comes to be included (as demonstrated in the history of the *Arabian Nights*). Hence the provisional structures of *Cosmicomics* and *Difficult Loves*, in which the implicit thematic or motific frame remains open to additions. Yet as the form of *Marcovaldo* demonstrates, Calvino was also drawn to the geometrical precision of the European framed collection, in which the tales are of a specific number and the structure is explicitly closed. Such features are exemplified in the *Decameron* and *Il Pentamerone*, which display their written status most overtly in the use of the frame as a means of limiting the text, presenting it as a self-contained object rather than an open anthology. This is particularly true of *Invisible Cities*, which follows the design of European story cycles in its numbered set of tales or cities (or invisible tales, as opposed to the visible tales of *The Castle of Crossed Destinies*) interspersed within the frame of the Khan and Marco Polo. *The Castle of Crossed Destinies*, Calvino's metafictional version of a narrative system such as he discovered in the folktale, echoes the framing scenarios of the *Decameron* and *Piacevoli Notti*, with its isolated group telling tales as a means of both identifying themselves and passing the time. It also parallels the traditional story cycle in the way motifs pass from tale to tale, interpreted according to context and representing a common store of units—in this case the tarots themselves, the potential story materials from which are realized the individual combinations. Interestingly, the reaction of Calvino's narrator when faced with the potentialities of the tarot system—what Calvino calls "a machine for constructing stories"—echoes the reaction of Calvino himself when faced with the seeming chaos of the folktale tradition: initial unease followed by a manic determination to chart the path of variants and versions.

Both *Invisible Cities* and *The Castle of Crossed Destinies* depict the relationship of teller and listener, albeit in the exploratory form of card player and interpreter, mime act or chess game. This written representation of oral narration follows the norm of the framed cycle, paradigmatically enacted in the relationship of Shahrazad and King Shahrayar in the *Arabian Nights*, a relationship echoed in Kublai Khan and Marco Polo, the former of whom commands Polo to "[t]ell me another city." References to the *Arabian Nights* abound in *If on a Winter's Night a Traveller*, the latter of which is a mix of the precision of the Italian story cycle with the looseness of non-European models. Chapter six of the main narrative refers to the legend of "an old Indian known as the Father of Stories," thought by some to be "the universal source of narrative material," the "reincarnation of Homer, of the story-teller of the *Arabian Nights*" (114); in the final chapter, the fifth of the readers which "the Reader" encounters in the library has collated "the various editions, the translations in all languages" of the *Arabian Nights*, yet has been unable to discover the ending of a story read as a child which he believes to be included in a particular version of the cycle (250–52). He proceeds to recite what he knows of the beginning of the story, which reads as one of the Harun al-Rashid tales, and the last line completes a sentence comprising the titles of the extracts the Reader has come across on his journey, thus completing a set of interlocking units—title: sentence; fragment: novel. What this elaborately demonstrates is that, in the last of Calvino's cycles, reading has taken over from listening, with the relationship between text and reader assuming the place formerly occupied by narrator and listener or audience. The performative aspect of oral narration, encoded in the folk-loric story cycle as a remnant of both the source of the narratives enclosed and the still socially prevalent means of narration, has been replaced by the silent and solitary act of reading, and the multitude of tellers, tales, and listeners that populate the *Arabian Nights* (and the Italian cycles) has become a proliferation of textual fragments and readers, including the Reader and us, the readers.

This is the final example of the assimilation of an idea from the folktale, and just as the potential embodied in the repertoire of tales is explored in the texts preceding *If on a Winter's Night*, so this "hyper novel" (Calvino's phrase) is the apotheosis of the textuality of the framed story cycle. It takes to an extreme the folk-loric cycle's reliance on the structural order imposed by writing, discarding the vestigial signs of orality. The frame, traditionally used to introduce and continue the relationship of teller and lis-tener(s) which generates the internal narratives, is replaced be the search for an increasingly elusive novel, and the internal tales form the first-chapter extracts of a disparate group of novels that become confused with the original text (which is, of course, *If on a Winter's Night*). The embedded-tale form is transformed into a series of potential novels-within-novels, and Calvino highlights the replacement of orally told tales with written texts by slyly resetting elements from the *Arabian Nights*. In the webs of intrigue encountered while searching for the missing novel, reference is made to the wife of a Sultan who has an "insatiable passion for reading," and who imposed a clause in her marriage contract stipulating that she "must never remain without books that please her." This obviously subverts the relationship at the heart of the *Arabian Nights*, with the Sultana as a contemporary Shahrazad empowered by her curiosity, just as the latter was empowered by her manipulation of the King's desire to hear the rest of each story. In the same way that the tales within the *Arabian Nights* include several Shahrazad-like characters who implicitly comment on the frame tale, so the Sultana is an echo of the main Shahrazad figure in Calvino's novel, the second Reader, Ludmilla. While Shahrazad tells the tales that form the cycle, Ludmilla appears to generate the genre of novel which appears as an extract by nominating the particular type of fiction she prefers in the preceding chapter of the main story; as the preference changes each time, so the extract follows. In addition, the description of the desired narrative given by Ludmilla always reflects in some manner on *If on a Winter's Night* itself, which certainly engenders "that sense of bewilderment a novel gives when you start reading it" (28); appears at times to "have as its driving force only the desire to narrate, to pile stories upon stories" (89); and succeeds in suggesting the putative objectivity of a text "where all the mysteries and anguish pass through a precise and cold mind, without shadows, like the mind of a chessplayer" (153).[44] A final twist is provided in the fact that the fragments all read as loosely generic exercises, including various types of thriller, thus setting up a duality between the overtly literary frame and the more populist fragments. The same is true of the Italian frame cycles, where the frame is either predominantly literary, as in the *Decameron*, or a literary adaptation serving as a frame, as in *Il Pentamerone;* while the internal tales are, at least in the case of

Basile, essentially folkloric. Once again, Calvino extracts a formal principle from the traditional material, extending it to function as a model—a model which adopts the historical discontinuities and anachronisms as a means of both inventing a new form and reinterpreting an old one. What was originally a means of unifying disparate material, of giving a semblance of order to a miscellany or anthology while allowing for addition and subtraction, provides a blueprint for a dismantled narrative form which both exhibits its workings and slyly evokes the tradition—both folkloric and novelistic—of narrative wholeness and closure. The experimental potentials of the premodern are recast as the historically resonant traditional basis of a postmodernist narrative.

In the final part of Mr *Palomar* reference is made to the manner in which an event occurring at a particular moment in the course of a life can change the shape of both what is to come and what has already passed, so that "events are arranged in an order that is not chronological but rather corresponds to an inner architecture" (111). My reading of Calvino has been explicitly organized according to such an inner architecture, initially suggested by the event of the production of *Italian Folktales,* and subsequently provided by the shifting presence of the folktale in his fiction. The tendency is to see such a presence everywhere and to allow the event to order all interpretation. I have attempted to avoid a simplistic ordering through the use of the notion of the folktale as a set of ideas or potentials, different aspects of which were pertinent to Calvino at different times, but which should not be seen as in any way cumulative. If the idea of the tale had a particular ideological weight in the fifties and early sixties, this was partly a result of historical particularities; if the mode of folkloric fantasy subsequently became more influential, this was in line with a shift in Calvino's interests, away from the neorealism of the early works towards a more idiosyncratic and autonomous conception of literature and the status of the writer; and if the formal symmetries of the tale tradition held sway over later works, this was in part the result of a further conceptual shift in relation to the production of literature, influenced by contemporaneous literary theory, science, and philosophy. In the fictions that result it is futile to suppose that the presence of the tale was dictated solely by other literary or social influences, or that these influences were themselves altered by the primary influence of the tale. The process is always reciprocal and to suggest otherwise is to veer into psychological biography, a form which Calvino himself regarded with suspicion.

Yet there is no doubt that ideas of the tale provide a means of viewing Calvino's disparate fictions en masse, as themselves a provisional anthology, just as the extremely varied influence of folk music on the original compositions of Bartók provides a means of charting other shifts in his technique and compositional intentions. If this means imposing some form of order, as in the trio of ideas explored here, then justification can be at least partly sought in the fact that the search for order and the fears this generates figure as leitmotifs in the texts themselves. Hence the various models of the later fictions; the reworking of previous tales into collections; the interest in science as a discourse which plays, in an exacting way, with models of the universe; and hence, perhaps paradigmatically, Mr. Palomar, a character always attempting to order, and thus understand, his environment, yet as interested in his failings—the process of the search—as his successes.[45] Calvino himself expresses his desire for order when faced with the ocean of stories in the Italian narrative tradition, and we feel his relief when order appears: not a limiting order but an order of combinations and permutations, a controlled proliferation in the Oulipian sense. It is tempting to see the tale itself as appealing to Calvino ultimately as a model of order, a tradition of narrative knowledge analogous with his other favored tradition of scientific knowledge; as a set of ways of knowing, expressing, and representing the world, which, like the models of Leonardo or Galileo, are interesting precisely because of their restrictive repertoire and archaic methods, suggesting the possibility of reinterpretation in new contexts. This is seductive but also a little glib. I prefer to leave it as a suggestion and use the loose framework of multiple ideas and potentials, which order the texts without undue neatness.

One reason for avoiding a perception of Calvino's narratives as models of order, as has been suggested by others, is that the metafictionality of the texts—the textual analogue of Palomar's critical self-awareness—undercuts the propensity of narrative to function as an ordered, disinterested medium.[46] Calvino repeatedly demonstrates the workings of his tales, from the frustrations with narrative representation expressed in *The Non-Existent Knight* to the teasing manipulation of our own readerly desire for closure in *If on a Winter's Night*. Narrative is itself an interpretation, always tendentious, yet it disappears in the representation of events and thus avoids being held responsible for its active presence. Calvino always holds narrative responsible, making its workings part of the story, and this is one of the reasons why the folktale can never sit unproblematically in its new historical and cultural context, never be for him a source of sentimental nostalgia but only a set of potentials to be worked through. It is this awareness of form as well as content that locates historically Calvino's attitude to the folktale, within a period in which narrative self-consciousness, including a knowledge of narrative as structure, has become a cultural dominant.

If reading Calvino's texts in this manner tends towards the explicatory rather than the agonistically analytical, this is partly a result of the sheer number of possibilities suggested by this particular act of creative appropriation, and partly because, as the above comment suggests, the reading is already tendentious. To concentrate on the traditional elements in a writer often held as quintessentially postmodern is to make a point that is central to this book. Calvino's personal library, his choice of a tradition, is indicative of an historically contingent experimentalism that is rooted in narrative history, albeit a history in which the dominant narrative model of the nineteenth century is polemically demoted. As is demonstrated by the frequent reference to his work in the writings of those other authors who have variously, and contemporaneously, turned to the folktale, Calvino offers a paradigm of such an influence.

Chapter 4

Narrative Turns

One of the aims of this book is to demonstrate the empirical fact of the folktale's multifarious presence in a significant range of recent fiction. The nature of this ostensibly anachronistic pairing of narrative types, most vividly worked through by Calvino, is the implicit question posed in the individual chapters. While each chapter attempts to establish an individual contextual framework, based on various interpretative approaches to the tales themselves, it would be disingenuous not to recognize a common set of concerns arising from the choice of these particular models by these particular fictions (or indeed, theories). In turning now to look at John Barth and Robert Coover—and in the final chapter, at Angela Carter and Margaret Atwood—and in seeking to establish a specific framework within which to read their appropriation of the folktale, the question of postmodernist fiction looms—a question I largely avoided in the preceding chapter in order to attempt a tendentiously focused account of Calvino's fictions via readings of the folktale alone. By choosing a canon of writers and fictions influenced by the folktale I am tacitly aligning myself with a conception of postmodernist fiction—or of one aspect of postmodernist fiction—as a self-conscious return to narrative, one example of which is the juxtaposition of a metafictional concern with the mechanics of narrative and a renewed interest in premodern—or, more broadly, pre-nineteenth-century—narrative forms and their various descendants. The meeting of

folktale and contemporary literature is a particularly striking instance of a return to storytelling, in which the distilled narrative
form of the tale—the perceived formal aspects of which I have
detailed in the preceding chapters—takes precedence as model
over both the extended structures of the classic realist text and
the extension of the tradition of psychological verisimilitude in
the static, interior dramas of the modernist novel.[1]

The argument for a return to storytelling is ostensibly circular.
Strands of recent fiction show a marked interest in the folktale;
therefore one of the characteristics of postmodernist fiction must
be a revived enthusiasm for story, as demonstrated paradigmatically in the tales of Calvino. This notion of a return or revivifica-
tion is necessarily predicated on the idea of a prior turning away
from or dissatisfaction with narrative. It is in this sense that the
postmodernist literature I am describing can be defined against
its modernist predecessor. Modernism's self-image in part comprised a polemically expressed dissatisfaction with received forms
of representation—in the case of the novel, linear, teleological
narrative conceived as a vehicle for the putatively realistic representation of human dramas. Narrative is above all else meaningful,
to the extent that it orders its constituent events into a unified
whole of implicit cause and effect passing from beginning to middle to end. It progresses, suggests continuity. It is precisely this
self-evident meaningfulness that is variously shunned in canonical novels of high and late modernism. Continuity, linearity, and
psychological causality now vie with discontinuity, stasis, repetition, "spiraling," and uncertainty.[2] To characterize the cultural
production of an historical period with such broad strokes, and
on such a level of formal abstraction, is necessarily to marginal-
ize those figures that do not fit. In the case of modernism it is
also to adopt the aesthetic credo of a select band of polemicists.
Nevertheless, as David Trotter has argued, the descriptive function of the idea of modernism—as opposed to its evaluative or
causative function—is still useful, not least because it allows for
the construction of localized literary histories such as I am attempting here: not developmental or teleological accounts, but

histories of shifts in the theory and practice of particular elements (4–5).[3]

The network of discourses alongside and against which the modernist text set about constructing its image of itself and its adversaries has been variously laid out: degeneration, with its ever-attendant ideas, both conservative and radical, of gender and ethnicity; increased colonial unrest alongside aggressive imperialism; the perceived threat of a burgeoning mass culture, heralding not least the end of Victorian publishing practices; a growing concern with alternative non-linear formulations of experience as suggested by psychoanalysis. In relation to such discourses, the received notion of narrativity as articulated in the realist novel was increasingly mistrusted, viewed as a falsifying, restrictive, pejoratively gendered convention. One alternative source of continuity was, of course, sought in the allusion to ritual, myth, and religion, with the attendant hierarchical conception of tradition and culture. More specifically, a use of various traditional narratives as symbols of transcendence, paradigmatically expressed in Eliot's description of Joyce's "scientific discovery" of the mythic model in *Ulysses*: "It is simply a way of controlling, of ordering, of giving a shape and a significance to the immense panorama of futility and anarchy which is contemporary history. . . . Instead of narrative method, we may use the mythical method . . . a step toward . . . order and form" (177). What is noticeable is that myth is here conceived as an alternative to narrative itself, precisely because it transcends both the fragmented moment and the relentlessness of historical progress; and yet this is achieved with recourse to terms such as "control," "order," and "shape" that could equally provide a critique of narrative. The fractured surface of the modernist text, which, Eliot suggests, reflects the alienated banality of its historical context, is theoretically transcended, not through allusion to mythic narratives as narratives, but as symbolic signifiers of wholeness and tradition, the locus of meaning in the text.[4]

Such a reading of modernism's disavowal of conventional narrative order as symptomatic, concomitant with a yearning to recoup the loss through allusion to past orders, has been interestingly glossed by Northrop Frye in terms of an underlying cyclical movement in literary history. Distinguishing between myth—"[t]he most important group of stories in the middle of a society's verbal culture"—and folktale and romance—"the more peripheral group," Fry comments that when "the elite literature," regularly drawing on myth, is in decline, "literature enters a transitional phase in which some of the burden of the past is thrown off and popular literature . . . comes again into the foreground." Hence "popular literature in this sense indicates where the next literary developments are most likely to come from" (7; 28–29).[5] One tangential possibility that this allows is a localized view of modernist and postmodernist literature in terms of their respective appropriation of myth and the folktale, with the concomitant cultural associations carried by each of these related narrative stores. The notion of an over-burdened Western high cultural tradition has figured significantly in attempts to define a contemporary literary sensibility, most notably in John Barth's companion essays "The Literature of Exhaustion" (1967) and "The Literature of Replenishment" (1980), and one route out of this perceived impasse has been via the use of alternative models and forms, including popular narrative genres marginalized by the cultural agendas and neuroses of high modernism.[6]

It is against the particular facet of modernism's self-image as sketched above that a certain type of postmodernist literature can be productively defined. In addition, if fiction has reengaged with narrativity in the wake of modernist rejection, the theoretical framework within which such a return might be placed can be found in those alternatives to the post-structuralist critique of narrative, the latter of which is in many ways itself heir to the modernist position. Post-structuralist conceptions of the content of the form of narrative have sought to theorize its ideological function as a primary means of socialization and a mythicized representation of the real: "narrative is revealed to be a particularly effective system of discursive meaning production by which individuals can be taught to live a distinctively 'imaginary relation to their real conditions of existence'" (Hayden White x). One of the most persuasive readings of the return to narrative in recent fiction has been Linda Hutcheon's concept of "historiographic metafiction," according to which it is precisely the constructed, mythical nature of narrative—the fictiveness mistrusted in early twentieth-century literature and the interpellative action of narrative critiqued in recent theory—that is manipulated to explore our appropriation of history as story, our ordering of past events into meaningful, generic patterns.[7] Works of historiographic metafiction hardly deny the shaping and situating action of narrative, but rather seek to use it to explore how we construct versions of the past, via a process of what Hutcheon calls "postmodern de-naturalizing—the simultaneous inscribing and subverting of the conventions of narrative" (*Politics of Postmodernism* 49). It is precisely in a recognition of the human desire for narrative, the propensity to succumb to its seductions, that we find a common thread linking postmodernist fictions with a range of theoretical discourses in which narrative has recently been explored. It is the self-evident chain linking contemporary narrative theory, narrative fiction, and the narratives of the folktale tradition into which I wish to inquire, both here and in the following chapter on the fairy tale and feminism.

Hutcheon's proposed genre is of a piece with what the psychologist Jerome Bruner nominates as a "paradigm shift" in attitudes to narrative in the 1980s. Elsewhere, Hayden White refers collectively to postmodernism as "informed by a programmatic, if ironic, commitment to the return to narrative as one of its enabling presuppositions" (xi); Fredric Jameson, introducing the narrative-based argument of Jean-François Lyotard's *The Postmodern Condition: A Report on Knowledge* (La condition postmoderne: rapport sur le savoir, 1979), comments on "the way in which narrative is affirmed, not merely as a significant new field of research, but well beyond that as a central instance of the human mind" (xi; a view repeated by Jameson in *The Political Unconscious* [13]); and Paul Ricoeur, commenting on his three-volume study *Time and Narrative* (Temps et récit, the first volume of which was published in 1983) goes as far as to say that the reconfiguration of abstract time as human time conceived as the ultimate result of narrative "reveals that the meaning of human existence is itself narrative" (Interview 17).

The purpose of this thumbnail sketch is twofold: firstly, to point to areas of theoretical engagement with narrative other than that strain of post-structuralism in which narrative is the suspect presumed guilty; and secondly, to demonstrate a shift away from structuralism as the dominant model, and so to suggest a further context for the fictions I will be reading in what follows. As Andrew Gibson has argued, the "revisionist narratology" of the 1980s produced by the likes of Peter Brooks, Mieke Bal, and Ross Chambers, while influenced by parallel developments in theories of the self and of gender, remained tethered to the "dimensions" of "narratological geometrics" (7–8). A properly post-narratological narratology is to be sought elsewhere: for example, in postmodernist narrative theory, Lyotard in particular, and in Ricoeur's monumental defense of narrative. Rather than abstract grammars we are dealing here with a pragmatics of narrative and a metaphysics of narrative. The development of the various structural models of narrative was based on the abstraction of a narrative grammar (*langue*) from any particular manifestation (*parole*). This abstraction was in turn predicated on a spatial hierarchy of "deep" and "surface" levels, with the former representing the achronological core. As we have seen, it was the apparent underlying similarity of Russian fairy tales that led to Propp's morphology, which itself built on nineteenth- and early twentieth-century attempts to catalogue types or motifs repeatedly combined in folktale traditions. Yet this founding example of the search for similarity in diversity, a basic methodological procedure in the subsequent development of narratology, is also the root cause of the abstract nature of the structural model—a model divorced from the historical, social, cultural, and economic specificity of any single telling. While such an abstraction is absolutely intrinsic to the synchronic nature of structuralist schemata, the two-leveled hierarchy of narrative grammar has been critiqued on the grounds of an inability to bridge the passage from story to discourse.

Such are the issues raised by Barbara Herrnstein Smith in "Narrative Versions, Narrative Theories" (1981). Significantly, she uses the "Cinderella" tale type (510A in the Aarne-Thompson catalogue) to demonstrate the problems inherent in a narrative model predicated on the idea of versions of a deep-structural story, such as that referred to by Propp as the ultimate object of his methodology. The realization of "the archetype of the fairy tale not only schematically . . . but concretely as well. . . . Rejecting all local, secondary formations, and leaving only the fundamental forms, we shall obtain that one tale with respect to which all fairy tales will appear as variants" (*Morphology* 89). The ideal of such an ur-version is problematic because it is destined to remain an unrealizable abstraction, and because it unavoidably ignores the relation between such a narrative and its various manifestations; as Herrnstein Smith comments: "what narratologists refer to as the basic stories or deep-plot structures of narratives are often not abstract, disembodied, or subsumed entities but quite manifest, material, and particular retellings—and thus versions—of those narratives, constructed, as all versions are, by someone in particular, on some occasion, for some purpose, and in accord with some relevant set of principles" (214).[8] The multiple contexts and conditions at play within any narration will always work against a hierarchical structuration of narrative, and it is a varied recognition of difference as opposed to similarity, together with a concern for narrative *in the world*, that is common to a particular strain of recent work on narrative.

This recognition has been marked by a move towards a conception of narrative less as model than as act—the methodological framework of structural linguistics replaced at least in part by the "ordinary language" speech-act theory of J. L. Austin and by Wittgenstein's anti-totalizing theory of the "language-game"— and it has been concurrent with an increasingly widespread concern with the role of narrative as a tool of meaning-making, indeed as perhaps the fundamental human act of meaning. The contemporaneous work of Jerome Bruner provides an introductory example of this development in the field of psychology. Proposing narrative as "one of the most ubiquitous and powerful discourse forms in human communication," Bruner argues for a shift towards a "cultural psychology" which would focus on "the processes and transactions involved in the construction of meanings," and in which "the organizing principle is narrative rather than conceptual" (*Acts of Meaning* 77).[9] This obviously echoes Herrnstein Smith's representative call for a pragmatics of narrative that would include the historical and cultural determinants of each narrative act, and Bruner similarly draws on speech-act theory as suggesting a context-based pragmatics; indeed, like Herrnstein Smith, he argues for a recognition of the specificity of any story and any interpretation of that story—their basis in a network of norms. At the heart of Bruner's enquiry is the interaction between our assimilation and manipulation of narrative norms and procedures and the possibility that we are in some way predisposed to organize our sense of reality in terms of narrative. Bruner is convinced of such a predisposition, of the infant's "entry into meaning" via "a 'protolinguistic' readiness for narrative organization and discourse" (*Acts of Meaning* 67–98). He cites a related shift in psychoanalytic theory towards a notion of "the self as storyteller," "a constructor of narratives about life," represented both by Donald Spence and, more radically, by Roy Schafer, the latter of whom concentrates not only on the content of the narratives we can construct about our past and our selves but also on the specific narrative form of these versions: on "the self as a telling."

It is this suggestion not only of a narrative representation but a narrative construction and constitution of the real—what Bruner refers to as "narrative realities"—that ultimately justifies the positing of a "narrative turn" following in the wake of structuralism. Its relevance here is that it provides a particularly apposite and fertile context for the postmodernist fiction of Barth and Coover, if not for postmodernist fiction as a distinct literary mode. One of the characeristics of narrative nominated by Bruner is "diachronicity," the "irreducibly durative" nature of narrative that Lévi-Strauss and Greimas sought to demonstrate is the surface manifestation of a deep structural set of logical, differential relations. If we take this as the endpoint of a staunchly abstract narratology then it is possible to encapsulate the paradigm shift in this area by turning to Paul Ricoeur's *Time and Narrative*. Ricoeur's hermeneutics of narrative, concerned, like Bruner and Herrnstein Smith, with "the entire arc of operations" involved in the construction and reception of narrative, is based on what he terms the "healthy circle" of narrativity and temporality: "between the activity of narrating a story and the temporal character of human experience there exists a correlation that is not merely accidental but that presents a transcultural form of necessity" (*Time and Narrative* vol. I, 52). In defining this notion of the narrative act, Ricoeur, like Bruner, tentatively posits a "prenarrative quality of experience," an "inchoate narrativity . . . that constitutes a genuine demand for narrative" (74). Significantly, it is because Ricoeur conceives of the human experience of being-in-time as the ultimate referent of all narrative that, as with post-structuralist theories of discourse, he does not finally distinguish between history and fiction, a fact which correlates with Hutcheon's definition of historiographic metafiction.

Ricoeur's conception of the "necessity" of narrative is based on his account of the three stages of mimesis which enclose the arc of the narrative act, beginning with the fact that human actions and events are "always already articulated by signs, rules and norms . . . always already symbolically mediated." It is the implicit temporality in the mediated nature of human events that forms the "primary interpretation" or "prefiguration" of the material of narrative that is subsequently "configured" in the process of emplotment. The act of emplotment is "the operation that draws a configuration out of a simple succession" and confers a potential meaning on individual events by dint of their situation within the scope of a story, a meaning which is greater than that of individual actions or sentences. While narratology isolates this action and seeks to provide a synchronic model of its functioning, Ricoeur goes on to include the final stage of the arc, the "refiguration" of the narrativized time in the act of reading or listening.[10] This final stage of emplotment is possible because of the manner in which narrative time is related to our sense of experience, including our prior experience of narrative: "the intersection, therefore, of the world configured by the poem and the world wherein real action occurs and unfolds its specific temporality" (71). In other words, there is a constant passage between the three stages of mimesis, the act of emplotment completed in its reception, which is in turn enabled by the correlation between narrative and our prefiguring of experience (52–87).

As Hayden White comments, Ricoeur's study posits narrative not as a false representation, such as that suggested by the refusal of narrative in certain modernist texts, but as exactly the opposite. Ricoeur conceives of narrative as an "allegory of temporality, but an allegory of a special kind, namely, a true allegory" ("The Metaphysics of Narrativity," *The Content of the Form* 171). Such a justification, only sketchily summarized here, is the natural companion to the pragmatics of narrative suggested by Herrnstein Smith and Bruner, and represents the fundamental defense of narrative in recent times. Yet this is not to suggest that Ricoeur ignores the criticism of narrative as consolation, of the configuring act as an example of what he calls "the violence of interpretation." For Ricoeur, such an objection is rooted in the twin notions that our experience of time is innately fragmentary and that narrative is the imposition of a hermetically sealed order: "so long as we place the consonance on the side of the narrative and the dissonance on the side of temporality in a unilateral fashion . . . we miss the properly dialectical character of their relationship" (*Time and Narrative* vol. I, 72). Not only is the notion of a disordered, unformed experience of time historically specific—Ricoeur proposes it as "one of the features of modernity"—but the newly created whole of narrative includes within itself the possibility of gaps, "contingencies and reversals."

Narrative is again defended, and it is the idea of the irreducibility of this newly created whole that is narrative—what Ricoeur calls "the new thing"—along with the possibility of difference within this whole, that links Ricoeur's hermeneutics to the more radical narrative pragmatics of Lyotard.[11] As is now familiar, the latter is based on what Lyotard views as a decline in the efficacy of the "grand narratives" of Western culture, such as have organized dominant philosophies of history and progress. Within the context of what I, after Bruner, am calling the "narrative turn," the pertinent aspect of Lyotard's analysis lies in his conception of these metanarratives as the ultimate source of legitimation for the multiple individual narratives of which they consist: their ability to transcend the status of narrative itself and appear as self-evident "truth." What *The Postmodern Condition* (1979) advocates, with reference to speech-act theory and language games, is the proliferation of individual narratives—*petits récits*—that have no recourse to legitimation via a putatively non-narrative "truth" but rather function as individual, localized experiments, acts or events. This suggestion is made with reference to scientific experiment, which Lyotard opposes to the narrative form of knowledge prevalent in traditional societies to the extent that the former has historically had recourse to metanarratives as the ultimate legitimation of its particular "truths." Just as Lyotard, in *The Postmodern Condition*, advocates an open-ended form of scientific endeavor, with experiment for its own sake and on its own terms—the scientist as participant in a language game, the aim of which is the generation of ideas—so in the related dialogue piece *Lessons in Paganism* (Instructions païnnes, 1977), he discusses the decline of the grand narrative of Marxism in terms of the proliferation of local, human tales—"clouds of narratives"—attesting to "the intimate and infinite power of stories." Again, like Herrnstein Smith, and Bruner, Lyotard is concerned with "all the complicated relations that exist between a speaker and what he is talking about, between the storyteller and the listener, between the listener and the story told by the storyteller." Conceived in this way, narratives exist as localized events within a series of like acts, without recourse to prior or future legitimation, such that "rather than asking if that story is more or less true than any other, you should simply note that it exists, that it is the product of an almost invincible power to tell stories that we all share to a greater or lesser degree" ("Lessons in Paganism" 125). This obviously raises the specter of relativism, and Lyotard is aware that texts such as "Lessons in Paganism" and

The Postmodern Condition appear to succumb to the "transcendental appearance" of granting narrative a privileged position among the human discourses ("Universal History and Cultural Differences" 314).[12] However, the crux of the argument that Lyotard proposes lies in the performative aspect of narrative and its syntagmatic status—the figural force of the narrative event and its radical singularity, Ricoeur's "new thing," that cannot be reduced to any non-narrative meaning or "truth." In Bill Readings's terms, "[t]he particularity of narrative replaces the unified narrative of multiplicity," foregrounding not similarity or theoretical interpretation but rather specificity and difference (85).[13]

How this conception of narrative can be thought through to literature is not immediately apparent beyond its radically antitheoretical stance, its distrust of theoretical unraveling or appropriation. It certainly does not fit with any notion of a human predisposition to narrative, and yet it does display parallels with the singularity of versions suggested by a pragmatics of narrative and the human time of narrative suggested by Ricoeur. What is certainly surprising is that Lyotard has repeated recourse to the form of oral storytelling in traditional cultures as a means of demonstrating his "pragmatics of narrative knowledge," in particular the form of introductory address used by the Cashinahua Indian storyteller (*Postmodern Condition* 20–23).[14] Lyotard demonstrates how the storyteller, the listener, and the tale (including the traditional hero of the tale who, it is implied, was also once narrator and/or narratee) are authorized by specific reference to their status within a chain of previous narratives. The narrative performance is an enclosed, self-legitimating event, and no aspect of this event—tale, teller, or audience—occupies a position outside the chain of narration. Thus the point at which we implicitly think any narrative is grounded—the "reality" of the referent, the autonomous subjectivity or authority of the narrator—is denied or, rather, relativized in relation to each point in the chain (Readings 67).[15] What Lyotard tacitly appears to suggest—or what we can extrapolate from his analysis of this facet of oral storytelling—is that the oral folktale provides a model of narrative performance (although he does

not differentiate between oral folktale and myth, the latter traditionally has the status of a factual, sacred narrative, and is thus un-
suitable for Lyotard's definitely secular, fictional purpose).[16] Ong
describes the status of words in primary oral cultures as "occurrences, events" that have, by dint of their evanescence, a particularly close relationship with time, and which are necessarily
"agonistically toned" (31; 43–45). This certainly reflects Lyotard's
advocacy of "an agonistics of language," and indeed oral narration
could be said to have a paradigmatic status with regard to the performative aspect of narrative pragmatics, much as the similarity
in diversity exhibited by the folktale had for Propp. While the
use of such a singular example is extremely problematic—Lyotard
himself admits such an instance cannot be "universalized," despite his use of it on several occasions, and I am wary of appro-
priating it here given the need for specificity when approaching
non-European traditional narratives—it does suggest a link, albeit
tenuous, with the possibility that particular aspects of the folktale
might provide a model for a pragmatics of narrative in the same
way that they did for narratology.[17]

In "Lessons in Paganism," Lyotard adds further definition to the
model of chains of narratives suggested by oral performance, with
reference to the "serial" as opposed to "parallel" assembly of stories. In the latter, the "flow of stories" is always organized around
a particular narrator or subject, and the narratives are linked by
prior and repeated, implicit or explicit reference to a point which
by dint of this authority stands outside of the narrative chain. The
paradigmatic instance of this process, at least for Lyotard, is of
course the grand narrative or metanarrative. Conversely, in the
serial chain of narration, narrative is inescapable:

> With the serial assembly process, the trademark stamped on
> the stories disappears. . . . And in fact there is no reason why
> the flow of stories has to be explained in terms of an initial
> and identifiable impetus. . . . If you give it an origin, you are
> simply telling a story which takes as its reference another
> story. . . . The series, together with the artificiality of the

references, constantly undercuts the overweening pretensions
of origins. ("Lessons in Paganism" 144)

Thus the concept of the serial chain is one of mobility, of the
interchangeability of reader/listener, narrator, and narrated; it is
one of narratives framed by narratives, and of one displacing and
being displaced by another without any form of hierarchy. For all
Lyotard's dismissal of theoretical discourse and for all his attempts
to provide examples of such a process, it remains highly abstract,
prone to the aforementioned charge of relativism; and yet if we
twist the context—a twist certainly in the spirit of the concept—
have we not already experienced this model of serial narration
in the form of the folkloric story cycle? The cycles of the *Arabian
Nights* and Somadeva's *The Ocean of Streams of Story* certainly provide specific examples of strings of tales and tales-within-tales, in
which narratees become narrators and which are always already
embedded within a story. In the case of the wonderfully convoluted history of the Sanskrit cycle we witness the incorporation
of narrative groups into the text and the subsequent splitting-off
of segments. The same is true of the *Arabian Nights*, but here we
have an even more "open" text, not only incorporating existent
material but impossible, ultimately, to delineate in terms of content. Each recension has its own history, its own narrative, but
apart from the identification of a core cycle and frame, none can
ultimately be dismissed as spurious. Unlike more recent elaborately written cycles, such as Jan Potocki's *The Manuscript Found
in Saragossa* (Le Manuscrit trouvé à Saragosse, 1797–1815, in part
stimulated by a fondness for the *Arabian Nights*), the material of
the *Arabian Nights* is not traceable to a named narrator but only to
a possible first appearance and then to the oral tradition. Similarly,
the introductory main frame of Somadeva's cycle situates the text
of which it is a part within a chain of prior narratives.[18]
    Both the *Arabian Nights* and *The Ocean of Streams of Story*
include what John Barth refers to as "serial primary frames," strings
of tales-within-tales ("Tales within Tales within Tales," *The Friday
Book* 226); indeed, such cycles are implicitly predicated on the

premise that what appears as a framed tale can equally serve as a frame tale (as demonstrated earlier, these frames represent in part the residue of an oral culture). While the tale of Shahrazad and Shahrayar ostensibly functions as the ultimate frame for the *Arabian Nights*, it is introduced as a tale itself and closer inspection reveals it to be caught in a web of frames.[19] Again, this suggests parallels with a pragmatics of narrative in which a recognition of framing—the story of the story, in all its aspects—is fundamental, along with the concept of narrative as a social act, which is also an intrinsic element of the folkloric story cycle.

The other related shift in emphasis common to recent narrative theories is the breakdown of the dualistic story/discourse model and a recognition of the contextual singularity of any telling: in terms of Ricoeur's conception, the rootedness of narrative in time and thus in an always changing configuration of elements. Herrnstein Smith makes this point with reference to the "Cinderella" tale type, in terms of the impossibility of revealing an ultimate ur-version and the concomitant fact that all of the multifarious tellings have been produced at specific times, for specific reasons, and according to specific historical and cultural norms; while the similarities are easily proclaimed, the differences may ultimately tell us more about the tale told (210–18). What is interesting here is that, as with the story cycle and the frame tale, the model that the folktale traditions provides has, as earlier demonstrated, also been used in the construction of a structural model of narrative: a hierarchical model of units, levels, and versions. Thus, if aspects of these traditions can provide paradigmatic instances, or at least convincing and productive examples, of a working narrative pragmatics, it appears they can also be used to chart the shifting, yet continuing, emphasis and methodology in narrative theory. One way of viewing this continuity would consider the fact that while narratology seeks to provide an ahistorical and ultimately logical structure for narrative, it is limited by the specificity of its source material, by the fact that its attempt at universality is in fact rooted in the staunchly ahistorical formalist interpretation of preindividualistic, apsychological traditional material. Thus narratology can be shown to have its own history, partly attempted in my first chapter. Changes in narrative theory are a principal problem in attempting to map narrative models in modern literature.[20]

The reverse side of this continuity is indicated by the fact that aspects of the tale traditions considered here provide a means of moving away from classical narratology while retaining the insights it offers. Continuity is also suggested by the interest in folktales in recent literature—literature which demonstrates links with the "narrative turn" sketched above. Again, we have a three-way passage of interconnections between aspects of the tale traditions, narrative theory, and the contemporaneous literature. Just as Hutcheon's aforementioned grouping of historiographic metafictions seeks to explain the links between certain recent narrative theory and fiction in terms of concepts of history—both the questioning of the content of the form of traditional narrative history and the concomitant blurring of the fact of history and the fiction of literature in terms of the common use of narrative—so my reading of a suggested "narrative turn" partly in terms of the folktale emanates from the use of the folktale in narrative fictions which demonstrate a similar concern with their formal aspect.

John Barth, Author of the *Arabian Nights*

> Does *The Thousand and One Nights* constitute a work?
>
> —MICHEL FOUCAULT

To place the fictions of John Barth within an interpretive context such as that sketched above is a first step towards comprehending the sheer proliferation of storytelling that ultimately characterizes Barth's output, particularly since the late 1960s. Malcolm Bradbury refers to him as "the postmodernist as pure story-teller" (231), for whom, in the words of one of the author's own characters, "the only entertainment better than a story is half a dozen stories" (*The Last Voyage of Somebody the Sailor* 21). In his influential 1967 essay "The Literature of Exhaustion," Barth characterizes the fragmented minimalism of Beckett as the endpoint of a stylistic development after which "it might be conceivable to rediscover the artifices of language and literature" (*The Friday Book* 68), and he proceeds to define "linearity" as one of the benign characteristics, as opposed to falsifying conventions, of literature: "to be linear, even continuous, is not necessarily to be wicked" ("The Future of Literature and the Literature of the Future," *Friday Book* 163).[21] To this extent, his work is of a piece with a Ricoeurean aesthetics of narrative as that which "contributes to making life, in the biological sense of the word, a human life," "a life *recounted*" ("Life in Quest of Narrative" 20, 31). I am concerned here with the later fictions of Barth, beginning with the suggestion of a shift in concerns signaled by the 1968 short story collection *Lost in the Funhouse* and the interconnected novellas of *Chimera* (1972), and developed in the more characteristically extended narratives of *The Tidewater Tales* (1987) and *The Last Voyage of Somebody the Sailor* (1991). In terms of the folktale, Barth's interest lies predominantly in the third category suggested in my reading of Calvino, that of form, and of one form in particular: the story cycle. His fictions return repeatedly to the story cycle and the frame tale, both as a means of narrative organization—the structure most suited to the proliferation of stories—and as that structure which can best enact narrative multiplicity as a *thematic* concern. And it is the *Arabian Nights*, into the textual space of which Barth has written so much of his own fiction, that would appear to encapsulate, for Barth, the confluence of narration as formal device as well as moral imperative.

Despite his affiliation with a group of American writers once both lauded and chastised as cutting-edge fictionalists—"the Generation of '31," to borrow Jerome Klinkowitz's only slightly doctored categorization ("John Barth" 424)—Barth is a writer who would seem willingly to have accepted the nineteenth-century ideology of the novelist, with all that implies of tradition, craft, and career. Hence it is fitting for several critics recently to have identified what amounts to a "late" style or period in Barth's prolific output—again, with the attendant connotations of both culmination and significant break. Klinkowitz refers to Barth's "seven-book canon" (430), from *The Floating Opera* (1956) to *Letters* (1979), positing *Sabbatical: A Romance* (1982) as "a reconstitution of Barth's technique" (432); likewise, having appropriated Harold Bloom's "Map of Misprision" to chart the course of Barth's fictions, Patricia Tobin takes *Sabbatical* as the point at which Barth "set sail for the beyond of Harold Bloom that is the postmodern literature of replenishment" (119). Whereas Thomas Carmichael bases his reading on the identification of a shift in Barth's writerly concerns, suggested by *Letters* but most apparent in *Sabbatical* and *The Tidewater Tales* (331–32), Tony Hilfer sensibly breaks up the rather unwieldy "seven-book canon" into a first phase of "postmodernism as black humor" and a second phase of "postmodernism as metafiction," with *The Sot-Weed Factor* (1960) as the transitional text (109, 129). For Hilfer the works following *Chimera*, particularly *Sabbatical* and *The Tidewater Tales*, represent a falling off, and thus, again, some form of break, albeit one negatively defined (133).

Along with such periodizations we have what amount to revisionist readings of Barth which seek to redefine, if not critique, his standing as an experimentalist (in the case of Tobin this has included establishing the manner in which Barth's postmodernism can be defined against a Romanticist conception of "absolute originality"). To varying degrees, and true to the implications of a late style, this process has involved a reassessment of Barth in the light of the characteristics of these later works: while Carmichael finds in *Sabbatical* and *The Tidewater Tales* a "return to realism" (330) which significantly tempers the putative relativism of the self-reflexive narrative, "successfully transform[ing] the imperatives of formalism in the service of contingency, history, and possibility" (337), it is in Nicholas Birns's extended discussion of Barth's oeuvre that a reassessment proper takes place. Birns seeks to draw attention to the "referential side" of Barth's output, which he feels has been sorely overlooked by a prevailing orthodoxy of interpretation, "a tyranny of textuality" (114) intent on merely bolstering "some idealized, commodified vision" of the role of Barth's texts in "postmodern culture" (115). As this suggests, Birns's piece is fiercely critical of "the innocent ideologues of metafiction" (129), and like Carmichael he is concerned to move away from what he characterizes as the conservatism of formalist readings. For Klinkowitz, however, it is not so much the literary critical establishment that has come to represent a conservative orthodoxy, so much as Barth's works themselves. Drawing on Barth's copious "Friday" pieces, Klinkowitz suggests that the author has repeatedly dismissed and distanced himself from the significant art movements of the postwar years, out of an essentially traditional (mimetic) conception of the art work, and an alignment "with a tenured academic community and a succession . . . of mainstream publishers," each with "a vested interest in representational literary art, as eminently teachable and saleable" ("John Barth" 431).[22]

While for some Barth's work has thus been significantly misappropriated in the name of an all too amorphous American avant-garde—a misappropriation made particularly apparent by the characteristics of the later works—for others it is not the literary critical milieu that is at fault but the works themselves, to the extent that they fail to address or take account of contemporaneous developments in artistic production (and thus, according to particular standards, fail on their own terms). In each case it could be argued that the perceived problem is not of Barth's making, given that his works have rarely exhibited the essentially modernist aesthetic of, say, Donald Barthelme or Walter Abish, and given his repeated disavowal of avant-gardism, as in his 1981 reference to himself as a traditionalist in modernist's clothing ("Tales within Tales within Tales," *Friday Book* 219). Nevertheless, for a writer whose works have exhibited extreme shifts of form, genre, and style, it would appear indisputable that Barth's work, post-*Letters* (an act of overt summation, among other things), has settled into what can best be described as a form of comfortable proliferation. The texts, from *Sabbatical* and *The Tidewater Tales* to *On with the Story,* (1996) are discursive, colloquial, variously autobiographical, concerned with the sea and the archetype of the sea journey, and concerned, above all, with stories: life stories, literary stories, and the idea of interaction between the two. As much as any alleged return to realism, it is the narrative expansiveness of these works that principally defines them. Indeed, narrative form is always on show in these texts, as the medium via which both characters and readers have access to the real. Yet it is not as much the notion of a narrative "turn" as it is a "return" that I am concerned with here, as suggested in Carmichael's and Birns's understanding of a late style which reflects back on earlier works, complicating straightforwardly chronological accounts of writerly developments. My account of Barth's later works involves his turning back to a founding influence of narrative expansiveness, the framed story cycle, most potently embodied in the *Arabian Nights*. It is an influence both positive and questionable, the charting of which is particularly useful in accounting for the sheer narrative prolificacy (and prolixity) of works such as *The Tidewater Tales* and *The Last Voyage of Somebody the Sailor*. If this reading is thus not revisionist in quite the same manner as Birns's, I nevertheless want to question the benignity of Barth's interactions with the *Nights*, which have on the whole been read in positive terms; if Barth is "the post-modernist as pure story-teller," I want to suggest that such purity is achieved at a price.

Contrary to inclinations suggested by the black comedies and mythopoeic epics which comprise Barth's early novels, his first sustained, if unsuccessful attempt at writing pointed in rather a different direction. In the fictionalized autobiography *Once Upon a Time: A Floating Opera* (1994), he refers to "my pseudo-Boccaccian tales" as "one hundred tales covering three hundred years of tidewater history, a kind of Dorchester County *Decameron*" (271, 245). And in a foreword added to a reprint of *Lost in the Funhouse* he refers to this aborted piece of juvenilia in the context of his interest in the "premodern tale . . . especially the tale cycle, as told by the likes of Scheherazade and Boccaccio" (v).[23] The shift performed by *Lost in the Funhouse* is thus more a reversion to an earlier model, a fact confirmed by an event that figures as a primal scene in Barth's development, one that he replays throughout the fictions involved here. In his 1965 essay, "Muse, Spare Me," he writes:

> As an illiterate undergraduate, I worked off part of my tuition filing books in the Classics Library at Johns Hopkins, which included the stacks of the Oriental Seminary. One was tacitly permitted to get lost for hours in that splendorous labyrinth and to intoxicate, engorge oneself with story. Especially I became enamored of the great tale-cycles and collections: Somadeva's *Ocean of Story* in ten huge volumes, Burton's *Thousand Nights and a Night* in seventeen, the *Panchatantra*, the *Gesta Romanorum*, the *Novellini*, and the *Pent- Hept-* and *Decameron*. (*Friday Book* 57)

This discovery is repeatedly evoked throughout the essays collected in *The Friday Book* and *Further Fridays*, as well as in *Chimera*, *The Tidewater Tales*, and *Once Upon a Time*.[24] On one level it represents the discovery of a personal canon, one which the self-consciously untutored Barth could claim as his own, with reference to "the massive eclecticism of the autodidact" and to Jorge Luis Borges's Bloomian truism that "each writer *creates* his precursors" ("Kafka and His Precursors" 108). Its resurfacing led to several essays on aspects of frame-tale literature—"The Ocean of Story," "Tales Within Tales Within Tales," and "Don't Count on It"—and, more significantly, to a new autobiographical strand in Barth's fiction, most explicitly displayed in *Once Upon a Time*. Yet it also represents Barth's own narrative (re)turn: a turning away from the mainstream of Western literature and a return to a founding influence, one in which narrative proliferation, as embodied in frames and cycles, is primary. It is the working out of the formal possibilities of this influence that I want to chart below.

It is no surprise that the 1960s-influenced experiments with recorded voice that Barth included in *Lost in the Funhouse* were prompted by this return, what Barth has referred to as "a more or less high-tech reorchestration of the oral storytelling tradition," a fact also reflected in the volume's organization as an interconnected series (*Once Upon a Time* 340).[25] The most explicit example of this is the first piece in the collection, "Frame-Tale," subsequently referred to by the author as "a paradigm for the book" ("It's a Short Story," *Further Fridays* 101): a self-assembly Möbius strip comprising the phrase "once upon a time there was a story that began." The first manifestation of Barth's interest in frames and cycles, not only does it reimagine a traditional form, it is also pure form, a *regressus ad infinitum* of narrative beginnings (perhaps suggested by Borges's reference to the probably apocryphal night in the *Arabian Nights* when Shahrazad begins to tell the frame tale of the *Arabian Nights* itself). It is this formalist propensity, coupled with a preoccupation with story cycles, which has come to differentiate Barth from others of the "Generation of '31," such as Robert Coover and Donald Barthelme. It also makes him particularly important within the context of a postmodernism defined by a renewed concern for narrative continuities. Yet given what was to follow, it is worth recalling Tony Tanner's prescient remark concerning the eponymous frame tale, made three years subsequent to the publication of *Lost in the Funhouse*: "inside that verbal circle, which moves but never progresses, Barth seems temporarily to have trapped himself" (258).

The next invocation of the story cycle in Barth's work is equally telling, in that it represents the companion to this nascent aesthetic of continuity: intervention, specifically intervention in the frame tale of the *Arabian Nights*.[26] "Dunyazadiad," the first novella in the three-part *Chimera*, revolves around a fictionalized reversal of the author's aforementioned discovery of the story cycle, and the concomitant literalizing of the storyteller Shahrazad. Here, it is she who discovers a fictionalized Barth in her own library-stacks, just as he discovered her in his. The version of Barth that appears in the novella—an author with writer's block—is in the process of imagining the story of a character who comes to believe that "the key to the treasure *is* the treasure," when he is miraculously transported to the Baghdad of the *Nights*. The transportation occurs just as Shahrazad, facing the problem of how to stop the murderous Shahrayar, utters the same formula at the conclusion of her attempt to solve her own problem by imagining her situation as a story. The novella thus enacts the possibility that to turn to narrative—for Barth reciprocally to reimagine his life story as a tale and Shahrazad's tale as a life story—is to imagine an alternative. That the *Nights* represents the distillation of various traditional oral tales is acknowledged in "Dunyazadiad" with reference to the fact that the only stories Shahrazad knows are "bedtime stories . . . the ones that everybody tells" (including her typically Barthian knowledge of *The Ocean of Story*). Barth's metafictional version of the frame tale involves the Barth character supplying Shahrazad with the required stories as they appear in his own copy of the text of the *Nights*, thus initiating an intertextual web. Barth the author intervenes in the frame of the *Nights* as part of his turn to premodern narrative forms. In the novella which enacts this turn, he depicts a version of himself as an author at "a turning-point," wishing "neither to repudiate nor to repeat his past performances," but instead "to go beyond them toward a future they were not attuned to and, by some magic, at the same time to go back to the original springs of narrative" (17). This results in his imagining his passing the traditional material of the *Nights* (in the Burton edition) back from the future to the teller of the tales, who fittingly retains her role as traditional narrator rather than inventor. The result for both characters is achieved by the same means: as the Barth character retrospectively comments, "he had gone forward by going back, to the very roots and springs of story. Using, like Scheherazade herself, for entirely present ends, materials from narrative antiquity" (36). Barth thus constructs a narrative out of his return to premodern narratives. In the process, he not only intervenes in a pre-existent frame tale, of which he tells several versions from differing points of view, but also narrates his version of the story of the frame tale itself. This is metafiction as continuity and intervention, at the level of both content and form. The model of the folkloric story cycle—the proliferation of serial frames and embedded tales as a literary enactment of oral storytelling—becomes the source both of thematic material and of a conception of narrative as a malleable space within which newly written interventions in traditional tales act as a mode of replenishment. Yet this enactment of narrative continuity, particularly the unproblematized and autobiographical nature of the intervention—aspects which are further realized in subsequent fictions—raises questions regarding the appropriative nature of the interactive relationship, questions which shadow the texts under consideration and to which I will return.

For the model of the *Nights* to be fully incorporated it is obviously necessary for Barth to construct his own story cycle, and this is one reason for viewing the "Dunyazadiad" novella as a transitional text or turning point. In addition, for the content of the narrative to be fully embodied in the form—what Barth refers to in *Chimera* and elsewhere as "the principle of metaphoric means"—requires, in Barth's case, a story cycle on the same scale as that of his models, the sheer size of the text a literal and metaphorical sign of narrative prolificacy and thus replenishment, those characteristics that serve as defining features of Barth's later work. To achieve this end he uses traditional devices, either from the *Nights*—the couple narrating into the night, as in *On with the Story* and parts of *The Tidewater Tales*—or from the European folkloric story cycle model—the group interchange of stories at a narrative gathering, as in *The Last Voyage of Somebody the Sailor* and, again, *The Tidewater Tales*. In this last-named novel, Barth constructs a huge postmodernist story cycle, comprising a formalized frame enclosing fourteen narrative days divided into two distinct weeks, thus following the European model of numerically symbolic and fixed tales within a closed frame. Moreover, the use of the *Nights* as archetype figures on various levels. Nights of narrative become days which consist of the day itself plus the stories told on that day; the two weeks coincide with the final two weeks of the female protagonist's pregnancy and the novel thus ends with the birth of both a child (twins, in fact) and the text itself, just as the *Nights* charts the course of three pregnancies and ends, according to certain traditions, with the injunction that the tales should be recorded. In both cases, the end is thus the beginning.

Narrative fertility is literally and metaphorically located by *The Tidewater Tales* in the oral tale tradition. What we read is the written version of the two week pre-delivery sailing trip of a couple, the male of whom is a writer of increasingly minimalist narratives, the female a co-founder of "The American Society for the Preservation of Storytelling" and Director of Folklore and Oral History at the city library, a role which involves "supervising oral history projects . . . collecting urban folklore and recording immigrant folktales," as well as driving "the Inner City Talemobile" and learning the skills of oral recitation herself (24–25). Her name, Katherine Sherritt Sagamore, is a typically Barthian echo of *Kathasaritsagara* (*The Ocean of Streams of Story*), which appears intermittently throughout the novel, and it is she who initiates the introductory challenge to her husband to tell their stories (reversing the ground situation of the *Nights*); or, more specifically, to narrativize their situation as a means of explaining their lives up to that point and, concomitantly, of taking them "forward." This "cruise through the Ocean of Story" is a patchwork of tales-within-tales, including the tales of the protagonists' past lives and the various narrative gatherings that take place during their trip, all of which are orally told at the time and subsequently recomposed and narrativized by the writer (Peter Sagamore), a deliberate enactment of the passage from the oral to the written. In a final twist on tradition, Peter and Katherine's retelling their lives as stories is meant to inform their children-to-be of their parental heritage. Thus the cycle becomes an elaborate children's story in much the same way as Barth, in "Dunyazadiad," has Shahrazad turn to the stories she was told as a child (68).

Elaborate as this may be, it is now familiar Barthian territory: narrativization as a means of imagining alternative versions, of continuing the story, and the oral/folktale tradition as the model for a narrative form in which this particular thematics of storytelling can be embodied. As with "Dunyazadiad," the companion to this (re)turn to narrative is the intervention in narrative tradition itself—replenishment via intervention—thus creating a form modeled on the story cycle, within which is framed the intervention within a specific cycle. Where the Barth character in "Dunyazadiad" has a symbolic form of writer's block, Peter Sagamore is suffering from the "Less is More" syndrome, facing the prospect that "he had written himself into a corner from which only silence could meaningfully issue" (37). Just as Katherine's professional involvement with the updating and continuation of oral traditions functions as a gendered sign of narrative fecundity, so Peter's literature parallels the Beckett/Barthelme axis of late modernist/postmodernist literary minimalism or exhaustion, and it is the literal and metaphorical route out of this perceived impasse via a turning (back) to narrative that forms a central strand of the novel.[27] Again, concomitant with narrativization as a means of imagining alternative versions—"the key to the treasure *is* the treasure"—is the inclusion of versions of pre-existent narratives. Barth expands his interventions here to take in two other influential models, the *Odyssey* and *Don Quixote*, including in his novelistic cycle meetings with fictional versions of the protagonists and swapping continuations of their stories—thus, again, literalizing fiction. In each case the characters stress the long literary tradition of such "follow-up stories" or "literary resurrections," which parallel Barth's own remark on the fact that "the eschewing of contemporaneous, 'original' material is a basic literary notion, by comparison to which its use is but an occasional anomaly and fad of the last couple of centuries" ("Muse, Spare Me," *Friday Book* 58). However, despite the manipulation in these episodes of textual anomalies or nascent metafictional elements, Barth is not a deconstructionist searching for fractures but rather a constructionist using these gaps as a means of entry and of achieving continuity with his own irreducibly metafictional perspective. While his "Frame-Tale" imagines an unending cycle of narrative, his conception of continuity is one in which intervention forms an integral part of tradition, and this is again one of the differences between Barth and other writers concerned with premodern narrative material, such as Robert Coover and Angela Carter, for whom intervention can also mean disruption and difference.

Other narratives serve as material and inspiration, but Barth's place in this chapter is secured by the fact that it is the *Nights*, as a framed story cycle, that is his primary formal model, and he returns to it again with *The Tidewater Tales*. As his conception of tradition is of an all-encompassing, but non-teleological, unfurling of narration, the narrative he returns to must now include the version of the frame story given in his own "Dunyazadiad"; hence the final narrative gathering in *The Tidewater Tales*, at which this particular version of Shahrazad's tale is told and expanded. On this occasion, it involves a further intertextual web spun around a retelling of the frame tale with reference to the "Dunyazadiad" version and a speculative explanation of the reason for the number of nights (an explanation which is itself a version of Barth's own essay "Don't Count on It"), followed by the post-*Nights* career of Shahrazad and her Sindbad-inspired desire to voyage. The result is her transportation to the time of the original Barth character from "Dunyazadiad" (now referred to as "Djean"), via the reverse of the process by which he was transported and with a different tag: "what you've done is what you'll do." As part of her sojourn in the present day she becomes involved in the annual convention of the "American Society for the Preservation of Storytelling," at which she orally narrates not only "a version of Djean's Key-to-the-Treasure story: the secret history of *The 1001 Nights*," but also the account of her life after that episode, which is, of course, what is orally passed on during the narrative gathering on the final night of *The Tidewater Tales* (525–613). Not only does Barth align Shahrazad with the oral axis of the novel, he also replays the trope of narrativization as continuity and a means of imagining multiple alternative versions. This process is additionally embodied in the fact that *The Tidewater Tales* interweaves on various levels with, and acts as a reimagining of, Barth's preceding novel, *Sabbatical*, which furthers the intertextual presence of his own narratives and the intermingling of these narratives with the *Nights*: his intervention in the frame tale of the *Nights* in "Dunyazadiad" is orally retold as an embedded narrative (a retelling of Shahrazad's own account) in *The Tidewater Tales*, which is in turn partly framed by *Sabbatical*.

Barth's subsequent novelistic cycle, *The Last Voyage of Somebody the Sailor* (1991), is the culmination of this approach, to the extent that it is the most formally elegant of his constructions, in(ter)ventions, and because it imagines the death of Shahrazad, the embedded narrator of the cycle, now storytelling for her death rather than her life, and framed, in this version, by the deathbed narrator (Simon Behler) whose life story is the subject of the novel. Again, it takes the theme of intervention both literally and structurally: the entire embedded narration takes place between the sixth and seventh (last) voyage of Sindbad, within which the Sindbad cycle is retold in full, together with the seven "voyages" of Somebody (Behler), whose presence in medieval Baghdad is explained via the nightly narrative exchanges. Somebody appears between the tellings of Sindbad's sixth and seventh voyages in the guise of a porter, and Barth thus uses the narratee of the original cycle—the full title of which is "Sindbad the Sailor and Sindbad the Porter"—as the companion narrator of his (again, minor incidents provide continuity). Beyond its use of the evening gathering, however, the novel itself is not modeled on the simple, single-frame structure of the Sindbad cycle, but rather on the multiple frames and embeddings of *Nights'* cycles such as "The Porter and the Three Ladies" and "The Story of the Hunchback."[28]

Once again, the novel explores the interrelated themes of orality, replenishment, tradition, and intervention. Barth's intervention in the Sindbad cycle includes Sindbad's own oral renarration of his voyages to the assembled guests, the latter of whom, like the novel's readers, already know the tales. In the formulaic interludes between the twin narrations, which also include a further serially embedded tale, Somebody transcribes the narrative exchanges, and the frame of the novel establishes the text as the oral retelling of these transcribed versions. True to the spirit of narrative pragmatics, Barth's characters are always performing. Barth again manipulates and enacts the traditional passage from the oral to the literary as part of the novel's structure, just as he reverses the historical passage of the *Nights* from East to West by having the American Behler narrate seven versions of key moments in his life story to the assembled guests at Sindbad's table, who duly marvel at the wholly unrealistic mode of Western storytelling.

In each of Somebody's tales, specifically referred to as "versions," he is aware of using a different narrative mode as the framework within which this part of his life can be, or was, read: in his early years he narrates to his stillborn twin sister; as an adolescent he imagines himself as the hero of his own generic story; and his third "voyage" includes the version of himself as a Tom Wolfe-esque New Journalist using autobiography as copy. Barth again fuses the theme of the human propensity to narrativize— the self as various generic fictions—and the structural reliance on versions. In this case, the multiple-identitied Somebody narrates to explain his appearance in Baghdad, just as Sindbad's own autobiographical voyages tell of his past life (again, Barth literalizes fictional characters), with the daytime interludes between narrative meals diminishing in number as the number of the parallel voyages increases. Barth thus creates a structure which enacts the gradual fusing of the two narrative worlds and in which intervention functions at the level of theme (the crossing of various boundaries: life/death, sea/land, sleep/waking) and form. In terms of its osmotic relationship with narrative tradition, the novel exists as an addition to the *Nights*, in the form of a hugely expanded retelling of one of its cycles, as well as a continuation, beyond the traditional dénouement, of the *Nights'* frame tale itself.

The exploration of narrative as an enabling space of possibilities, transformations, and interventions, demonstrates particularly vividly Ricoeur's notion of the second stage of mimesis—the act of emplotment—as the work of the "productive imagination," both "intellectual and intuitive." As structuralism sought to demonstrate, this imaginative act is always governed by rules, what Ricoeur calls "traditionality," yet this tradition is built through the interplay of application and innovation: "not the inert transmission of some already dead deposit of material but the living transmission of an innovation always capable of being reactivated by a return to the most creative moments of poetic activity" (*Time and Narrative* vol. I, 68). The degree of innovation is governed by the paradigms of the specific traditions, with "[t]he folktale, the myth, and in general the traditional narrative" standing at the opposite pole to the contemporary novel in terms of "application" and "deviation" (69–70). In Barth's postmodernist story cycles we witness the potential continuity that exists between these two extremes: the innovatory aspect of the traditional and the traditional basis of this particular brand of innovation. Barth's texts enact the idea of the interplay of tradition and innovation, through a narrative intervention which serves as the embodiment of the productive possibilities of narrative. Subsequently, Barth's postmodernism—a term with which he has repeatedly aligned himself—is defined by its traditionality.

Yet having attempted an exposition of Barth's formal strategies, we need to return to the question of the nature of the interaction enacted in such texts. In contrast to my reading of Calvino's fictions, Barth's writerly idea of his chosen aspects of the folktale tradition appears problematic, precisely because of its unproblematized nature. As I have sought to demonstrate, this idea of tradition is based on continuity, and on intervention within this continuity as integral to tradition. The process of intervention which his novels enact is fundamentally seamless. The narrative prolificacy and nascent metafictionality of the traditional material are exploited as replenishment, just as the resultant contemporary narratives reveal themselves as grand elaborations and expansions of an unfurling tradition. The problem lies in the absence of disruption or discontinuity, not because of the contemporaneous high critical status accorded these aspects but simply because they are an integral element of the process of intervention and of the history of specific stories. To silence them is, in Ricoeur's terms, to foreground the synthesizing, concordant nature of narrative—the space it creates for intervention—to the detriment of any productive sense of discontinuity or space for contingency; or again, according to Tobin's suggestion of a postmodernist aesthetic based on a dialectical relationship between "continuity and rupture" with regard to narrative precursors, Barth could be said to sidestep the possibility of generic and historical differences that would trouble the seamlessness of the narrative. One feature of Barth's later work which results from this appropriation is the homogeneous narrative tone and style, particularly apparent in *The Tidewater Tales* and the later framed story collection, *On With the Story*. Because Barth uses aspects of his particular narrative tradition which create continuity with his own aesthetic sensibility, he always *appears* to find what he knows will be there, and concomitant with this is the undoubtedly wish-fulfilling autobiographical relationship established in "Dunyazadiad" and *The Tidewater Tales* between the writer-character and Shahrazad. As Heide Ziegler has commented, this fictional version of literal intervention, which in The *Tidewater Tales* rather uncomfortably results in consummation, is not just a betrayal but also a limiting, just as his attempts to explain literally the exact number of nights in the *Nights* is a reduction of its historical resonance (Ziegler).

This is not to accuse Barth of Orientalism or, as Ziegler does, of Westernizing the frame tale. As I have demonstrated, the convoluted history of the *Nights* unavoidably includes its European manifestations, both in translations and in the pervasive influence of its form. While this does not mean we can ignore the specificity of the various Middle Eastern and Indian traditions of which its material may originally have been a part, it would be specious to single out Barth for continuing this long history of interaction. He has himself answered the possible charge of artistic Orientalism, quoting Said on the fact that "[t]here is nothing especially controversial or reprehensible about such domestications of the exotic; they take place between all cultures, certainly, and between all men"; again, to criticize Barth's strategies from this angle would be to ignore a history of creative interaction and, indeed, would trivialize Orientalism as a specific form of colonialism ("4 1/2 Lectures: 3: The Arabesque," *Further Fridays* 318–20).[29]

The possibility of a sceptical rather than approbatory reading of Barth's strategies lies rather in the problems implicit in the relativizing of historical positions caused by such a stress on the irreducible potentialities of narrative: the disappearance of the alterity of historical material. Calvino, for example, in the early short stories and *Marcovaldo*, uses this historical distance both formally and thematically, in the sense of authorial detachment, the self-enclosed minimalist structures, and in the mixture of archetypal flatness and psychological depth in the characterization. This raises the broader issue of postmodernism as an essentially ahistorical eclecticism, referred to earlier with reference to Lyotard's advocacy of the idea of unbroken strings of self-legitimizing local narratives; indeed, his idea of the serial chain of *petits récits* might be compared with Barth's ongoing free play in the ocean of narrative tradition, although the latter's enthralment to oral and literary precedent is markedly at odds with Lyotard's continued advocacy of the avant-garde as the locus of postmodernist artistic practice.

However, this is to shift the argument away from an account, such as that attempted here, of Barth's texts as generated out of an idea of the folktale. Given that the full flowering of his interest in the story cycle, the *Nights* in particular, has coincided with a significant number of similarly influenced texts by other authors, we might at this point introduce contrasting textual interactions: Salman Rushdie's repeated recourse to, but not intervention in, the *Nights* and *The Ocean of Streams of Story* as representing precolonial traditions of storytelling, the fluidity of which offer an ongoing challenge to, and means of critique of, political and cultural orthodoxy;[30] or Naguib Mahfouz's *Arabian Nights and Days* (Layali alf lela, 1982), a text which creates and maintains a distance between the reader and the world of the tales via narratives which are neither short story nor folktale, but rather suggestive of both without attempting a seamless fusion. The result is a pervasive *strangeness* that maintains a distance between the material and its present manifestation. In each case the defining status of the cycle as an oral, communally produced work is productively preserved. Conversely, it is the comfortable proliferation and the stress on continuity that causes Barth to iron out such potentially fertile disruptions.[31] In the essays collected in *Further Fridays*, he writes of how he views the *Nights* as a "Roman" ("4 1/2 Lectures: 4 1/2: PM/CT/RA," *Further Fridays* 344), a "splendid maxi-novel about Scheherazade" ("It's a Long Story," *Further Fridays* 80). To conceive of the *Nights* as a novel is an index of the process by which Barth's late style contains the productive differences that palpably separate the form of the novel, however conceived, from the framed story cycle. The result is a homogeneity of text and intertext, the literary and the oral, the novel and the folktale.

Attempting to articulate the mobility of form, of part and whole, that characterizes the *Nights*, Nicole Ward Jouve writes of "interpenetration," "that combination of distinct identity (the story and its difference from other stories) and flowing in and out" (183): "the stories ceaselessly rupture the unit. And so, there is no risk of totalizing, by which I mean the drive to homogenize experience by making what is diverse and specific into a unified whole, which is the overwhelming temptation of the Book" (186). Conversely, referring to Borges's "Pierre Menard, Author of the *Quixote*," Barth comments on its distinctly postmodernist exploration of the idea of innovation from transplantation. In particular, the manner in which Borges manipulates the idea of the contemporaneity of anachronism. Barth nominates his own version: "I myself have always aspired to write Burton's version of *The 1001 Nights*, complete with appendices and the like, in ten volumes" ("The Literature of Exhaustion," *Friday Book* 69). Though he disclaimed *needing* to write it, the fictions discussed here could be read as the record of just such an attempt, in which the *idea* of an interactive transplantation is relegated in favor of unproblematized intervention. The result, it could be argued, is not a multiplicity of versions but rather the continual expansion and retelling of a single narrative, a single Book: Barth's *Arabian Nights*.

"Familiarity Breeds Consent": Robert Coover and the Fairy Tale

It is with the fictions of Robert Coover that I turn to the fairy tale as a specific genre of the folktale. While in the final chapter

I place readings of the "Bluebeard" tale type within the context of the history of the fairy tale itself, here I am concerned with the extent to which Coover's use of the fairy tale can fruitfully be placed within the context of a pragmatics of narrative. As I have suggested, Barth's highly selective use of the folktale can be read partly in terms of the third idea or potential suggested in the discussion of Calvino (in Chapter 3): the idea of formal innovation based on particular aspects of the folktale tradition. In contrast, Coover, Barth's near-contemporary, is concerned with the idea of the tale as an ideologically coded form of narrative; not in terms of a national tradition, as in Calvino, but as a pervasive form of popular culture. Where Barth's interventions are based on continuity, Coover's is an aesthetics of multiple disruptions, but one deeply informed by a concern for the human propensity to use narrative as an ordering system, a means of reading the real.[32]

It is this concern for narrative that sets Coover apart from his other near contemporary, Donald Barthelme. Barth, Barthelme, and Coover represent three relatively distinct faces of postmodernist fiction. Barth is, by his own admission, "a traditionalist in modernist's clothing." Barthelme's only tradition is that of modernist experimentalism, his short stories presenting a collage of absurdist and surrealist techniques. Coover can be placed between these two poles, less traditional than Barth but sharing with him a preoccupation with those narrative structures largely shunned by Barthelme. One element linking Barthelme and Coover, however, is their frequent allusion to the forms and materials of American popular culture, and it is within this context that they refer to the fairy tale. Theirs is the fairy tale of Walt Disney, a form of narrative defined by its role in popular entertainment rather than by its status as originally oral tale or as the historically dominant literary version of a series of tale types. They thus refer to the most popular tales—"Snow White," "Little Red Riding Hood," "Beauty and the Beast"—precisely because of their iconic status, but unlike Angela Carter and Margaret Atwood, do not turn to the folktale tradition for alternative versions or forgotten narratives. It is for this reason that I have placed specific discussion of the fairy tale as a genre of folktale in the following chapter, according to what I have found to be the most productive and apposite contextualization of the respective fictions.

The use of the fairy tale in Barthelme's first extended work, *Snow White* (1967), is indicative of this particular mode of appropriation, as well as of the similarities and divergences in Coover's and Barthelme's use of intertextual material. The three-part series of prose fragments, based loosely on Snow White's stay with the seven dwarfs, has engendered much critical commentary. Its bleakly comic depiction of the stagnant relationship of a group of neurotic men with an increasingly dissatisfied Snow White and an anachronistic hero-figure has been read variously as an anti-fairy tale, a critique of the deadening effect of contemporary mass culture, and a feminist retelling that highlights the fetishization of Snow White and her own dawning sense of being both a product and a construction of gendered cultural norms.[33] Yet in each case the reading is predicated on a limiting of the sheer multiplicity of the text—of what it itself refers to as "audacity" (114). Barthelme's use of collage, jargon, typographical experiments, and quotation, creates a text that is both over-abundantly meaningful and provocatively meaningless; it relies on the "stuffing" or "sludge" of everyday language and on the now famous "dreck": "matter which presents itself as not wholly relevant (or indeed, at all relevant) but which, carefully attended to, can supply a kind of 'sense' of what is going on" (96, 106). At the center of this textual turbulence is the significantly static section of the "Snow White" narrative in which the heroine stays with the dwarfs, an episode the absurdly anachronistic material of which functions in the manner of the huge body of the titular absence in Barthelme's next extended work, *The Dead Father* (1975). Barthelme himself has commented on his use of such bases: "[w]hat's attractive about this kind of thing is the given—you have to do very little establishing, can get right to the variations" (Interview 42). These variations can of course be read in terms of the basic intertext, and certainly the text demonstrates the fact that "[i]mages fray, tatter, empty themselves" ("The Falling Dog" (1970), *Sixty Stories* 173).

Yet one question raised by such eclecticism concerns the extent to which the resultant text can be read solely, or even largely, in relation to the "Snow White" narrative, beyond "the given"— just as contemporaneous jazz versions of the Disney *Snow White* song "Someday My Prince Will Come" waste little time in moving far away from the source melody.[34] To revert to the latter as the hermeneutical key is to tame the disconnectedness of the text, its audacity; part of the effect of *Snow White* is precisely to trouble, perhaps by provocation, such attempts at intelligibility, and as I am concerned here with an investigation of the relationship between text and folktale intertext, such an interpretation of *Snow White* would be, for this reader, too comfortable.[35] Something is always lost in a reading which focuses primarily on an intertext, and such a reading should thus be based on the extent of this loss.

Barthelme preferred writing short stories, as the sectional structures of his tentative experiments with extended narratives indicate. In one of them, "The Dolt," he writes that "[e]ndings are elusive, middles are nowhere, but worst of all is to begin, to begin, to begin"; and it is this difficulty with narrative that marks a significant difference between Coover and Barthelme ("The Dolt" (1968), *Sixty Stories* 96). At the time Barthelme was writing *Snow White*, Coover was also turning to the fairy tale as a source for *Pricksongs and Descants* (1969; the majority of these stories were written before Coover published his first novel, *The Origin of the Brunists*, in 1965) which, as a collection, represents a source book of formal possibilities. However, the majority of Coover's subsequent work demonstrates a turning away from the fractured and fragmented prose pieces suggestive of an aesthetic connection with Barthelme, towards the extended narrative, and more specifically to the narrative exploration of narrative forms. His earlier two novels, written after the stories, already demonstrate this interest. *The Origin of the Brunists* explores the production and workings of religious myths, while *The Universal Baseball Association, Inc., J. Henry Waugh, PROP.* (1968) focuses on one man's construction of an alternative reality in the form of an imaginary baseball league, and the working through of the league's inter-

connected narratives. *The Public Burning* (1977), which fiction-
ally explores the historical era and character of Richard Nixon,
is a paradigmatic example of historiographic metafiction; and *A
Night at the Movies* (1987) uses the generic norms of popular cinema both within its individual pieces and as a unifying structure.

Coover's own comments bear out the narrative preoccupations
exhibited in his fictions and are strikingly similar to the contemporaneous comments of Barth on a turning to premodern sources.
Referring to "art forms that have been shunted aside by the developments of the last three hundred years," Coover speaks of research "into the mechanics of the narrative form" that preceded
and helped crystallize his approach in *Pricksongs and Descants*: "I
turned to the ancient fictions to research what had already been
done and to see what new ideas they might engender. *The Arabian
Nights*, I discovered, was a gold mine of formal possibilities." Allied with this are two other preoccupations. Firstly, Coover speaks
repeatedly of the human propensity to use story structures to organize experience and construct meaning: "There's no sense in
decrying this fact; on the contrary, it is a useful—even necessary—
means of navigating through life . . . we fabricate; we invent con-
stellations that permit an illusion of order to enable us to get
from here to there. . . . [I]n a sense, we are all creating fictions
all the time, out of necessity (Interview, 1973, 151–52)." Coover's
own predisposition to narrative forms—"[t]he central thing for me
is story. I like poems, paintings, music, even buildings, that tell
stories"—is thus allied with an interest in the processes of narrativization as meaning-making (Interview, 1979, 69). This suggests
links with the aforementioned "cultural psychology" described by
Jerome Bruner, but it is the accompanying emphasis on the fictional nature of narrative against the historical fixing of narrative
as seeming "truth"—myth or metanarrative—that is particularly
pertinent to his fiction writing, and that suggests broad parallels
with that aspect of Lyotard's work detailed earlier. In dedicating
the "Seven Exemplary Fictions" of *Pricksongs and Descants* to Cervantes (another influence shared with Barth), Coover, in know-
ingly grand terms, advocates the manner in which the dedicatee

"struggled against the unconscious mythic residue in human life," using "familiar mythic or historical forms to combat the content of those forms" (61–62). In other words, "if some stories start throwing their weight around, I like to undermine their author-ity a bit, work variations, call attention to their fictional natures" (Interview, 1979, 68). These various narrative processes are en-capsulated in *The Universal Baseball Association*, in which the pro-tagonist, Henry Waugh, constructs an imaginary baseball league, complete with players whose histories and life stories increasingly impinge on Henry's everyday existence. Together with the de-tailed portrayal of this constructed environment, Coover's novel explores a number of central themes: the desire for order, the con-struction of fictions (to satisfy this desire), and fiction's colonizing of the real. Coover points to the benign effects of this process: a folk singer (Sandy) casts the events of the league in mythic terms, with a particularly gifted player immortalized as "Aladdin," "The boy with the magic arm": "[i]n a way, Sandy did them a disservice, provided then with dreams and legends that blocked off their per-ception of the truth. But what was the truth? Men needed these rituals . . . that was part of the truth" (103). The process is be-nign as long as it continues to function as process. Conceiving the idea of writing "a compact league history" (a "factual" account of his fictional construct, an idea which reverses the workings of historiographic metafiction), Henry is struck by the necessity for change within order: "it [the history of the league] needed a new ordering, perspective, personal vision, the disclosure of pat-tern, because he'd discovered . . . that perfection wasn't a thing, a closed moment, a static fact, but process . . . and the process was transformation" (211–12). Yet the final chapter, set one hundred league-years on and with the ontological frame of Henry's reality now conspicuously absent, depicts the previously described events of the narrative in the form of a once-yearly ritual re-enactment, in which masked rookie players take the roles of the legendary heroes in front of a baying audience. Process has frozen into myth, and the narrative fictions that we witness Henry constructing are now fought over in various interpretations of the "truth" of the events. As one sceptical character comments, this appears to be "[c]ontinuance for its own inscrutable sake" (239).

The workings of this novel encapsulate Coover's double-edged attitude. He uses narrative both as a reflection of the narrative construction of reality and as a means of revealing the fictional nature of particularly pervasive narratives that have taken on the mantle of truth—"static facts." Such a qualified justification for the self-conscious use of narrative is emblematic of the postmodernist return to storytelling: an awareness of the shared commonality of story structures that is reflected in the use of popular genres and a manipulation of the desire for pattern depicted in the double-voiced layers of metafiction. Given this stress on the constructedness of narrative, it is unsurprising that what Coover discovers in his own "narrative turn," specifically in Ovid and the fairy tale, is the transformational aspect: narrative as a space in which the processes of change are enacted, as stated by Henry Waugh. Obviously, the literal transformations that underpin the fairy·tale (and the *Metamorphoses*) vividly enact this idea, but on a metaphorical level this transformational aesthetic is interpreted by Coover as the antithesis of static and ahistorical narrative, and of the tendency to continue using entrenched stories that have taken on the appearance of self-evident truth: "the basic, constant struggle for all of us is against metamorphosis, against giving in to the inevitability of the process" (Interview, 1973, 152). Whereas Barthelme uses a static point in his chosen fairy tale, Coover characteristically focuses on points of change, or, more specifically, on the moments prior to the transformational or initiatory encounter around which the tales pivot: Little Red Riding Hood on the verge of encountering the wolf or Hansel and Gretel nearing the witch's house. Yet both "The Door" and "The Gingerbread House" (in *Pricksongs and Descants*), which draw on these aforementioned tales, break off at this pivotal point and thus omit the turn of events that marks the successful dénouement in the fairy tale. In Coover's fragmented versions, these transformational points remain untamed, as if to suggest not generic outcomes and explanations but rather multiple possibilities: about to enter the house, Little Red Riding Hood realizes that "though this was a comedy from which, once entered, you never returned, it nevertheless possessed its own astonishments and conjurings, its towers and closets, and even more pathways, more gardens, and more doors" ("The Door," *Pricksongs* 13); and Hansel and Gretel are similarly left at the liminal doorway, "[s]hining like a ruby, like a hard cherry, and pulsing softly, radiantly. Yes, marvellous! delicious! insuperable! but beyond: what is the sound of black rags flapping?" ("The Gingerbread House," *Pricksongs* 59). The suggestion of a multiplicity of narrative routes and a concomitant open-endedness is echoed in other pieces in the collection, most notably "The Babysitter" and "The Elevator," which also consist of discrete fragments of prose and which similarly avoid closure through the suggestion of multiple possibilities. As one of the characters in another of the fairy tales in *Pricksongs and Descants* comments, " 'there are no disenchantments, merely progressions and styles of possession. To exist is to be spell-bound' " ("The Magic Poker," *Pricksongs* 22).

However, this manipulation of the fairy tale also demonstrates the ideological intent of Coover's transformational aesthetic, his interest in the historical provenance of the material. As is the case with Barthelme, Coover uses the most popular tales, a popularity which is reflected in, and has been furthered by, what have become the standard interpretive readings of the fairy tale as a literary genre for children. Tales that focus on transformational encounters have come to be seen as enacting and encoding the successful passage from childhood to adulthood, the socialization of the protagonist that is symbolized in the marriage or happy conclusion. Pivotal points in the narratives thus function as the endpoint of the child's development, beyond which all is certainty: sexuality, morality, societal role. Such a reading, to which I will return, represents a consensus view of the literary fairy tale that settled into place in the nineteenth century and which persists, albeit modified, in such recent texts as Bruno Bettelheim's *The Uses of Enchantment: The Meaning and Importance of Fairy Tales* (1976). As summarized by Bettelheim, fantasy and the seemingly

disruptive elements of the tale are deemed necessary precisely because they are worked through and neutralized in the reassuringly
realistic and didactic dénouement. Narrative and process are sur-
mounted by meaning and morality, as enshrined in the twentieth
century in the ideology of Disney: the fairy tale as a medium for a
putatively timeless message of good behavior and successful maturation.

Contemporary literary fairy tales are in part a reaction against
this dominant ideology, as will be seen in more detail in the following chapter on feminist reimaginings. For Coover, it is the fact that
the self-evident truth of such readings denies the transformational
energies contained within the tales, or rather, that the transformation around which the tale is organized is taken as an endpoint
which acts as both the true meaning of the tale and the end of the
narrative: the fairy tale as "static fact." His own fractured narratives work against this in a number of ways. As demonstrated, they
break off at the main point of narrative tension, thus suggesting
possibilities of continuation rather than the onset of closure; the
pieces are structured along the lines of a prose cubism, in which
multiple perspectives are set out without resolution; and most im-
portantly, the characters in the tales are tellers themselves, so allowing for the question of interpretative strategies to be included
within the space of the narrative itself. In "The Door," which fuses
motifs from "Little Red Riding Hood," "Jack and the Beanstalk,"
and "Beauty and the Beast," Coover casts Jack as the father of the
girl, and the tale opens with his musing on "the old songs, the old
lies": "he'd given her her view of the world . . . not really thinking it out, she listening, he telling. . . . He'd pretended to her that
there were no monsters, no wolves or witches, but yes . . . there
were" (Pricksongs 10). Given a scurrilous soliloquy, the Grand-
mother character reminisces on a life spent according to fairy tale
expectations: "yes knew all the old legends I did and gave my heart
to them who hadn't heard them? . . . [O]nly my Beast never became a prince. . . . I have suffered a lifetime of his doggy stink. . . .
I have watched my own beauty decline . . . and still no Prince"
(Pricksongs 11–12). Using fairy tale characters as the repository of

their own tradition allows for the suggestion of alternatives beyond the limits of the standard dénouement, while the idea of
the fairy tale as historically sanctioned lie is itself complicated by
an undercutting of the archetypal characterization. The Grand-
mother's ribald thoughts end with the suggestion that she is in
fact the wolf in disguise—"bring me goodies! for I have veils to lift
and tales to tell"—and Jack is schizophrenically aware of his own
duality: "[t]his was the hard truth: to be Jack become the Giant,
his own mansions routed by the child he was" (*Pricksongs* 12, 9).
Similarly, "The Magic Poker" sustains the multiple possibilities of
the eponymous object, as opposed to enacting transformation as
the revelation of a sole latent meaning.

The unresolved excess that keeps the symbolic economy of the
narratives in a state of flux is accompanied by a similarly excessive
use of language. All the pieces in *Pricksongs and Descants* contain
linguistically extravagant references to sex and violence, often
as an expression of the desire of the characters straining at the
boundaries of the fragmented prose, and encapsulated in the recasting of the volume's title as "death-cunt-and-prick-songs." In
"The Dead Queen" (1973), an expansion of the "Snow White"
narrative written soon after the publication of *Pricksongs and Descants*, Coover luridly describes the death of the Queen, followed
by the blackly comic antics of the dwarfs during the explicitly
detailed consummation of the marriage of the heroine and the
Prince. Such linguistic excesses not only work against the historical process of bowdlerization that culminates in the cartoons
of Disney—again, a process described in more detail in my final
chapter—but also work with the other elements of Coover's aesthetic to avoid the appearance of mere critique: to necessitate the
use of narrative in the reconstruction of the tales as suggestive
of multiple alternatives and possible transformations. In Coover's
version of "Snow White" it is hence the Queen who appears as
the motor of the narrative, sacrificed in the inevitable need for
final, irrevocable closure such as that described above. The death
of the Queen allows Snow White to attain perfection, but it is
perfection as stasis, and Coover focuses once again on this anti-

transformational ideology. The Queen becomes the doomed artistic force behind the plot, one whose subversive invention is retrospectively acknowledged by a Prince who is now faced with an inviolable cipher: "she foresaw the Hunter's duplicity, the Dwarfs' ancient hunger, my own weakness for romance. Even our names were lost, she'd transformed us into simple colors, simple proclivities, our faces were forever fixed and they weren't even our own!"(305). As such, she is comparable with the much-maligned fox of the fable tradition—that "cartload of mischief"—who is reassessed in Coover's *Aesop's Forest* (1986), in terms similar to those of the Queen: "[h]ave to admire the sly bastard: in his way, he's an artist"(9–12). While the "The Dead Queen" suggests the transformational aspect of the passage into adulthood, Snow White is in fact a frozen, idealized, perpetually adolescent symbol; a static, untouchable "truth," whereas the Queen's plots, albeit impotent, represent an attempt to disrupt the standard narrative—impotent, of course, because caught up in the gendered moral logic of the narrative itself.[36] At her funeral, the dwarfs sing "a lament for the death of the unconscious," and thus for the pre-transformation fantasy of the plot that is tamed and fixed in the dénouement.

Yet it is in the extended narrative of *Pinocchio in Venice* (1991), in which a similarly aged hero is turning back to wood, that Coover uses the narrative form itself as an integral thematic element. As in Barth's work, where the earlier short pieces prepared the way for his expansion into the story cycle, so Coover's early, more formally experimental work can be viewed retrospectively as a series of fragmented explorations of pre-existent narrative material; indeed these fairy tale pieces work because, as Barthelme says, their popularity allows for a more extreme manipulation of readerly expectations. *Pinocchio in Venice* is the first full-length narrative in which Coover uses pre-existent literary material, as opposed to those earlier novels in which the framework is provided by narrative structures imposed on the real. As such, it reads as a summation of this aspect of Coover's work, and central to this is his choice of source text. While it would obviously be possible to trace the complicated histories of each of the individual fairy tales used by Coover in his short stories, and suggest the possible relation of that history to the new text—a subject which I explore in the following chapter in relation to the "Bluebeard" tale type—we can broadly summarize such a history as the passage from oral tale, via literary versions, to widespread dissemination in countless anonymous children's books and, in some cases, films, pantomimes, and dramatic adaptations.[37] In the case of *Pinocchio* this history is supplemented by the fact that the text is not a children's literary version of a folktale but rather a nineteenth-century literary narrative for children in which the fairy tale has already been absorbed and sublimated, a process which has continued in the form not only of countless bowdlerized versions but also of the famous Disney film (Disney's second feature-length cartoon, released in 1940, following *Snow White and the Seven Dwarfs* in 1937). Coover's object, *Pinocchio*, thus already consists of multiple layers or sedimented histories that are potentially available to disrupt the aura of timelessness which envelops the modern Disney(esque) versions. Whereas in the earlier stories Coover suggests various descants to an implied source narrative, here the extended narrative allows for the simultaneous inclusion of the multiple layers of *Pinocchio*'s heritage and history: melodies and descants appear simultaneously.

The relevance of *Pinocchio* in the context of a survey of the folktale in recent fiction is that it stands in for the role played by the folktale, as literary fairy tale, in the rise of a literature specifically for children. The relevance for Coover is that *Pinocchio* represents another object of popular culture, with the added layer of filmic distillation. The rise of children's literature is tied chronologically to the rise of the literary fairy tale. While some have speculatively identified the publication of Charles Perrault's *Histoires ou contes du temps passé* (1697) as the birth of children's literature, the identification of the latter as a distinct genre, and so field of publishing, is more usually dated around the middle of the eighteenth century, thus coinciding with the gradual shift in emphasis in the French vogue for literary tales towards versions specifically intended for the moral instruction of children. With the advent of Romanticism there developed concomitantly a tacit link between the folk/fairy tale and the child, in terms of origins: the tale as relatively untainted repository of a nation's narrative heritage, and the young child as having privileged access to this original state. While in the eighteenth century the fantastical elements of the tales were thought by some either to be morally dangerous or at least unhealthily entertaining, the shift towards a benign view of imagination and untainted innocence meant that the fantasy was seen as essentially "true" by nineteenth-century standards, representative of the pre-literary state of our common heritage, both culturally and individually.[38]

It was within this historical context that Carlo Collodi's *Le avventure di Pinocchio* was written and published in Italy (1881–1883).[39] Collodi had previously translated Perrault's tales in 1875, together with those of Mme d'Aulnoy and Mme LePrince de Beaumont (the latter's 1756 version of "Beauty and the Beast" is one the earliest examples of the fairy tale as a vehicle intended explicitly for the moral instruction of the young).[40] Like these literary fairy tales, Collodi's story has gone on to achieve a popularity signified by its breaking free of its moorings in the form of numerous shortened, simplified versions, of which the Disney cartoon is only a particularly prominent example. What I want to highlight, however, is the extent to which, just as Coover's *Pinocchio in Venice* is a tendentious reading of *Pinocchio* and its various reworkings, so Collodi's story is a reading of the literary fairy tale, or rather, a distillation of certain aspects of that genre as it appeared to the author in the latter half of the nineteenth century.[41] From the beginning, Collodi manipulates fairy tale elements. The story opens with a simultaneous evocation and refusal of conventional fairy tale subjects and the central characters of the puppet and the Fairy are similarly double-edged. Like the canonical fairy tales I have been discussing, *Pinocchio* ends with a pivotal transformation—perhaps the most overtly symbolic transformation in all of the literature influenced by the fairy tale—and this is certainly one of the dominant themes in Coover's choice of intertexts. Yet as Nicholas J. Perella points out, "it is not Pinocchio's social status that changes. The puppet's transformation is the result of his unalterable acceptance of a rigid work ethic. . . . In this respect, *Pinocchio* as a whole is an anti-Cinderella story" (27–28). Perella goes on to comment that the Fairy combines characteristics of the literary fairy tale stepmother and godmother, an example of the story's fusion of fantasy with a didactic reality deemed necessary for educating the young in the newly unified Italian state. Indeed, the fantasy element is given a markedly un-Romantic reading in *Pinocchio*, aligned as it often is with the wayward and disruptive. Despite the use of fairy tale elements, Collodi's text is a linguistically sophisticated amalgam of a number of influences, with the overall intention of instilling bourgeois family values and an unidealistic zeal for hard work in its young readers and listeners.

The end of Collodi's story initiates Pinocchio's human life. Not a beast returned to human form but a beastly puppet finally accepted as worthy, he has been transformed into a real boy. In conventional fairy tale fashion, the story thus ends with certainty, as Pinocchio's disruptiveness is tamed, and he himself is literally transformed. The beginning of his morally approved life is the end of the narrative within which all social disruptions have been both enacted and neutralized. The process of maturity via narrative has been completed, unless, of course, the transformation should prove reversible, as is imagined in Coover's *Pinocchio in Venice*. Like Coover's Aesop, whose death functions synecdochically for "a time when all comforting covenants are dissolving," his Pinocchio is at the end of his life, a life spent in the studious pursuit of the absolute and the avoidance of process and mutability. I have suggested above that Coover's conception of narrative is based on an acceptance of the inevitability of process—narrative as a space in which process is enacted, and as a form which always undermines the static and the seemingly immutable—and it is this conception that finds ultimate embodiment, literally and metaphorically, in the physical fact of Pinocchio.

Following the chronology of his life from conception in 1883, Pinocchio's aged body is now rotting, or rather, reverting to wood, and the narrative follows his return to Venice (a piece of poetic re-location on Coover's part) to write the final part of his final work: the "vast autobiographical tapestry" to be titled "Mamma."[42] Just as Coover's protagonist is gradually revealing his former self, so his text is a version of this protagonist's "autobiographical tapestry," woven from the strands of Collodi, Disney, and the rigorous academic adult life that Coover imagines for him. Thus Coover develops his interventionist strategy of using characters as the repository of their own tradition: his Pinocchio is *the* Pinocchio, has lived the life of Collodi's book as well as the subsequent Disney version; he is a character who knows his own tale and its various retellings, a literal palimpsest. (As such, he is perhaps the most striking example of the reverse of the fictionalized biographies of historiographic metafiction.) In Coover's *Pinocchio in Venice*, the Disney film figures as a version of an early autobiographical work by Pinocchio himself—"The Wretch"—which Hollywood duly recasts, citing "the need for metaphoric coherence and condensation . . . the alleged infantilism of the American public . . . a growing dissatisfaction with Fascist Italy and with theology in general" (96). Disney's "timeless classic" is thus simultaneously fictionalized and historicized as the text wonders, as much about itself as about its chief protagonist, "what is it he remembers? His own life or the film of it, the legends?"

Where Coover's use of the fairy tale in his stories is dictated by popular versions, with little concern for the folkloric origins of the narratives, here his use of Disney is allied with a far more prominent appropriation of the Collodi original. In fact, *Pinocchio in Venice* is densely allusive, acting not only as a continuation and reinterpretation of the original story but also a re-enactment and "fleshing out." To this extent it is possible to see a nascent form of hypertextuality at work in the novel, a view prompted by Coover's developing interest in the workings of hypertextual narratives, and in the implications of the latter for a conception of narrative per se. A similar effect—related to those hypertextual editorial projects in which the texts in question are viewed as in process, and so offered in a non-hierarchical body of states of composition, multiple versions, and formats—is produced by Coover's *Briar Rose* (1996). Here, the space of the heroine's dreams (a motif lifted from Charles Perrault's telling of the tale) and the space of the wall of briars that surround her, in which the hero is caught, become textual spaces in which multiple versions and analogous narratives, both fictional and theoretical, circulate and interrelate.

In the case of *Pinocchio in Venice*, Coover's text literally incorporates Collodi's, just as Pinocchio's body contains its multiple histories, and this simultaneity acts again to lift the new text above the level of mere exuberant critique: as the aged Pinocchio experiences the return of the repressed, so the text he inhabits exhibits its multiple histories. As well as the parodic general allusions—"pull a few strings," "like gold coins on a magic tree"—the text uses countless specific elements from Collodi, elaborating on minor details such as the painted fireplace and kettle on Gepetto's wall, indicating poverty in the original and referred to by Coover's Pinocchio as the "trompe l'oeil" that gave him his first experience of what was to become the core of his academic career, the visual arts (41–42). Each character met by the decaying Professor is either a literal or metaphorical relative of his counterpart in the original, and again Coover expands on minor roles, frequently using chunks of Collodi's text verbatim. This strategy is further developed in *Briar Rose*, in which narrative is relegated—or rather, stalled—in favor of a nonhierarchical series of prose fragments offering different aspects of "the eternal city of the tale," a synchronic space comprising tale types, literary variants and analogues, critical commentaries, and theoretical appropriations (57).

Similarly, the intertexts of Collodi and Disney are incorporated into Coover's tapestry, laid out across a Venice which serves, like Pinocchio in *Pinocchio in Venice*, as the literal and metaphorical site of all the character's adventures (an embodied "eternal city of the tale"): the Field of Miracles, the island of Busy Bees, Funland, as well as a more general "fairyland," a "city of endless illusions," which Pinocchio himself comes to realize are a series of "overlays, a montage, variations on a theme"—just as the various manifestations of the Fairy in *Pinocchio* and *Pinocchio in Venice* flash before the dying character in the final chapter as "a kind of moving montage." Pinocchio stands as the now decaying embodiment of a life lived according to the absolute precepts of the Fairy, and Venice metaphorically acts as the equally crumbling embodiment of Beauty and Truth: "the immense integral Self that is this enchanted city." It is to this embodiment of a timeless idea of absolute values that Pinocchio has dedicated the majority of his post-Collodi life, in order to act out his debt to the Fairy, "the social order [he] embraced": "[e]ven these musings on Palladio and Venice, eternity and history, purity and its pursuit have really been little more . . . than coded meditations on that guiding spirit" (183). However, this pursuit of purity is a turning away from process and thus from Pinocchio's own roots in the process of transformation. "The Wretch," "his first essay in unabashed autobiography," is also the first of his advocacies of the unified self, an "assault upon all the modern and eventually postmodern . . . denials of what in a famous coinage he called 'I-ness.'" Coover thus weaves a thematic web around Pinocchio's human life, a life devoted to Wholeness, Beauty, Truth (and explicitly shunning Cooveresque strategies of irony, parody, and sarcasm, "the final recourse of the mental defective"), those static facts which extend the ideologically coded static fact of the dénouement of Collodi's narrative (32).

It is this stasis that Pinocchio finds in the religious art of the Renaissance—he likes pictures "[b]ecause they don't move"—and his devotion to the various guises of the abstract ideal is characterized explicitly in two key passages as a repression of narrative: "[t]he quest for the abiding forms within life's ceaseless mutations was *his* quest. . . . [H]e too, rejecting all theatricality, sought repose in the capricious turbulence—freedom, as it were, from *story*"; "the professor, in his dedicated pursuit of ideal forms, has always rejected the theatrical, the narrative, indeed *all* arts with concepts of time other than eternity" (115, 175–76). Yet this pursuit is a denial of Pinocchio's narrative status, a status which his initiatory transformation sought to erase but which is physically returning in the form of his body's reversion to its original form. It is this original, pre-transformation narrative that is literally re-enacted in the layers of Coover's intertextual landscape, with the return to process embodied in Pinocchio's increasingly wooden frame; and just as Coover's Prince Charming comes to acknowledge his unalterable enthralment to a frozen, culturally sanctioned ideal which he has helped to realize, so the aged Pinocchio, living through the palimpsest of his own life, comes to understand his enthralment to the frozen ideal of the Fairy, "[s]ociety's little helper! Civilization's drill sergeant!"

Coover is writing against the moral edifice of traditional children's literature, represented in the sedimented, layered history of *Pinocchio* itself. Against the cleansed truth of the fairy tale dénouement he musters a formidable arsenal of mischievous excess, scatology, scurrilous linguistic punning, phantasmagoric crudity, an explicitly sexualized account of Pinocchio's relationship with his guiding light, and a detailed portrayal of a rotting body in the process of reverse transformation. Pinocchio makes a final attempt to accept his origins as a marionette, an elaboration of the specifically popular art of puppet theater within which his character is rooted but which represents all he has rejected—and which is also paralleled in the anarchic Venetian masked Carnival: "[i]t is time made real, it is movement, it is passion, it is life." If *Pinocchio in Venice* energetically dismantles the ideological certainties of Disney by historicizing its sources, it also deflates the simplistic, ahistorical idea of a civilizing maturation embodied in the didactic "truth" of the irrevocable transformation of the fairy tale ending. All that has been repressed in that ending returns in Coover's Venice literally to pick away at Pinocchio's flesh.

Pinocchio is a character tied to his story. It is a story that Coover reads as profoundly anti-teleological, as this radically appropriated character comments: "[t]here are always endings, but there are not always conclusions," and it is the idea of the subservience of individual stories, including fairy tales, to the greater, non-narrative conclusion of moral or meaning that Coover is writing against. That he attempts this in a narrative that incorporates

Collodi—not in the sense of the simplified slimming-down of Disney and others but as a massive expansion, retelling, reinterpretation, continuation—means that his narrative tells a multiplicity of stories about a character who is reassessing a life spent turning away from narrative. The resultant complexity—and my reading is a tendentious taming of a sometimes deliberately excessive complexity, not least in its demotion of the textual *Death in Venice* against which the literal dying of the novel is arranged—is thematic, in that it is the antithesis of the singular meaning of Pinocchio's transformation, a freeing of the desire, fantasy, and multiplicity that this truth seeks to shut out.[43] It is as if the text is speaking to Pinocchio in a voice lifted, fittingly, from one of its author's own fairy tales: "'Oh no, my dear, there are no disenchantments, merely progressions and styles of possession. To exist is to be spell-bound'" ("The Magic Poker," *Pricksongs and Descants* 22).

Chapter 5

CRAFTINESS AND CRUELTY:
A READING OF THE FAIRY TALE AND ITS PLACE
IN RECENT FEMINIST FICTIONS

If the fictions of Barth provide a form of maximalist counterpart to the minimalism of Calvino—both in their different ways manipulating narrative as *combinatoire* and drawing on the conventions of the framed cycle—then those texts of Coover that are influenced by the fairy tale provide a bridge to the subject of this final chapter: recent feminist explorations of, and interventions in, the genre of the fairy tale. The reworking of fairy tales by the likes of Angela Carter and Margaret Atwood has certainly been the most prominent example of the influence of the folktale on recent fiction, allied as the fictions in questions undoubtedly are with contemporaneous feminist analyses of the genre of the fairy tale. Thus my focus now shifts from readings of single authors in terms of specific folktale characteristics to the interaction between a range of writers and a comparatively clearly delineated type of tale.

As a specific type of folk narrative, one containing an element of magic or enchantment, the genre of the fairy tale can be conceived in several interrelated ways: as a canon of narratives expressing a particular mode of thought, a collective form of knowledge; as a series of individual tales, literary but anonymous; as an historically defined subgenre of the folktale; and as a literary genre complete with various generic characteristics.[1] Recent work in this field has tended to concentrate on the first of these elements, looking at rewritings as a reaction to an ideology that is seen as enshrined within the traditional fairy tale and thus viewing the reworking of any individual narrative as primarily part of this overtly ideological project. In the related critiques of the tales themselves, the common approach is to treat them collectively, as a form which embodies and prescribes a particular set of culturally dominant ideologies centered on the codes and paradigms of patriarchy. They are read as suggesting and symbolically rewarding gendered patterns of behavior particularly pertinent for young readers, depicting as they often do the transition from adolescence to maturity. The revision and retelling of the canonical fairy tales in new fictions thus becomes one aspect of the deconstruction of narratives of patriarchy, allowing for a critique of the way such narratives function and including illustrations of the effects of, and alternatives to, such historically dominant codes of behavior.[2]

I return to this critical work in my later discussion of recent feminist fiction, but for the purposes of the first part of this chapter I have set it aside—not in order to downplay the importance of such an ongoing project but simply to offer a different critical angle on the subject, enabled by exactly this body of critique but also dictated by its position within the context of a study of folktales and contemporary literature. In attempting an alternative to the more holistic feminist critiques, which view traditional fairy tales en masse as historically sanctioned paradigms of successful female socialization, my aim is for an approach that is more specific, focusing on the work of contemporary writers in this area as a re-energizing of what has become a staid genre, a static group of narratives. As Jack Zipes has suggested, "[p]erhaps the major social critique carried by the fairy tale genre can be seen in the restructuring and reformation by feminists of the fairy tale genre itself" (*Penguin Book of Western Fairy Tales* xxviii); it is a dual focus on both the aesthetic and the historical side of this equation—the importance of the fairy tale as an historically determined genre of writing as well as a cipher for moral prescription and proscription—that makes it possible to approach this region of contemporary fiction productively from a different direction.

To take this step beyond revision, I have followed three principles: firstly, rather than focusing on the values contained within the canonical fairy tale I have turned to the history of the tales themselves, in particular their passage from the oral to the literary and across national boundaries. This process problematizes the question of the ultimate meaning of any particular tale, its status as a fixed, self-contained narrative, and is thus related to ideological critiques of the core body of fairy tales. Following on from this, I have chosen to focus on one specific tale, together with its closely related tale types, in order to avoid some of the generalizations to which related criticism in this area has been subject, as well as to illustrate the multiplicity of material and meaning contained within a particular folk narrative. Patient submissiveness, as a putative paradigm of female behavior, is in fact endorsed by a very limited number of fairy tales. As Alison Lurie, among others, has sought to stress, such tales, although enshrined as canonical, are "from the point of view of European folklore . . . a very unrepresentative selection," reflecting more "the taste of the refined literary men who edited the first popular collections of fairy tales for children during the Victorian era" ("Witches and Fairies" 6); the fairy tale is, indeed, "one of the few sorts of classic children's literature of which a radical feminist would approve" ("Fairy Tale Liberation" 42).[3] There is undoubtedly a harsh misogyny present in folk narrative traditions, a misogyny characteristic of much traditional literature, and of literature closely related to or influenced by such material. Yet a more inclusive conception of these traditions suggests that other character types do exist, and it is this drawing out of marginalized folk narratives as a way of challenging orthodox readings that I wish to follow here.[4]

Finally, I raise the question of the status of contemporary retellings and fairy tale influenced feminist fictions. Postmodernist fiction can be at least partly defined through its exploration and manipulation of the conventions of popular literary genres; to place fairy tale related fictions within this context—to read them as narrative fictions rather than simply critiques—is to draw out the aesthetic components that can be ignored in more singleminded ideological criticism: questions of style, intertextuality, and generic subversion. The fictional texts can thus be read in terms of what the folklorist Wolfgang Mieder refers to as "innovative survival forms of the fairy tale," the result of an interaction between tradition and innovation comparable with that referred to, with reference to Barth and Ricoeur, in the previous chapter (xii).

One of the major successes of the feminist critique of fairy tales has been its narration of the historical construction of the ideology of the canonical tales. This process has brought to the fore the tendentious nature of the seemingly universal and natural, the product of what Jack Zipes has termed "bourgeoisification": the manner in which, during the eighteenth and nineteenth centuries, certain tales, in (re)written form, came to embody a set of conservative, Christian, bourgeois values, and were thus gradually assigned a new role in the socialization process (aided by the relegation of the fantastic in literature in favor of the seemingly more mature mode of realism). The tales gradually become static, seemingly ahistorical, analogous to a Barthesian contemporary myth in which the historically specific comes to stand as the timelessly natural (Zipes, *The Brothers Grimm* 148–50). The feminist project has thus been to rehistoricize these narratives and deconstruct their ideological underpinning. However, by approaching this area from the angle of the folklorist or historian of folk narratives it is possible to undercut the fixedness of these narratives at an earlier point, as well as to begin to think about contemporary retellings as part of an ongoing process of revision and revivifying. While the ideology of the tales has been shown to be historically determined, it is also important to engage with both the history of the tales themselves and the fairy tale genre; to move away from a definition of the tales as, according to the Grimm brothers, "a genre whose narrative stood beyond time and place" (quoted in Bottigheimer, "From Gold to Guilt" 199), and away from critical approaches which seek to treat the tales "flattened out, like patients on a couch, in a timeless contemporaneity" (Darnton 13).

To return to the source of what we know as the fairy tale conceived as a literary genre would appear to be to return to Perrault's *Histoires ou contes du temps passé*, first published in 1697. Not only does this collection of eight tales contain three of the limited number of narratives that have since become synonymous with the fairy tale—"Cinderella," "Sleeping Beauty," and "Little Red Riding Hood"—it has also been read as marking an epochal shift from the relative obscurity of the oral tradition into the mainstreams of social and literary history, namely, the institutionalization of a genre and its paradigmatic expression. Thus Michel Butor remarks that "Perrault's tales . . . permit us to observe the precise moment when the transition occurs from folklore to book, when the oral tradition calls writing to its rescue in order to perpetuate itself" (211)—a view with which Peter Brooks concurs: "[t]he act of transcription, both creative and destructive, takes us from the primitive to the modern, makes the stories and their themes enter into literacy, into civilization, into history" ("Toward Supreme Fictions" 11). Even in the most basic sense, accounts of this seemingly momentous shift are flawed, ignoring as they do (to choose one example) the publication, in 1550 and 1553 respectively, of the two parts of Straparola's *Le Piacevoli Notti*, a collection of seventy-four tales that includes forerunners to some of Perrault's narratives and which was translated into French as early as 1560.[5] Yet this error masks another more problematic assumption. To state that Perrault's volume marks such a "precise moment" is to place a boundary between the oral and the literary, to install a literal turning point that marks a fixed border between traditions of storytelling and types of story. As I attempt to illustrate throughout, such boundaries are always fatally flawed, to the extent that they seek to impose a hierarchical and static fixity. Conversely, the history of the tales—the history of a type of narrative—points towards a fluidity in which boundaries are blurred, one in which "each tale can be seen to consist of interpenetrating layers of narrative," thus problematizing any attempt to co-opt the fairy tale as in some way inherently illustrative of a particular set of values (Bottigheimer, "Tale Spinners" 141).

What is at stake here is the extent to which it is possible to narrativize the history of the fairy tale, to provide a unifying account that neatly orders the process of the dissemination of tales. Just as

the diverse conceptions of narrative that I summarized in the previous chapter are rooted in an acknowledgment of the partial and
provisional, so it is only possible provisionally to account for the
complex, layered nature of this specific field of storytelling. For example, while the aforementioned existence, in French translation,
of Straparola's collection legitimizes the possibility of Italian influence on the late seventeenth-century vogue for fairy tales in Paris,
the fact that Basile's equally important collection, *Il Pentamerone*
(1634–1636), was not available in French at the time does not
mean that it did not cross regional borders in the form of oral versions. Similarly, the influence of an oral tradition of storytelling
problematizes the concept of narrative authenticity upon which
the neatly conclusive account of tale dissemination is based, in
that it foregrounds the act of telling itself. An oral tradition posits
a series of storytelling events, a chain of (re)creative acts whose
very specificity—teller, audience, setting—denies the possibility
of establishing an original version, even before we consider the
probable influence, at various stages, of written texts. This oral
tradition is central to any theory concerning the literary fairy tale,
not only before but also after tales have been transcribed, indicative of the interplay between the oral and the literary that is a
primary characteristic of the genre.[6]

In terms of its history, the folktale tradition can be imagined as
a series of shifting icebergs, with the texts of, for example, Perrault
and the Grimm brothers as merely the visible tips, signs of far more
expansive bodies of storytelling. Perrault's collection was part of
an historically significant outburst of tale-telling that occurred in
the fashionable salons of Paris in the late seventeenth-century,
giving rise to the notion of the tales as a distinct literary genre: *contes de fées*. The chain of storytelling that produced this vogue has
its origins, at least in part, in the passage of tales from the lower to
the upper classes, a pivotal process in any shift into the domain of
the written, rather than solely the spoken, word. The frontispiece
of Perrault's collection depicts a female servant in the process
of telling stories to a huddle of children, thus recording the role
played by servants of various types—governesses, nurses—in the

dissemination of tales. As Joan DeJean comments, "the tales of my mother the goose were still a part of oral tradition, still the property of the substitute mothers, the nurses, who recounted them to their charges" (*Tender Geographies* 54); and it is important in the construction of this particular chain of storytelling to recognize the presence of both the oral tradition and the female teller at this stage: "the predominant pattern reveals older women of a lower status handing on the material to younger people . . . sometimes, if not often, of higher position and expectations, like future ethnographers and writers of tales" (Warner, *From the Beast to the Blonde* 17).[7]

The central role played by women storytellers continued as tale-telling became a fashionable part of the salon culture of aristocratic Paris. From the time of the inauguration of the French salon tradition in the form of the *ruelle* (or alcove, between bed and wall) of Catherine de Vivone, Marquise de Rambouillet, this interior space was to a significant extent the domain of women, an "alternative space" (DeJean, "The Salons" 297)—in part a compensation for the denial of entry into the official realm of the Academy—in which stories, issues of the day, politics, and sexual relations were debated in the form of the artful conversation: as Marina Warner points out, "[i]f the *académies*, controlling the written word, were dominated by male authors and thinkers, then the *ruelles* were the sphere of women, where they presided over the spoken word and its uses" (*From the Beast to the Blonde* 50). Fittingly, it was within this oral environment that the remembered tales of childhood came to be retold as part of the conversational games that constituted the culture of the salon. They were manipulated as a form which could be used to elaborate on contemporary issues, including questions of particular pertinence to the educated aristocratic women who formed a large part of the groups: questions of education, of childbirth and, particularly, of the institution of marriage. Motifs and plots were elaborated and improvised upon in displays of the art of conversation—part entertainment, part tendentious debate.

Following this percolation of narratives, the tales began to appear in print. In 1651, Madeleine de Scudéry—prolific author and, in her youth, frequenter of the salon of the Marquise de Rambouillet—introduced the conversation, or conversational style, into her writing as a reflection of this particular milieu, "a gesture of homage . . . to the art of conversation in which they [women] had excelled in the salons." In a similar fashion, the fairy tale, transferred between different types of oral culture, now assumed its place in Parisian culture as a literary form (DeJean, *Tender Geographies* 47). Given this rootedness in the oral—whether the lower class traditions of storytelling or the artful conversational games of the *précieuses*—it is fitting that the first magic tale to appear in print at this time, "L'île de la Félicité," was written by a frequenter of the salons, Marie-Catherine d'Aulnoy, as part of her first novel, *Histoire d'Hypolite, comte de Duglas* (1690). Other "salon women," such as Henriette Julie de Murat and Marie-Jeanne L'Héritier (the niece of Charles Perrault), soon followed Mme d'Aulnoy into print with their elaborate and often extended variations on familiar narratives, while Mme d'Aulnoy herself went on to publish two volumes of fairy tales between 1697 and 1698. The fairy tale had become fashionable as a literary form, the symbol of a specifically modern, non-classical style of writing which tacitly demoted the arguments of the "Ancients." The fact that it was women who were the main initiators and practitioners of the form highlights the position of this newly created genre within the contemporary cultural milieu: slightly subversive, marginal, symptomatic of modern ideas; produced by, and producing, an alternative space, yet simultaneously staunchly aristocratic in outlook and patriotic in its suggestion of a specifically French, rather than a broadly Western Classical, tradition.[8]

As we now know, it was the tales of a male author—indeed, the only prominent male author among the new tale-tellers—that were eventually to become synonymous with the rise of the literary fairy tale. Perrault's narratives are not representative of this new genre, neither in their explicit appeal to a younger audience nor in their economy and brevity of style (two characteristics which at least partly account for their success in the subsequent history of the literary tale as a children's genre). While this may suggest a closer association with oral sources, it is more likely that Perrault's tales are as much stylistic constructions as the extended embellishments of his female contemporaries: as Dorothy Thelander comments, "even the most literary of these stories seems to have been made from bits and pieces of folktales . . . [and] there is no reason to believe that any of the authors accurately reproduced peasant sources" (470).[9] In fact, the characteristics of the tales of Mme d'Aulnoy and Mlle L'Héritier—the fusion of the oral and the literary, the mixture of simplicity with aristocratic mannerisms and the construction of tales from disparate motifs—are more indicative of the hybrid nature of the fairy tale tradition than Perrault's shorter and plainer versions.[10] As the narratives pass into a new context they both gain and lose certain elements, and it is this accumulation of layers that complicates any characterization of the genre. Institutionalized as a literary genre, the fairy tale retains the mark of its parallel existence as a related oral form, with the oral roots of storytelling present in the process of transmission: the conventions and expectations of the specific setting and audience, including the influence of the conversational style. The same is of course true of the story cycles of Chaucer, Boccaccio, Straparola, and Basile, where the physical act of telling is incorporated into the form of the written text, signaling the close proximity of the two modes of narration.

This interplay of tradition and innovation proceeds into the eighteenth and nineteenth century, during which time the notion of a literature specifically aimed at the moral education of children (the history of which was sketched in the previous chapter with reference to Coover and the fairy tale) and the concept of a readily available, authentic national folk culture gradually take shape. It is the latter that forms the philosophical basis of the second major written document—in historical terms—of the folktale tradition: the Grimm brothers' *Kinder- und Hausmärchen*, the second point at which the streams of storytelling coalesce to form an influential set of texts. Yet the history of the several editions of this collection is as illustrative of hybridity and intertextuality as that of the

French salon tales. While Perrault's tales were soon reprinted—in Holland, for example—the new French literary genre was rapidly shorn of its extravagances and appearing in much simplified versions in chapbooks of the time: the *Bibliothèque bleue*, distributed by itinerant pedlars to peasant communities, thus transplanting an altered set of tales back into the oral tradition to be adapted and retold.[11] While it is probable that these versions were circulated outside France, they certainly appeared in German versions of the French chapbooks, the *Blaue Bibliothek* series, and this is one of the facts that has led to speculation as to whether the type of tale exemplified by the literary fairy tale—the written, adapted version of the oral wonder tale—actually existed in Germany as part of the oral tradition before the mid-eighteenth century: as H. V. Velten comments with reference to Perrault's tales, "the stories were popular in Germany for approximately a hundred years before the first genuine German fairy tales appeared in literature" (5).[12] The implications of such a suggestion are indicative of the shift that has taken place in Grimmian studies, away from a view of the collections as a distillation of relatively unadulterated Germanic narratives, towards an idea of the tales as hybrid literary creations.

It was the Grimm brothers themselves who sought to characterize their project as the recovery of an indigenous, specifically authentic narrative tradition, in which the presence of ancient German myth was tangible and which thus provided a link with the wellsprings of a national culture: in the (translated) words of the preface to the second volume of the first edition, "[e]verything that has been collected here from oral tradition is . . . purely German in its origins as well as in its development and has not been borrowed from any sources."[13] Such claims obviously rest on the notion of authentic sources and once again the female narrator was invoked as the central figure in the transmission of tales. The Grimms suggested the ideal of the female peasant storyteller, a character privy to the oral tradition of the spinning room, the "places by the stove, the hearth in the kitchen," where tales were exchanged as part of a daily routine (204). They cite one of their

most important informants, Dorothea Viehmann—a major source
discovered after the publication of the first volume of the first
edition—as just such a "type," including a detailed description
of her storytelling technique; indeed, it was a portrait of Frau
Viehmann, drawn by the Grimms' younger brother, Ludwig Emil,
and used as a frontispiece in numerous later editions, that came
to signal generic peasant authenticity as, for example, the English
figure of "Gammer Grethel."[14] However, subsequent studies show
Dorothea Viehmann to have been not only the literate wife of
an artisan but also a descendant of Huguenot immigrants, many
of whom had come to Germany after 1685 to escape persecution
under the increasingly prescriptive monarchy of Louis XIV. Similarly with another major source, the contentious figure of "Old
Marie," originally thought to have been the widow of a village
blacksmith and thus suitably in tune with the tradition of the
folk. It is now known that a large majority of references to this
source actually denote the eldest daughter of the Hassenpflug family, wealthy family friends of the Grimms. The Hassenpflug's were
of Huguenot origin, prone to the influence of local tales and literary versions, and the contributions of "Old Marie" have been
shown to exhibit marked similarities with the literary fairy tales
of Perrault and d'Aulnoy (McGlathery, *Grimms' Fairy Tales* 46).[15]

This is not to suggest that the Grimm brothers—founding figures in the area of folktale scholarship—were unaware of parallel
traditions: in the preface to the first volume of the first edition
they characterize their material as "never fixed and always changing from one region to another, from one teller to another" (208).
Complimentary reference is made to Perrault and to the rich Italian tradition of Basile and Straparola, and in later editions Wilhelm openly attests to his belief in the Indo-European ancestry of
the tales (209–10). Also, if both the original and simplified versions of French literary fairy tales influenced the Grimms' sources,
it is equally true that in later editions of the tales they drew on
"the robust, gutsy, rough-hewn tradition of early German literature" in the form of the *Schwank*, chapbooks containing coarse
tavern-tales aimed at both educated and uneducated (and rife

with misogyny; Bottigheimer, "From Gold to Guilt" 199–204).
Yet the narrative purity of the tales is not only open to question
via the sources: a simple comparison of the prefaces to the first and
second editions reveals a subtle but definite shift in attitude, from
a stance for which "the value of a true, unadulterated recording"
is paramount, to a justification of the need for minor alterations.
In the second edition, as well as the elimination of "every phrase
not appropriate for children," reference is made to the fact that
"many stories have been told more directly and simply," illustrating "the kind of attentiveness and tact required to sort out what is
pure, simple, and yet intact from what is inauthentic" (220). The
authenticity thus subtly begins to tilt towards the manufactured,
in response to two central impulses: firstly, the desire to appeal
to a bourgeois readership, in particular to children, for whom the
Grimms intended the volume as "a manual of manners" (in the
first edition these manners were referred to as implicitly resulting
from the naturalness of the tales, but were subsequently imposed as
part of the editorial process); secondly, the ambition to embody
a pre-existent notion of the folktale tradition as the collective
expression of an untainted imagination at one with nature, a Romanticist spirit of spontaneity. In spite of his frequent criticisms
of the speciousness of contemporaneous folktale volumes, Wilhelm, the chief editor, has increasingly been perceived as a self-
conscious manipulator of folk narratives, constructing what has
been referred to as the genre of the "Grimmian fairy tale" or, more
generally, the *Märchen*.[16] As early as 1929, Elisabeth Freitag was
uncovering specific examples of embellishments and alterations
over the course of the early editions, as McGlathery summarizes:

> Among the stylistic changes cited by Freitag were addition of
> alliteration, repetition of words, onomatopoeia, direct speech,
> and diminutives. She pointed also to increased attention
> to depicting household matters and life's material needs, as
> well as less open mention of sexual matters, elimination of
> vulgar expressions, and a greater role for prayer and piety.
> (McGlathery, *Grimms' Fairy Tales* 42)[17]

Yet even before such overt changes crept into the editorial process, the Grimms were operating with an unavoidable set of preconceptions with regard to their material, its sources, and its potential audience, preconceptions which are a part of the multiple "filters" involved in the necessarily complicated passage from the oral to the literary.[18]

While some critics use the evidence of increasing editorial interference, together with the sullied nature of the Grimms' sources, to point to the contaminated status of the tales (a charge repeatedly made in John Ellis's vehement critique of the Grimms' methods, *One Fairy Story Too Many* (1983)), this only suggests a prior state of uncontamination, as well as the largely unrealizable possibility of exact and complete transcription, and thus implies exactly the same notion of purity as that claimed by the Grimm brothers with reference to "an inexhaustibly rich ideal type" (215). As I have sought to demonstrate, folk narrative traditions are criss-crossed with numerous currents that leave their mark, often glancingly, on individual tales. This includes the oral traditions themselves, which are prone to the influence of literary versions of tales as well as to original literary texts. Indeed, the worldwide dissemination and popularity of the hybrid forms of the Grimms' fairy tales has led to their passing back into various oral traditions, to be re-shaped in the process of retelling, just as the French fairy tales seeped into the German narrative pool.[19] To talk of an authentic tradition is always to create a fiction, one based on pure origins and mythical bearers—hence the political manipulation of the folktale in Hitler's Germany, where cheap editions of the Grimms' collection were printed in vast quantities during the war years (Bottigheimer, "The Publishing History of Grimms' Tales" 91–92).[20] Just as there is not a purely German canon of tales so there is not an inviolably patriarchal set of narratives.

The implications of these various historical instances are manifold, not least for the interpretation of specific tales and their retellings. As they demonstrate, the fairy tale is a hybrid form on a number of levels, constructed of a series of shifting intertextual strands, with each tale functioning as a narrative chameleon able to assume and discard the social color of its current setting in a complex interplay with tradition. It is possible to contextualize contemporary retellings or modifications of motifs as part of an ongoing historical process which involves the choice or uncovering of specific strands within this movement (possibly to counter others that have gained dominance), continuing a tradition which is not so much characterizable as variations on a theme but rather as the theme of variation itself. Thus, just as Marie-Catherine d'Aulnoy molded folk forms and motifs to fit currently prevalent social concerns (at least as perceived by her intended audience), so the use of fairy tale material in contemporary narratives is a continuation of a process of adaptation and innovation, one which relativizes the claims of any particular version to the status of "original," or of any interpretation to the status of "true." As Robert Darnton says, "[f]olktales are historical documents. They have evolved over many centuries and have taken different turns in different cultural traditions. Far from expressing the unchanging operations of man's inner being, they suggest that mentalités have changed" (13).[21] It is this approach to the area that avoids the "over-simplification" remarked on more than fifty years ago by J. R. R. Tolkien: "the cauldron of story has always been boiling, and to it have continually been added new bits, dainty and undainty" (26).

One of the ramifications of the intrinsic hybridity of folk narrative history is the need for specificity when reading the tales themselves, in order to encompass the competing currents present within any particular tale type. While this approach goes against the grain of recent critiques of canonical fairy tales that take a broadly collective approach to the genre, each tale or motif serving to illustrate an underlying trend or ideology, it nevertheless has a similarly undermining effect on the claims to universality of individual versions or interpretations. Mieder comments on the need for such an approach in the realm of folkloristics, where "variation is intrinsically related to tradition": "If we want to study the cultural significance of traditional stories . . . it is of the greatest importance that their existence with and without their textual changes be studied diachronically and synchronically" (xi).[22] It is the relativizing action of this mode of reading that is most crucial, the manner in which a concentration on individual strands of folk narrative history enables dominant versions and interpretations to be unraveled from within the tradition itself.

For the purposes of this chapter I have chosen to map the web of connections that surround the story of "Bluebeard" and its related tale types. This reading functions on two levels: *vertically*, or paradigmatically, in terms of the various manifestations of this specific tale, and *horizontally*, or syntagmatically, in terms of the close proximity—in spatial terms, to the left and to the right—of two closely related tale types.[23] The choice of a limited group is in line with the pragmatic turn in narrative theory sketched in the previous chapter, in which the specificity of the individual narrative is valued over the deep structural similarities between a broad range of examples. While such a view theoretically suggests the need for individual treatments of each tale, the folk narrative tradition is characterized by interconnection and thus an approach which recognizes the fluid nature of the tale pool while attempting to delineate specific knots of narrative material represents a practical midpoint between methodological extremes. The text of any folktale is already a hybrid construct produced through the various stages of the passage from the oral to the literary; the study of such an isolated text would certainly provide insights but would have the adverse effect of installing one manifestation of a tale as *the* version, and would be of little use in establishing an informed and fertile context for the reading of subsequent retellings.

"Bluebeard" (AT 312) is particularly appropriate in this context, not only because of the role it has played in recent feminist fictions, but because it is an example of a tale that was included in the first edition of the Grimms' *Kinder- und Hausmärchen* (as "Blaubart," No. 62 in the 1812 volume of the first edition), but subsequently dropped as exhibiting too strong a French influence.[24] Yet its presence is still strongly apparent in the Grimms' chosen versions of its related narrative types—"The Robber Bride-groom" ("Der Räuberbräutigam," KHM 40) and "Fitcher's Fowl" ("Fitchers Vogel," KHM 46)—both of which became part of the their final canon. It is this marginal status that gives "Bluebeard" its fascination. While it was included in Perrault's *Histoires ou contes du temps passé* (as "La Barbe bleue") it has not gone on to achieve the status of tales such as "Cinderella" or "Sleeping Beauty." Rarely appearing in children's story collections and yet to be awarded the accolade of a popular animated cartoon version, it stands at the edges of Perrault's volume and in the margins of the Grimms'.[25] This position is further enhanced by the story's liminal status as a genuine fairy tale, containing no discernible fairy tale elements—at least in the Perrault version—other than the magic key, and certainly no quest or romance motifs.

Approaching "Bluebeard" *vertically*, what is immediately apparent is the relative lack of variants, together with the pre-eminence of Perrault's version: an artful, discreetly literary tale which manages to capture a folk-like quality while simultaneously illustrating his skill as an adapter.[26] The tale opens with a classic fairy tale duality, placing the lone male figure, wealthy but unattractive, against the female community of mother and two daughters. The "frightfully ugly" male protagonist is characterized as fundamentally lacking, a lack which parallels the abundance of beauty in the world of the daughters. What this opening motif illustrates is the close relationship between "Bluebeard" and the "Beauty and the Beast" narrative type (AT 425C), both of which are variations on the animal bridegroom theme. The pivotal difference is of course that the male character is a figurative rather than a literal beast, reflecting the more darkly realistic mode of the tale (although a German version casts the Bluebeard character in the form of the devil, which fits with several European variants of the "Robber Bridegroom" and "Fitcher's Fowl" types ["The Girl Who Married the Devil," Ranke 42–44]).

Being a fairy tale, it is the younger daughter who is gradually seduced by the wealth of Bluebeard, his hospitality causing her to conclude that "the beard of the master of the house was not as blue as it used to be and that he was a very worthy man." This motif of wealth occurs in many of the variants, and if the extravagant descriptions seek to purvey the lure of abundant riches, the fact that this form of abundance is set against the abundance of beauty in the daughters—each acting as the counterpart lacking in the life of the other—tacitly suggests an inherent link between worldly wealth and the male world, and physical or familial security and the female environment. It is this male world that the youngest daughter is drawn to, her optimism sullied only by the passing reference to his previous wives and the fact that "nobody knew what had become of them." It is in a French variant ("Blue-Beard," Bødker et al, 158–60) that the number of seven previous wives is specified, and this has become the agreed, if not symbolic, number, appearing repeatedly in later retellings—most notably Béla Bartók's one-act opera, *Duke Bluebeard's Castle* (A Kékszakállúherceg vára, 1911), based on Béla Balázs's symbolist "mystery play."[27]

What follows constitutes the motific heart of the "Bluebeard" tale, embodying the classic fairy tale sequence of prohibition-violation. Just as the male character—Bluebeard or Devil—has come to represent masculinity in the schematic folkloric characterization, so now he proceeds to stamp his mark of patriarchal authority in the form of a prohibitive law. This is emphasized by two details: Bluebeard is leaving on a "matter of great consequence," a matter which takes place in the distant world of business of which the female protagonist need know little, and the law or taboo is symbolized in the shape of the keys, the smallest one of which carries the prohibition, a fact which is repeated in all variants. The size of this key, along with the size of the "little room" and the relative insignificance of the injunction, is set against the boundless freedom given in all other respects: "[h]ere are the keys to my two great storerooms . . . these are the keys to the strongboxes . . . this is the passkey to all the apartments." Yet the key's small size appears to contradict the seemingly excessive punishment its misuse carries: "if you dare open the door, my anger will exceed anything you have ever experienced." The word of the law is thus characterized as curiously illogical, literally out of proportion, and it is this very incongruity that encapsulates its status as law and as an embodiment of the unquestionable condition of access to the realm of the law. In the violation which follows, the central motif is the bride's insatiable curiosity, now made to appear all the more unwarranted in the symbolic economy of the tale by the wealth of freedoms already granted to her. In Perrault's version we hear of how "her curiosity increased to such a degree that . . . she nearly tripped and broke her neck," while the pivotal gendering of curiosity is stressed in an alternative French variant in which both the bride and her "sister Ann" enter the room together, "even though it was forbidden" ("Blue-Beard," Bødker et al). This motif is chosen as the tale's lesson in one of the two verse morals appended by Perrault, in which he warns that

> [c]uriosity, in spite of its charm
> Too often causes a great deal of harm
> . . . With due respect, ladies, the thrill is slight.

It is this forbidden room which constitutes the tale's literal and metaphorical core, consisting of the bodies of dead women suspended from the walls. This is the secret that the law seeks to hide, the embodiment of the law and the cost of failure to abide by it: the test and the punishment.

It is thus fitting that it should be the symbolic key itself which refuses to conceal the violation, stained as it now is with blood (blood which draws into the foreground the sexual undertones that are scattered throughout the narrative and which have played a central role in literary adaptations). Bluebeard returns earlier than expected to find that his bait has been taken: "[y]ou wanted to enter the room! Well, madam, you will enter the room and take your place among the ladies you saw there." At this point the girl's curiosity translates into cunning, her piety in the face of death masking a mind busy concocting a means of escape. That the bride manipulates the social signs of femininity here in order to trick her husband—signs which are the counterpart to the curiosity he

has seemingly come to believe is an intrinsically female biological inheritance—is neatly brought out in the alternative French
variant, in which, having being told by her husband to "put on
her prettiest dress, to go on a journey," she proceeds to use signs
of femininity to play for time: "I must get my prettiest blouse. . . .
I must get my prettiest stockings. . . . I must get my prettiest hat"
("Blue-Beard," Bødker 158–59). In a further French variant cited
by the Opies from an oral version recorded in 1886, the wife's
delay is excused by the fact that she is putting on her wedding
dress, the traditional garment of those approaching death by ex-
ecution, an act intended to deceive Bluebeard into thinking his
wife is resigned to die (Opie 134).[28] As expected, this ploy works
and she and her sister are saved by their brothers, the tale ending
in a wash of traditionalism in which the now-wealthy widow buys
commissions for her brothers to become captains, arranges a marriage for sister Ann, and finally herself marries a man "who made
her forget . . . Bluebeard."

The step towards reading this tale type *horizontally*—in terms of
its closely related narrative neighbors and the manner in which
those variants cut across, comment on or subvert the tale they
intersect—is authorized by Aarne and Thompson's listing of one
of these, the Grimms' "Fitcher's Fowl" ("Fitchers Vogel," KHM
46), as a "Bluebeard" variant, tale type AT 311. Just as the 1812
volume of the Grimms' tales included "Blaubart," whose close
affinity to the Perrault narrative led to its subsequent rejection,
so it also included "The Castle of Murder" ("Das Mordschloss,"
No. 73 in the 1812 volume of the first edition), a tale of Dutch
provenance which fuses an expression of AT 311 with AT 955, this
second being the other major variant that constitutes the "Bluebeard" trilogy under discussion. "The Castle of Murder" was also
dropped in subsequent editions, but its existence serves further to
highlight the interrelated nature of these tales and their various
expression.[29]

Attempting broadly to characterize the nature of the various
national narrative traditions (and aware of the composite nature
of the tales that constitute any such tradition), Darnton sees the

French propensity for humor, domesticity, and everyday craftiness
as indicative of a concern for the natural world, while finding in
the Germanic tradition a tendency towards the mysterious, the
fantastic, and the macabre: the otherworldly as opposed to the
down-to-earth (21–22; 34; 44–46). This is strikingly evident if
we read "Fitcher's Fowl" as a version of a Germanic "Bluebeard,"
a reading sanctioned by its textual history. Here, the male se-
ducer is a wizard who preys on "beautiful girls," merely having to
touch them to gain control. This parallels the figure of the devil
in the aforementioned non-Grimmian German "Bluebeard" variant ("The Girl Who Married the Devil," Ranke 42–44), a figure
who also appears in the Italian version of "Fitcher's Fowl," "Silver
Nose" (Calvino, *Italian Folktales* 26–30); further variants cast a
midget in this role ("The Tale of the Fäderäwisch," Ranke 40–
42). These components highlight the macabre and beastly element variously present in this tale group, enhanced in AT 311 by
the characteristic fairy tale forest. As in AT 312, much is made
of the riches contained in the male protagonist's home, "magnifi-
cently furnished" in "Fitcher's Fowl," and with "each [room] more
beautiful than the other" in "Silver Nose." Similarly, the core of
the tale is an elaboration on the prohibition-violation binary, here
repeated once for each daughter. While in each variant the keys
are present, as both narrative device and possible symbol, individual manifestations include intriguing and colorful additions:
in "Fitcher's Fowl" the girls are given an egg, and it is this which
becomes indelibly stained with blood; in "Silver Nose" the devil
places a different flower in each successive girl's hair, the petals
of which are scorched by the flames in the forbidden room; and
perhaps most revealingly, in a Spanish variant, "The Merchant
and His Three Daughters," the girls are each given "a beautiful apple" which is dutifully dropped and bruised on entry into
the room ("The Merchant and His Three Daughters," Bødker
173–74). While the blood on the key is suggestive, the egg and
apple variants of this motif enhance the symbolism, suggesting
archetypes and thematic connections—of sex, sexuality, and bib-

lical precedents—which have been unraveled in recent explorations of this knot of tales.

At the heart of the prohibition-violation cycle is the ubiquitous "room of blood," entry into which is an inevitable consequence, within the structural economy of the tale, of the equally ubiquitous female curiosity.[30] Confirming Darnton's characterization, the German variant is suitably explicit concerning the contents of the room, in which stand "a huge basin full of blood . . . full of chopped-up dead people," "two sisters hanging from the ceiling—long, stiff, and dead." In a more metaphysical vein, the Italian "Silver Nose" includes a forbidden door that leads directly into Hell and "a crowd of damned souls in agony inside the fiery room." While "Fitcher's Fowl" does not specify the sex of the victims, the Spanish variant refers to "the corpses of young girls, all with their heads cut off," and another German variant describes a room containing only the bodies of the elder sisters. This echoes the dead wives lying at the heart of the "Bluebeard" tale type, with the gruesome addition of anonymous female victims. Given that this further polarizes the role and status of the female characters in the thematic structure of the narrative, it is appropriate to find a further clarification of the role of patriarchal law, in the form of the wizard's summary: "[s]ince you have entered that room against my will . . . you shall enter it again against yours." Just as there is an apparent disjunction between key and punishment at the same point in the "Bluebeard" tale type, so here we encounter a paradox: the room can be entered, but only on the terms laid down by the law, a law which is embodied in the injunction against entry.

Yet if these versions of this tale are both more violent in their depiction of women's bodies—each including a description of the death of the first two sisters—and more explicit in the statements they appear to make about the status and character of women (at least as they figure in the tales' textual environments), they simultaneously expand on the inconspicuous motif of cunning subversion present in the "Bluebeard" tale type. This acts not only to provide a counterpoint to an increasingly oppressive atmosphere but also to draw out and comment on the role of this element in both narratives. While in the "Bluebeard" tale type the youngest daughter is usually the only one of the two sisters to be seduced, the "Fitcher's Fowl" group sets her actions against those of her two elder sisters, both of whom fail the test and are cast into the room. Yet the point is not that the third and youngest daughter, that generic staple of the fairy tale, is immune to curiosity—this motif is common to both tale types and is always explicitly referred to. The difference is that the third daughter—"Sly Lucia" as she is called in "Silver Nose"—quick-wittedly guesses the nature of the egg/flower/apple gift and thus avoids allowing it to be indelibly marked. And it is by craftily appearing not to have succumbed to what is perceived as a distressing female trait that this daughter gains the confidence of her husband/master. The law is ostensibly kept as well as secretly broken, and the locus of power, albeit a necessarily devious and clandestine form of power, shifts to the woman: "[h]e now no longer had power over her and had to do as she told him." It is at this point that the tales, read collectively, seem unconsciously to hint at a connection between female curiosity and female craftiness. The various versions offer different accounts of this section of the narrative, but all are characterized by further examples of the third daughter's artfulness in rescuing her sisters and outwitting her captor. In "Fitcher's Fowl" this involves actually piecing together her disembodied sisters and smuggling them home in sacks thought by the wizard to contain laundry. Yet perhaps the most subtle of this character's smart ploys occurs in the first half of an Italian version, "The Three Chicory Gatherers." In this relatively distant variant the malevolent character is cast as a dragon and the test involves eating a part of the body of an earlier victim. The body parts have the power of speech and act like the key in "Bluebeard," thus revealing to the dragon, on his return, that the girls have been unable to eat them (Calvino, *Italian Folktales* 500–503). While the youngest, Mariuzza, is equally unable to indulge in her captor's cannibalism, she grinds the prescribed foot with a pestle and hides the powder in a stocking underneath her dress. When the dragon returns and inquires of the foot's whereabouts, it dutifully admits to being "[o]n Mariuzza's stomach," and she is entrusted with the keys to the dragon's home—a wonderfully devious example of the duping motif, stressing the inhumanity of the male protagonist and amplifying the less prominent role of female cunning in the "Bluebeard" tale type.

While Perrault's "Bluebeard" concludes with a wash of generic neatness—male rescuers, remarriage, and secure futures—here the role of the first of these is minimal, the clever third sister constructing a simulacrum of herself in the form of a doll or decorated skull in order to allow her to enact the final escape. This distinctly folkloric motif provides another instance of the darker atmosphere of this tale type, as well as possibly revealing the literary provenance of Perrault's ostensibly comforting dénouement. Here we do not learn that the sisters proceed to forget their experiences and remarry, and one consequence of this is that the energy, both mental and physical, of the pivotal youngest sister is not dissipated but lingers as one half of the dual heart of the narrative, alongside the forbidden room and its contents: a woman's active craftiness and women's dead, or inactive, bodies.[31] It is also pertinent to note that the tradition spawned by Perrault's "Bluebeard" is the only one in which the rescuers are specifically and solely male, thus further suggesting the need for an informed reading of this version.[32]

As mentioned above, the Grimms' first edition contained a tale which was an amalgam of the "Fitcher's Fowl" narrative, AT 311, and what in later editions became "The Robber Bridegroom" ("Der Räuberbräutigam," KHM 40), identified in the Aarne-Thompson index as AT 955. It is this last tale type which completes the knot of narratives under discussion, each of which acts as a variant and commentary on the other—an intertextual play of motifs. While the "Fitcher's Fowl" tale type is the darker, more fantastic version, "The Robber Bridegroom" elaborates on the more realistic of the various narrative components, a fact which possibly accounts for the prevalence of this tale type in the English tradition, most notably in the form of the witty and poetic "Mr.

Fox" (a tale thought to predate Perrault's "Bluebeard").[33] Such a characterization is confirmed by the placing of this tale type in the "Romantic tale or novelle" section of the Aarne-Thompson index, whereas the other two narratives are placed in the section devoted to magic or wonder tales. However, as was suggested earlier, the broader generic grouping of these tale types as fairy tales is problematic, particularly in the case of AT 312, precisely because of their close proximity to the form of the novelle.

The first half of the tale is an unremarkable variation on the familiar introductory motifs: a strange, rich suitor becomes engaged to a girl (usually at her father's behest) whose suspicions are aroused, or whose suspicions increase, when he fails to invite her to his home. The girl then either extracts an invitation or travels of her own accord through a dense forest to arrive at the house; here she is warned by a bird that this is the home of a murderer, and so discovers, either in the cellar or in "the Bloody Chamber," what is the most explicit expression so far of this motif. In "Mr. Fox," Lady Mary finds "bodies and skeletons of beautiful young ladies all stained with blood," while in "The Robber Bridegroom," the girl, after being instructed by an attendant old woman to hide, is witness to a ritual dismemberment carried out by the murderous gang: "They were dragging another young maiden with them; they were drunk, and paid no heed to her screams and lamentations. They gave her some wine to drink, three glasses full, one of white and one of red and one of yellow, and that made her heart burst. They then tore off her pretty clothes, laid her out on a table, hacked her fair body to pieces and sprinkled them with salt." Again, at least half of the variants specify women as the victims, with the male protagonist in one American version having a penchant for "broilin' women's breasts in front of the fire" ("Old Foster," Angela Carter, *Second Virago Book* 10–12). Just as the more explicitly descriptive passages in the "Fitcher's Fowl" tale type (in comparison with "Bluebeard") are accompanied by more inventive counter-strategies, so the even more gruesome details in this group are accompanied by correspondingly suggestive twists on the theme of cunning. As the robbers chop up their victim a finger flies into the lap of the hidden heroine, which she takes with her on her escape. On the wedding day that follows, the guests take part in a feast of tale telling; called upon to contribute, the bride opts instead to tell a dream she has had the previous night, a dream which is actually an account of her trip to her husband's den, and as the story reaches the moment when the finger is chopped off, the bride miraculously reveals the real finger and the guests dutifully kill or arrest the offender.

This motif of cunning, indeed metafictional, storytelling as a means of escaping fate and revealing the villain occurs in an interesting range of variants.[34] The dream ploy appears in "The Robber Bridegroom" and the American "Old Foster," while the Italian "The Marriage of a Queen and a Bandit" contains, not a fictionalized dream-version of actual events, but an invented dream as a goad to elicit a real means of escape (Calvino, *Italian Folktales* 606–9). In the English "Bobby Rag" (Katherine Briggs 375) the dream is prefaced by a song, while in "The Girl Who Got Up a Tree" (Briggs 405) and "Mr. Fox's Courtship" (Briggs 448) it is replaced by the equally tangential means of a riddle. What all these versions illustrate is the use of cunning female storytelling, of wit and sly artifice, to subvert a bad end. The elaborate tale-within-a-tale acts as an oblique version of the truth, the only option open to a girl who is literally caught in the story, just as the only option open to the youngest sister in the previous tale type was to appear to adhere to, while secretly transgressing, the law. The character's life story is dictated by her father and her future husband, up to the moment at which she, as narrator, literally takes control of the plot. From that point on it is dictated by her, history becoming herstory, a straightforwardly linear narrative turning into a metafictional version and a subversive reading of the narrative within which it occurs. At the crucial moment, the narrative is broken into from outside, in the form of the detached finger, graphically demonstrating the fact that the slanted version of the tale which has just been told is in fact both the real story of a series of deaths and a method of evading death itself.[35] This echoes and returns us to the "Bluebeard" story, thought by some to be an incomplete and modified legend based on the character of the Breton Comorre the Cursed, murderer of four wives before he met Tryphine, the latter of whom managed to escape, while pregnant, with the help of one Gildas the Good (who was later canonized). Whatever the link between fact and folktale fiction— an almost impossible gap to bridge with any degree of specificity or certainty—it provides an instance of the history that often lies embedded within the fabric of the folk narrative, a sometimes harsh historical reality that can call for devious interventions.[36]

What this selective survey illustrates is that the fixed, literary form of any particular folk narrative is always partial, always provisional, a point on a narrative path that is crossed by various other routes.[37] Inscribed within Perrault's stylized "Bluebeard" is the explicit violence of "Fitcher's Fowl," a violence which amplifies the suggestions contained by the artfulness of the French version, taking away the potentially mitigating specificity of the wives and problematizing Perrault's insistence on reading the tale primarily as a cautionary exemplum of women's curiosity. Similarly, the relatively subdued motif of craftiness found in the "Bluebeard" tale type is developed in the variant narratives into a far more subversive, less circumscribed energy, to the point at which this craftiness becomes a challenge to the tale within which it is contained, a variant version in itself. As with the hybridity implicit within specific folk narrative traditions, so the multiple versions latent within the interstices of ostensibly stable tales are similarly available to threaten and challenge a prescriptive interpretation or a putatively authentic reading; again, the challenge comes from within the traditions themselves.

These readings demonstrate the benefits of a motific interpretation of folk and fairy tales, based on a provisional acceptance of categorization into tale types. The motifs that constitute the tales suggest options for interpretation, and it is a specific alignment of these options that gives rise to an individual reading. Not surprisingly, the three interrelated thematic elements that are suggested by a reading of the tale types in question revolve around sexual politics, and it is predominantly for this reason that the constituent tales have played a prominent role in feminist revisions of the fairy tale.

As was the fashion at the time, Perrault added verse morals to his tales, both as an example of his literary acumen and to point up the intent of the story in relation to prevailing aristocratic mores. As we know, in the case of "Bluebeard" he picked an element that was to become the central tenet for future readings:

> Curiosity, in spite of its charm,
> Too often causes a great deal of harm.
> A thousand new cases arise each day.
> With due respect, ladies, the thrill is slight,
> For as soon as you're satisfied, it goes away,
> And the price one pays is never right. (Zipes, *Beauties* 35)

The second verse moral proceeds to point out that husbands no longer "insist on having the impossible," thus supplementing the suggestion that the tale's didactic relevance to a modern audience lies in its warning against the dangers of female curiosity.[38] By shifting the emphasis away from other possible motifs—the forbidden room, the wife's means of escape—the tale becomes one of a failed test of obedience. Yet the girl's curiosity regarding the contents of the room, her desire for knowledge, appears on closer inspection to reveal a more disturbing trait. We have already noted the tell-tale blood on the key, and when this is coupled with Perrault's verse comment on Bluebeard as a man who is "jealous and dissatisfied," it becomes clear that the "impossible" wish he no longer insists upon is fidelity. Following this path of interpretation, the wife's cognitive curiosity becomes a sign of sexual curiosity, centered on an overbearing desire to use the "little key" to enter "the little room at the end of the long corridor on the ground floor." While this may seem rather crude, it represents what is without doubt the dominant interpretation. Maria Tatar has charted the shift in interpretations and literary retellings away from the fact of a tale whose central male character, in all versions of all related types, is a serial murderer—and so prime material for any moral commentary—to a reading in which the wife is the chief locus of evil in the narrative. For example, in Ludwig Tieck's five-act drama based on the tale (*Ritter Blaubart*, 1797), the wife, on seeing the bodies in the room, exclaims "O Curiosity . . . damned, scandalous curiosity! There's no greater sin than curiosity," implying that this supposed defect is the root cause of the crimes on display (quoted in Tatar, "Beauties vs. Beasts" 135).[39] Tieck's Bluebeard proceeds to suggest that this feature has been an inherent part of the female character since Eve's fatal curiosity brought sin into the world, a remark at least partly sanctioned in folk narrative terms by the aforementioned substitution, in one variant, of an apple as the tell-tale sign. This fatal flaw appears several times in the history of the fairy tale, most revealingly in the *locus classicus* of the genre (in literary terms), Apuleius's second century "Cupid and Psyche" (from *The Golden Ass*), in which Psyche's overeager desire to *know* her lover almost leads to her death. (As an antecedent of the "Beauty and the Beast" tale type, "Cupid and Psyche," at least as it appears in early modern versions, is a constituent of the same narrative web as "Bluebeard," albeit more distantly than the other types I have drawn on.) In the Grimms' version of AT 710, "Our Lady's Child" ("Marienkind," KHM 3), the forbidden room and the motif of transgression by curiosity lead to the heroine's punishment, which in this case is to be struck dumb until she truly repents of what is explicitly intended to be read as a sin.[40]

However, I want to retain the focus on versions and interpretations of "Bluebeard" and its closely related types. In more recent commentaries there has been relatively little change. Despite tempering his reading with references to the danger of male possessiveness, Bruno Bettelheim finds in the tale a challenge to female fidelity: he assumes that "[t]he behaviour of Bluebeard's bride suggests two possibilities: that what she sees in the forbidden closet is the creation of her own anxious fantasies; or that she has betrayed her husband, but hopes he won't find out." The fact that the behavior of this character is a product of her discovering the dead bodies of her predecessors is seemingly ignored—pathologically ignored, given the prevalence of this interpretation—leaving the way clear for Bettelheim to speculate on the assumption that "everybody had a high time" while Bluebeard was absent. The inevitable result is a conclusion, written in 1977, which in no significant sense differs from Perrault's moral of 1697: "Women, don't give in to your sexual curiosity; men, don't permit yourself to be carried away at being sexually betrayed" (299–303).[41] As Tatar points out, this tide of interpretation succeeds in "converting a dramatic encounter between innocent maiden and barbaric murderer into a moral conflict between corrupt woman and corrupted man," using biological essentialism and determinacy to legitimize the most extreme behavior ("Beauties vs. Beasts" 136).[42]

Yet as will be apparent from a broad reading of narrative traditions and individual tales within these traditions, the putatively self-apparent nature of this interpretation—the seamless join between tale and commentary that is sanctioned through historical persistence—is simply one version of the story, a version which in this case has more to do with legitimizing male fears and sanctioning a particular morality than with the persistently disturbing elements of this knot of tales. As I have attempted to suggest, the historical fixity of these readings is open to question precisely from the other strands at play within the narratives themselves. The orthodox interpretation is based almost wholly on AT 312, and on a critical reading of the female curiosity motif, bolstered by archetypal extrapolations via Eve and original sin. Yet the parallel motif of female craftiness and cunning that we have seen to be particularly prominent in AT 311 and 955—thus amplifying the less explicit versions in AT 312—finds alternative resonance in the suitably folkloric figure of Shahrazad. While we can detect echoes or antecedents of the Bluebeard/wizard/robber bridegroom characters in King Shahrayar, it is the parallel with Shahrazad's manipulative tale-telling in the face of death that stands out, link-ing her with the female character in the "Robber Bridegroom" tale type and, by extension, her other cunning cousins.

The craftiness in AT 955 is not merely an alternative to, but rather an inscription within, the much maligned curiosity along-side which it occurs, and if cunning in this instance is a response to death, a means of evading death and undermining the power of the villain, curiosity is as much a part of this life-giving tactic. There is of course an umbilical link between curiosity and story-telling or narrative—storytelling as a means of explanation—just as there is a metaphorical link between storytelling and death. It is only through death as the ultimate ending that a narrative achieves its fully transmissible form: "[d]eath is the sanction of everything that the storyteller can tell. He has borrowed his au-thority from death" (Benjamin 94).[43] Yet it is the evasion of death through storytelling that is represented here, an evasion that plays on the curiosity that the narrative form evokes and which here turns back on itself. In a reading of the three interrelated tale types, the curiosity elicited by the robber's bride (witness the rob-ber's increasingly worried but eager interjections) acts to undercut the status of the malignant curiosity attributed to her near relative in "Bluebeard" and "Fitcher's Fowl." This tale-teller manipulates the curiosity she evokes in order to avoid death, a death which in this and the other tales is depicted as a direct result of just such curiosity.

As in the *Arabian Nights*, the actual or threatened death in "Bluebeard" stories is resolutely gender specific. Attempts to read any of the tales as elaborations on the theme of death in gen-eral, such as that by Derek Brewer—"[d]eath is the horrible little room behind all images of wealth and splendor. Death is so to speak an absolute prohibition that we have to break"—are thus simply milder variants of the orthodox interpretation commented on above (40). All three tales revolve around gender and the control of female characters, which is why the tactics of subver-sion resorted to by the women are necessarily devious, subverting simultaneously from the outside, in the unorthodox mixture of reality and seeming illusion—the use in "Fitcher's Fowl" of simulacrum and artifice—and the inside: the tale told as entertainment at the wedding feast, the apparent adherence to the law or the tactical manipulation of cultural signs of femininity. Just as these women are assigned to a dark, disembodied place in the story, so it is from a parallel position of marginality that the history of their deaths, and the craftiness of which its telling is an example, emanate.[44] These multifarious tactics are wittily subversive in the face of adversity, using invention to halt the chain of deaths that lie in the prehistory of each narrative.

In the two motifs, curiosity and cunning, we find a set of potential strategies of interpretation, two of which I have traced: a relatively narrow, prescriptive reading of the former and a more folkloristically inclusive reading of both. Just as it is possible to disassemble orthodox interpretations by pointing to injustices in the symbolic weight the tales are made to carry, so it is possible simultaneously to undermine a group of readings while suggesting an alternative, a silenced voice or narrative that has lain to one side of the officially sanctioned commentary. It is the fact that this maintains the play of motifs and variants that makes it especially applicable to recent retellings, which themselves constitute versions that do not function solely as revisionist glosses but as artful narratives in their own right, interventions within the historical process of oral and literary negotiations.

The third major motif in this trilogy of tale types is the variously depicted forbidden room, around which the curiosity and craftiness revolve. It is this presence that gives rise to the necessity for strategies of escape, and yet it is exactly this disturbing presence that has been interpretatively neutralized or ignored in the historically dominant readings. However, this is a space that cannot be erased. Its uncanniness echoes that of other forbidden rooms, other tropes of confinement, and it is the re-placing of this room at the literal and metaphorical center of the narratives that marks the dominant theme of recent versions, to which I now turn.

"Curiosity ... Is Insubordination in Its Purest Form"[45]

Look. It was like this. Or rather it was more like this, or parts of it were like this, or this is one part of it.

— SARA MAITLAND, "THE WICKED STEPMOTHER'S LAMENT"

As will be apparent from earlier references to Tieck, Maeterlinck, and Balázs, the literary "survival form" of my chosen knot of folktales constitutes a tradition in itself, and more recent adaptations are as much a reaction to these versions as to the folktales on which they are based. The majority of these treatments take Perrault's "Bluebeard" as their main source text, yet as I have suggested, this tale is always caught within a narrative network—a position which needs to be borne in mind at those times when the prevalence of Perrault's tale may seem to be erasing the voices of its relatives.

Within the interpretative context of literary adaptations, Tieck's Bluebeard drama exemplifies that dominant strain in which Bluebeard's wife is perceived as the corrupting force and the murderer himself as tortured, if extreme, victim. Fifty years on, we find a broadly similar reading of the folktale in Thackeray's droll social comedy, "Bluebeard's Ghost" (1843), which casts a mildly mocking eye over its source material; yet underpinning the parodic tone lies the now familiar attitude towards the character of Bluebeard's wife.[46] And similarly, a further fifty years on, in Anatole France's *The Seven Wives of Bluebeard* (1909), we find the continued dominance of this attitude, with a dénouement centering on a plot to murder Bluebeard himself, and thus inherit his fortune, together with his wife's eagerness to reach the lover who is waiting in what is in this instance an unforbidden room.

Both Thackeray and France treat the fairy tale very much as a minor genre, a result of the nineteenth-century relegation of the tales to the nursery. Despite the less than serious tone, however, these retellings follow the lead of Perrault's verse moral, seeking to rehabilitate Bluebeard via the portrayal of a female protagonist who is either murderously over-curious or a manipulative adulteress—cognitive curiosity suggesting or merging with sexual curiosity—while the male character is either simply over-zealous, misguided or genuinely blameless. Each version builds on the implicit and explicit morality of Perrault, elaborating or extending, but never challenging, the now canonical account of the tale, and creating in the process an orthodoxy of interpretation that adopts the guise of an ostensibly neutral expression of an inherent truth. The current of this particular tale is thus brought to a standstill by the sedimented weight of concurrent interpretations.

Above all else, it is this sense of fixity that I want to hold as representative in the following discussion of feminist adaptations—representative of the weight of a relatively strictly defined, moralistic institution against which a range of writerly strategies have been aimed. Feminist adaptations can be read as part of a broader project of cultural critique that has sought to unravel the implicit assumptions underlying the historically dominant narratives of Western culture, what Sandra Gilbert refers to as the "revisionary imperative," a project that has played a considerable role in feminist theory and fiction over the last four decades and one which seeks, as Gilbert summarizes, to "review, reimagine, rethink, rewrite, revise, and reinterpret" historical and cultural events and documents (32). It is within this context that feminist fairy tales have been, and are, received and interpreted, a context analogous to Stanley Fish's conception of an "interpretive community," out of which the meaning of any individual work is constructed.[47] As I suggested in relation to Perrault and the Grimms, context is always telling in the construction and reception of both the fairy tale and its explicitly literary offspring, and it is the position of feminist fairy tales within an "interpretive community" that frames and supplements whatever political efficacy they may have.

The manner in which gender is represented—implicated and constructed—in the texts under consideration is the dominant concern, hence the renewed interest in "Bluebeard" and its related types. As the historically dominant trend in "Bluebeard" adaptations and interpretations demonstrates, fairy tales have served both to embody and to enforce prevailing assumptions about gender, and it is to unravel and challenge what Gilbert refers to as "the nexus of genre and gender . . . the secret intersections of sexuality and textuality" that recent fairy tale writing has set out. If the resulting texts are postmodernist—playful, (self)referential, drawing on norms of the genre in a fusion of the "popular" and the "literary"—this is an oppositional postmodernism, in which the aesthetic concerns raised by the genre are allied to a degree of ideological questioning that serves both to deconstruct and to revive what has become a static, mythicized group of tales.

The feminist reworking of the fairy tale has taken place in several modes, from the complex, extended treatments of Angela Carter, Margaret Atwood, and Tanith Lee, to the irreverent takes on canonical tales that can be found in, for example, the Attic Press series of "Fairy Tales for Feminists" and the work of the Merseyside Fairy Story Collective.[48] In broad terms, the various strategies constitute a re-energizing of a tradition and a subversion of traditional interpretations. The newly composed tales seek to change the direction of both particular stories and of the genre as it is known, giving a voice to an often passive, silenced presence, a voice that speaks both against the grain of the narrative and through the breaks and gaps in the overlaid moralities of previous generations. This is achieved by pulling submerged stories through these gaps, stories both in the sense of alternative life stories and submerged, parallel folk narratives. The paradigmatic figure for these tellers is thus the robber's bride-to-be, who retells the story from her own perspective and so alters its direction while maintaining the narrative momentum. While the most effective of these retellings raise the same issues of textuality and representation as the postmodernist narratives of Coover and Barthelme, it is questions of gender that they place to the fore, drawing out the unspoken rules of the genre in its canonical nineteenth-century form and sharpening the blunted contours of the tales. Implicitly manipulating the revisionary status of narrative itself—the sense in which narrative is always a remembering and a re-telling that seeks to bring about some form of change—contemporary feminist fairy tales enact a process of remembering, repeating, and working through, in which the tales are taken out of a cycle of repetitive orthodoxies of interpretation. To use Peter Brooks's formulation, this process marks a move from passive to active repetition (*Reading for the Plot* 98).

One of the most striking recent literary versions of "Blue-beard" is Joyce Carol Oates's "Blue-Bearded Lover" (1988), a tiny, gnomic tale which depicts the stifling attention of Bluebeard and the price of acquiescence. The wife in this version accepts the prohibition as "a token of [her] lover's trust," and Oates provides a telling metaphor for both her fate and the presence of the previous wives in the form of Bluebeard's description of the stars: "When we stood at night beneath the great winking sky he instructed me gently in its deceit. The stars you see above you, he said, have vanished thousands of millions of years ago; it is precisely the stars you cannot see that exist, and exert their influence upon you. . . . But if it is a power that is known, are the stars invisible?" (182–83).[49] This astronomical theme echoes an earlier adaptation, Sylvia Townsend Warner's "Bluebeard's Daughter" (1940), in which the rival curiosity of the heroine and her husband is not condemned but ultimately accepted as a mark of their humanity. They come to the conclusion that " 'since we cannot do away with our curiosity, we had best sublimate it, and take up the study of a science' "; they settle on astronomy (185).[50] Yet the tale ends equivocally with the faint suggestion that Bluebeard's daughter simply becomes her husband Kayel's wife, acting as the wind beneath the wings of his celebrated scientific discoveries (scientific knowledge functioning here as synonymous with the traditionally male spheres of activity, and thus comparable with the unidentified world of "business" the folkloric Bluebeard leaves his new bride in order to attend), and it is this strand that is drawn out in Oates's darker vision. Her tale focuses on the suffocating effect of subservience in a way that hints at the dream motif in "The Robber Bridegroom": there, the girl's ability halts the inevitable outcome and amplifies the cunning of Bluebeard's wife; here, we have only the muffled ghost of this talent in the girl's dreams, which she remembers as being "of extraordinary beauty . . . and magic, and wonder": "[h]ow is it that you of all persons can dream such dreams, he says,—such curious works of art! / And he kisses me, and seems to forgive me" (183). This sense of entrapment, hinted at in Warner's tale and amplified in Oates's, is also the theme of Sylvia Plath's "Bluebeard," a short piece of mid-1950s juvenilia in which the fatal offer of the key is rejected:

> in his eye's darkroom I can see
> my X-rayed heart, dissected body:
> I am sending back the key
> that let me into bluebeard's study.

An alternative strategy is to undercut the gothic seriousness of the tale—not, as with Thackeray, in a continuation of the standard interpretation but precisely to mock the grounds on which it is based. Hence Suniti Namjoshi's characteristically pithy take on "Bluebeard," "A Room of His Own" (1981), in which the lack of curiosity shown by the villain's wife—who feels he is "entitled to a room of [his] own"—so incenses Bluebeard that he kills her, pleading provocation at the trial (*Feminist Fables* 69). Similarly, Donald Barthelme's "Bluebeard" (1987) conjures with the historically dominant motif of female curiosity, albeit in a more tangential manner, whereby the source text is merely the most prominent reference point in a textual mass of often absurd possibilities. The tale is told retrospectively by Bluebeard's wife, and, structurally at least, follows the broad path of the original narrative. Set in France in 1910, like all the folkloric variants of this tale type it involves reference to great wealth, here in the form of the extravagant and explicitly male commodity of decadent high art. Barthelme litters the text with echoes of earlier versions: Bluebeard always returns "suddenly . . . unexpectedly" and has "veins of silver" in his nose (invoking the Italian Bluebeard, "Silver Nose"); a reference is made at one point to a certain "Thérèse Perrault," and the narrator refers to herself as the seventh wife. Yet the main intent of the narrative appears to be to play on the wife's curiosity and the motif of the key as narrative devices, one metaphorical, the other literal, both serving to generate narrative momentum through desire. As in Namjoshi's account, and despite her husband's repeated warnings, the female character is uninterested in the contents of the room; once her generically jaded curiosity is aroused—after the thought occurs that the room may contain something other than dead bodies—a series of events leads to the presence of no less than fourteen duplicate "forbidden" keys. The narrative is freighted with immanently symbolic artworks and historical figures vying for the accolade of narrative key, together with the now familiar adulterous subplot. However, read within the context of feminist interest in this tale, the highly ornate nihilism that permeates Barthelme's narratives here becomes a parodic mocking of any singular interpretation, not least the accumulative tradition that would see Bluebeard as more sinned against than sinning. Like Namjoshi, but to different effect, Barthelme evokes this tradition just as he mocks its highly moralistic pretensions, making the ostensibly self-apparent appear absurd. It is thus meaningfully unsurprising that his forbidden room contains "gleaming in decay and wearing Coco Chanel gowns, seven zebras" ("Bluebeard" 97).

In their various ways these versions shift the perception of the related tales away from a critical reading of female curiosity in order to reinstall the forbidden room and the concomitant actions of the male protagonist at the heart of the narratives. Such a process of reinscription is most extensively enacted in the versions by Carter and Atwood, to which I turn in the final part of this chapter. However, to give a sense of the range of feminist engagement with the fairy tale, and in order to include representative examples of other strategies of revision, we must briefly look beyond the "Bluebeard" nexus.

Oates's "Blue-Bearded Lover" illustrates a central concern in feminist fairy tales, the sense of being caught within a story (to borrow the title of a collection of contemporary literary tales) and, by extension, within the cultural norms and expectations encoded in, and by, this closed narrative. Thus, in Sara Maitland's elegiac "Rapunzel Revisited" (1993) we meet the heroine as she re-enters the landscape of the original tale at a later stage in her life, the happy ending of the story having worked itself out. She is left with brittle hair and osteoporosis, together with a vague sense of betrayal, hinted at in the passing reference to the manner in which her husband suppressed the fact of her humble origins. Yet none of these thoughts are allowed to coalesce into anger as Rapunzel has never had any sense of her life beyond a series of prescribed patterns: "The story has fixed my seeing" and "it is impossible for me to shape my future, although that is what I came here to do. I have been the child, and the beloved and the queen and the widow. I have come to a place where I need a new way of seeing and I am so entangled in the old ones, unbrushed and unbraided, that I cannot let down my hair and haul up a future" (191).[51] The narrative acts in two ways: as an extension of "Rapunzel" itself, depicting a character lost outside the passive role of heroine in a world in which there is literally "no plot, no narrative," and as a realistic portrait of a late middle-aged woman who has played the part of child, wife, and mother, and has now arrived at the endpoint of a series of socially prescribed roles. This sense of entrapment is once again illustrated in Namjoshi's understated summary of the tale, "Rescued" (1981): here, Rapunzel escapes her entrapment by the witch through her imagination, dreaming of a rescue and—ironically in the light of Namjoshi's "Bluebeard" narrative—"a room of her own" (87). Yet the tale suggests the circular nature of this form of escape, sanctioned by the traditional structures of the fairy tale genre and thus reliant upon a "[p]rince who is extremely powerful and extremely strong" to transport the heroine to a castle in which she is once again confined.

In the same manner as the "Bluebeard" adaptations, these tales function as artful reworkings of particular narratives—Maitland's elegant first-person stories and Namjoshi's jack-in-the-box fables—and as critiques of the roles and functions assigned to women in the canonical fairy tale. They are, to varying degrees, polemical, uncovering the inadequacies of the tale tradition read as a set of behavioral models. They thus form part of that particular branch of feminist practice referred to by Elaine Showalter as the "feminist reading or the feminist critique . . . in essence a mode of interpretation" (245). In the realm of fairy tale adaptations, the interpretation takes the form of a fiction, one which serves as a commentary on, and a version of, the source tale(s), a practice which Alicia Ostriker (writing about contemporary poetry) refers to as "revisionist mythmaking," defined as "a vigorous and various invasion of the sanctuaries of existing language, the treasuries where our meanings for 'male' and 'female' are themselves preserved" (315). As I have demonstrated in the case of the "Bluebeard" tale type, a prevailing orthodoxy of interpretation has governed a significant range of fictional and critical readings; hence the challenging of what has, by dint of mere repetition, come to seem interpretively neutral. At their best, these "survival forms" work against the process of ossification. As Ostriker comments, "they are enactments of feminist anti-authoritarianism opposed to the patriarchal practice of reifying texts." Feminist retellings act as a continuation of a history of narrative flux in which a host of contesting versions hover around any particular manifestation. The new tales work precisely against the notion of interpretive truth, making submerged or silenced elements or readings part of the story, there to be questioned but not ignored. To use Adrienne Rich's phrase, this is "writing as re-vision."

As indicated by the historical rise of the fairy tale, the ideology of any story, at least as it appears to us, has been overlaid and amended by successive generations of transcribers and writers, from Perrault to the Grimms, from Andrew Lang to the hordes of anonymous adapters producing countless versions of the famous tales for children. However, while the fairy tale as an historically limited canon does enshrine a broadly definable, gender-based set of functions, the essence of the genre can equally be located in its aesthetic, an aesthetic of transformations. As Peter and Iona Opie write, it is the magic of these transformations that "encourages speculation" (18)—speculation which exploits what Jack Zipes refers to as "the liberating potential of the fantastic" (*Fairy Tales and the Art of Subversion* ch. 7), and which sanctions and enables the exploration of alternatives and inversions. Hence Patricia Duncker's comment on the roots of what some have characterized as anti-fairy tales:

> One of the interesting contradictions in the traditional fairy
> tales was the genuine instability of the society reflected within
> them. Frogs could be princes, miller's sons could get to be
> rich kings. The one thing that could not and did not change
> was women's subordination to men. . . . By transforming
> women's definitions of themselves, feminist fairy tales at a
> stroke complete a pattern of subversion implicit in the old
> stories. (*Sisters and Strangers* 155)

This imagining of alternative versions implicit within the rules of a genre based around wish-fulfilment is perhaps most apparent in "reversal tales," in which existing narratives are used not so much to illustrate modes of entrapment as to imagine alternatives which build on the enchantment and wonder of the fairy tale genre, and serve to reimagine what is theoretically a utopian form (that is, according to the logic of its own transformational aesthetic). While such tactics are to some extent limited—both Showalter and Duncker point to such limitations as the intractability of material and reliance on pre-existing models—they are nevertheless liberating to the extent that they lay claim to a traditionally prescriptive, and proscriptive, genre. Again, the discursive contemporaneity of such versions is a continuation of a literary fairy tale tradition based on the annexing of tales for the purposes of demonstrating, however implicitly, a particular *Weltanschauung*.

The most striking group of "reversal tales" are those which depict women's friendships as an alternative to the traditionally assigned roles. Sara Maitland appropriates the figure of the witch from "Hansel and Gretel" as a "crazy, ancient and unseen" "Angel Maker" (1987), a genuine witch doctor who aids women, at various times, through abortion and artificial insemination, helping to combat nature and retaining a special love for her Gretel.

Such a rehabilitation of the fairy tale wicked witch is indicative of reversal stories, as is the related theme of lesbian relationships. Namjoshi's "In the Forest" (1981) similarly imagines a Gretel who stays on to live with the witch, commenting that "it is distinctly possible that in this wild witch's world she stands a better chance" (*Feminist Fables* 93). This echoes the relationship between witch and Rapunzel hinted at in Maitland's aforementioned "Rapunzel Revisited": the heroine's reminiscences there involve the recollection of a witch who was "not my servant, nor my mother," a curiously detached figure committed to the younger girl in a way the latter can still only vaguely comprehend: "[d]id she imprison me or protect me? Did she love me or hate me?" (189–91). This suggestive undercurrent, present in both of Maitland's stories, is realized in Namjoshi's overtly lesbian rewritings, and in the American poet Olga Broumas's *Beginning With O* (1977). Making strategic use of nature imagery, Broumas draws out the relationship between witch and Rapunzel to imagine a couple that shun societal norms of age and sexuality in a utopian dream of transgressing prescribed roles ("Rapunzel," Broumas 59–60). Both Namjoshi and Broumas rewrite "Beauty and the Beast" as a lesbian narrative, the latter characterizing the Beast as one woman's internalized desire ("Beauty and the Beast," Broumas 55–56), while the more straightforward intervention of the former pivots on a change of sex for the Beast: " 'the Beast doesn't change from a Beast into a human because of its love. It's just the reverse. . . . It loves Beauty, but it lives alone and dies alone' " (*Feminist Fables* 23).

These tales form just one mode of the process of reversal, challenging as they do what Patricia Duncker sees as "one of the cornerstones of patriarchy": the divisions and rivalries, enshrined within traditional fairy tales, between mother, daughter, and sister, generative of an atmosphere of "women, beware women" ("Reimagining the Fairy Tales" 7). Lesbian rewritings question normative definitions of female relationships and sexuality, imagining alternative communities to those depicted within the standard fairy tale world. These reversals stand alongside parallel explorations by the likes of Angela Carter, who draws out the eroticism

and subversive violence in the tales, and the more light-hearted
send-ups of the Attic Press "Fairy Tales for Feminists" series, which
includes such self-explanatory swipes as "Rapunzel's Revenge" and
"Snow-Fight Defeats Patri-Arky."[52] As Maitland says of "the old
stories," "although they do not lie, they omit," and it is the gaps
in the narratives that are filled by such alternative takes. This is
not an instance of a series of smaller narratives eroding a master
narrative but rather of a series of submerged versions problematizing and historicizing a tradition of storytelling. Perhaps the best
summary of such strategies is A.S. Byatt's "The Story of the Eldest Princess" (1992). Byatt challenges prescribed patterns, an act
represented here in the quest of an eldest daughter who becomes
aware of the orthodox nature of her role—"I am in a pattern I
know"—and thus provides a running commentary on the tale as
it unravels. It is the girl's awareness of the standard interpretations that allows her to by-pass the traps in the familiar tests, to
arrive at "the Last House," where, unsurprisingly, she meets an old
woman who prompts her to tell her story: "[y]ou had the sense to
see you were caught in a story, and the sense to see that you could
change it to another one . . . for many things may and do happen,
stories change themselves, and these stories are not histories and
have not happened" (26). Using language redolent of the self-
consciously pared-down text of the literary fairy tale, Byatt gets
to the heart of the tales of reversal; in the process she brings back
into my own narrative the figurehead of retellings, the robber's
bride-to-be (AT 955), a parallel character cognizant of her allot-
ted role and who similarly resorts to an alternative story as a means
of escape and a challenge to the orthodoxy.

   The literary texts I am including here, as "survival forms" of the
fairy tale, function by association or allusion: the "source" narrative, or more precisely an idea of it, becomes the object of scrutiny
out of which the fictional reading grows, and onto which it is
mapped. The tales presume a shared knowledge of both the specific source and the associated generic norms, and the new reading
stems from the resultant intertextual tension between assimilation and dissimilation (Hebel i). However, such textual relations

are complicated by the fact that the source texts in this case are folktales and thus highly unstable narratives that already exhibit a complex intertextuality. Consider the following passage from Roland Barthes's "From Work to Text," in which the notion of "text" is "enunciated": "The intertextual in which every text is held, it itself being the text-between of another text, is not to be confused with some origin of the text: to try to find the 'sources,' the 'influences' of a work, is to fall in with the myth of filiation; the citations which go to make up a text are anonymous, untraceable, and yet already read: they are quotations without inverted commas." (*Image Music Text* 160). This condition of pure intertextuality, synonymous with the text itself, is equivalent to the narrative boundary crossing I read as implicit in the folktale tradition. The history of the tales—the passage of anonymous, communal narrative traditions across national boundaries, between social classes and in and out of the pages of literary editions—is bound up within each particular narrative. The temporary stasis of a single variant is built out of the contesting voices of closely related characters and motifs from variant tale types and parallel traditions. There is no founding version in this story pool but only, to adapt Barthes, "a serial movement of disconnections, overlappings, variations"; each manifestation is an implicit reading of a strand of tradition and is in turn already read by the tales within that strand. Discounting the educational additions of various editors, there is no teller as such, beyond the unreachable "original" narrators. Behind each tale is not an authorial meaning or a true and final interpretation but another set of tales (versions of the same tale, to the extent that we can only know these stories through literary transcriptions). It is the position of any tale within this web that ultimately negates any interpretative closure. If "[i]nterpretation makes art manageable, comfortable," then the folk narrative tradition exhibits an edge of discomfort in its challenge to standard notions of interpretation and explication (Sontag 8).

Recent adaptations can thus be seen as part of a history constituted of retellings, in which the inherent allusiveness of each story avoids a hierarchy of interpretation, positing instead a series of constructed meanings which disqualifies any seemingly final, normative reading. It is in this way that fictional critiques of the fairy tale tradition—stories, poems, novels—are particularly effective, functioning both from within the tradition as I have described it— as "survival forms"—and from a critical standpoint outside. Thus, as I suggest throughout this chapter, the fairy tale patron of feminist versions is the cunning figure of the robber's bride-to-be— to choose the example of the craftiness motif most pertinent to narrative fiction—whose inventive plotting creates a tale-within-a-tale that is paradigmatic. A source narrative is retold in order to draw out the submerged voice, a voice which functions not to erase the tale of which it is a part but to cut across, comment on, and recast it—just as, as a folktale, it is implicitly already traversed by related variants.[53] While mindful of an overly anachronistic reading of this character, it would be disingenuous not to remark on the nascent metafictional aspect of her strategy. What is particularly exposed in contemporary feminist retellings is the manner in which ostensibly universal gender roles are constructed within the source tales, as part of a broader examination of the manner in which conventional notions of gender can be viewed as fictions open to deconstruction. The strategy of self-referentiality, which functions as a means of simultaneously evoking, while undermining or problematizing, an element within a narrative, thus allows a deliberately tendentious adaptation to lay bare and examine a particular aspect of the construction of gender within the source tale(s): as Gayle Greene writes of women's fiction which manipulates existent literary narratives, "[m]etafiction is a form of literary criticism, a fictional expression of critical positions and assessments, and feminist metafiction is a form of feminist literary criticism" (7–8). Again, the fictional adaptation functions as critique and new version or "survival form."

I want briefly to pause at this stage to consider an additional reason why the heroine of "The Robber Bridegroom" is particularly pertinent. One significant gap in the narrative turn I sketched in the previous chapter—the shift away from an abstract, universalizing theory of narrative towards a pragmatic concern with the contextual specificity of narrative acts—was the contemporaneous feminist revision of the tenets of narratology, which has sought productively to reconcile the manifest differences in methodology between the formalism of narratology and the political and historical concerns of feminism. This has involved both an acceptance of the uses of narrative poetics and a critique of its shortcomings, and as the following statement by Susan Sniader Lanser demonstrates, such a revisionary project shares much common ground with the pragmatics of narrative suggested by Herrnstein Smith:

> a historically-situated structuralist poetics may offer a valuable
> differential framework for examining specific narrative
> patterns and practices. The exploration of narrative structures
> in women's writings may, in turn, challenge the categories and
> postulates of narratology, since the canon on which narrative
> theory is grounded has been relentlessly if not intentionally
> man-made. (*Fictions of Authority* 6)[54]

The central feminist critique of narratology is aimed at undermining its putative universality by demonstrating the gendered nature of its source texts and resultant concepts, and by stressing the need to recognize the role of gender in the elaboration of the various stages and participants in the narrative act. As a folktale, "The Robber Bridegroom" is representative of the kind of text particularly conducive to traditional structural analysis. As my first chapter sought to demonstrate, one of the founding source texts of narratology was the folktale, specifically the Russian fairy tales used in the construction of what Lanser refers to as "Propp's androcentric morphology," and it is precisely the ignoring of the gender of the constituent elements of narrative that is problematized by the *mise en abyme* told by the heroine in "The Robber Bridegroom" ("Toward a Feminist Narratology" 612). She tells a version of her own story—a retelling of the tale in which her telling is embedded—which cannot adequately be understood unless its context, and her gender, are considered, and which thus reflects both on the tale as a whole and on any analysis of the tale which ignores this fact. This is a single, simple example, but again it serves to demonstrate the significance of this protagonist. The feminist revision of the fairy tale, both in fiction and criticism, has been a critique both of the historically rooted normative reading which seeks to appear as universally applicable, and of readings, such as those of some of the founding texts of narratology, in which gender is neutralized. A female protagonist/narrator who tells an implicitly gendered version of the story of which she is a part can thus be seen as a significant model for recent feminist tale-tellers, for whom the context of gender is simply unavoidable in the telling and in the world of the tale.

Read as postmodernist narratives, feminist fairy tale variants foreground the process by which motifs and allusions are simultaneously evoked and subverted, making explicit the process of intertextual interpretation implicit within the folktale tradition itself (and, in the case of Carter and Atwood, manipulating this tradition of narrative instability). The historically defined generic norms of this tradition act in a similar way to the generic landscape and characterization of science fiction or the detective novel, in each of which gender plays a central role. Just as the manipulation of a known genre reveals the manner in which norms and expectations are pitched as part of a constructed textual environment, so the allocation of roles along the lines of gender within this construct appears equally manipulative, equally illustrative of a world functioning by historically contingent rules. It is the intersection of the textualities of gender and genre that provides a window on the social construction of roles, both now and throughout the history of any genre, and this is particularly apparent in the more self-conscious of contemporary fictions.

Critics such as Linda Hutcheon and Susan Rubin Suleiman have written of intertextuality and generic metafiction as strategies of postmodernist feminist parody which belie any notion of empty or nostalgic pastiche (what Jameson refers to as "blank parody" [*Postmodernism* 17]), conceiving of the play involved in parody, at least within the context of contemporaneous "interpretive communities," as fundamentally oppositional in orientation.

These strategies are thus part of a broad postmodernist critique of representation based on a "general cultural awareness of the existence and power of systems of representation which do not reflect society so much as grant meaning and value within a particular society" (Hutcheon, *Politics of Postmodernism* 8). As Suleiman comments, the rewriting of old stories is practiced as much by feminist historians, psychologists, and literary theorists as by writers of fiction, each of whom enacts the idea that "the stories we tell about reality *construe* the real, rather than merely effect it. Whence the possibility, or the hope, that through the rewriting of old stories and the invention of new forms of language for doing so, it is the world as well as words that will be transformed" (143; 235 n.10). This is, to use Donna Haraway's suggestion, "feminist theory as a storytelling practice . . . a multileveled story told from quite particular locations" (32).

I have traced a thin line through this area of theoretical enquiry and debate in order to provide a framework within which to set the more overtly complex intertextual and metafictional webs of the extended feminist fairy tale adaptation, in which the presence of the source tale is more diffuse than in the compact form of the short story. Nevertheless, this is another "survival form": rather than explicit rewritings, the texts set up networks of allusions and motifs which create a number of contesting narratives, often suggesting a structure modeled on the/a fairy tale. I have chosen to illustrate this area by focusing on two authors—Angela Carter and Margaret Atwood—and on a novel and a relatively extended short story by each. In both cases the short story is an explicit reworking of the "Bluebeard" narrative, while the novel is open to interpretation as an extended fairy tale and, through specific allusion, as a reading and retelling of the "Bluebeard" tale type (plus, as always, its related variants). As well as providing another mode of intertextuality—within one writer's work—the juxtaposition of the direct and the diffuse, the explicit and the allusive, demonstrates the range of treatment of the fairy tale evident in contemporary fiction, and the allure this tale type still holds.

Angela Carter's collection *The Bloody Chamber* (1979) has come to stand as perhaps the paradigmatic instance of contemporary feminist tale-telling. All of Carter's fictions are influenced, to varying degrees, by the fantastic world of the wonder tale, as well as by the cultural associations of non-canonical forms, and it is in an earlier novel, *The Magic Toyshop* (1967), that we find both the first manifestations of an interest in the proto-gothicisms of "Bluebeard"—an early example of Carter's idiosyncratic attraction to the sensual, physical world of the tales—and in the sexual politics at play in this textual landscape. If "The Bloody Chamber" constitutes Carter's notion of a postmodernist—she might have preferred "mannerist"—fairy tale, then *The Magic Toyshop* is, as she says, "a malign fairy tale" in the form of a novel (Interview 80).[55]

The title of "The Bloody Chamber" invokes "Bluebeard" variants such as the American tale "The Bloody House" and the British "Robber Bridegroom" variant "The Cellar of Blood," thus signaling both the status of the tale as an explicit and expanded rewriting of a particular tale type and an awareness of the hinterland of folktale tradition. Alternatively, *The Magic Toyshop* is a novel which, read structurally, has a fairy tale simplicity: three orphans living in an isolated, seemingly fantastical house, with an ogrish stepfather and a cowering stepmother. The three orphans recall folkloric groupings of three siblings, and the conventional folk narrative device of repeating an action three times is mirrored in the plot of the novel, revolving as it does around the three occasions on which Uncle Philip is absent—the third of which, naturally, precipitates escape. The potential for spotting embedded fairy tale plots is tempting: the novel functions as a "Cinderella" story in reverse: the orphans abandonment by/to a wicked step-parent in a dark and unknown setting parallels "Hansel and Gretel," and the narrative pivots around a denial of the generic certainties of "Beauty and the Beast" and "Sleeping Beauty." While these elements combine to construct a reading of the generic norms of the fairy tale, the novel also strongly conjures the character and setting of "Bluebeard" and its variants.

Carter uses Bluebeard's castle as the archetypal gothic nightmare, drawing on the aforementioned tradition of symbolist adaptations in which the castle serves as the objective correlative of masculine oppression and isolation. Soon after arriving, Melanie explores the new home, "walking along the long, brown passages, past secret doors shut tight. Bluebeard's castle" (82). She repeatedly walks "past all the closed doors of Bluebeard's castle" (146), and finding—so she thinks—a "freshly severed hand" in a kitchen drawer, imagines that "Bluebeard was here" (118). Carter also signals her awareness of the status of "Bluebeard" in relation to parallel tale types via allusions to the British "Mister Fox," a "Robber Bridegroom" variant: "Bluebeard's castle it was, or Mr Fox's manor house with 'Be Bold, be bold but not too bold' written up over every lintel and chopped up corpses neatly piled in all the wardrobes and airing cupboards" (83).

The coded environment serves to foreground the generic types that constitute the protagonists: Uncle Philip, always appearing in doorways and thus associated with the shut (forbidden) doors of the house, is a tyrannical Bluebeard whose voice is the law and around whose absences, as in the folk narrative, the plot unwinds; Melanie, taken to this house as she enters puberty, is a potential female victim of the patriarch and so takes on the character of the inquisitive folktale heroine: arriving at the house "[s]he wanted to . . . find out what lay behind all the doors" (58), thus exhibiting a curiosity later fed by her night-time spying on the Jowles' folk group and, through Finn's spy-hole, on the brothers' bedroom. Allusions to Eve, the archetype of female curiosity, further the intertextual gendering of traits: Eve is summoned in "The Bloody Chamber" (as is Pandora) where the bride is indelibly marked for her inquisitiveness by the enchanted key, while in *The Magic Toyshop* Melanie imagines herself as the banished Eve, punished for her first night-time transgression in her parent's bedroom only to re-enact that moment with Finn at the novel's close: "[a]t night, in the garden" where "[n]othing is left but us" (199).

"Bluebeard," together with its knot of tale types, thus figures as a resonant intertext in *The Magic Toyshop* and as the specific source narrative(s) in "The Bloody Chamber." However, just as the identification of allusions as an end in itself is a tautological interpretative process, so it is necessary, in order to engage with the manner in which such allusions *function* in the texts, to see them as "already read"; it is within the intertextual space of the narrative that this reading takes place: as Bacchilega says, Carter's is a "metafolkloric or archeological project" (*Postmodern Fairy Tales* 124). Both of Carter's texts offer a tissue of coded references, through which the original tale is filtered in "The Bloody Chamber," and together with which the allusions to it intermingle in *The Magic Toyshop*. To highlight one strand, Debussy and Wagner, whose broadly late-Romantic aesthetic influenced the literary "Bluebeard" adaptations of Maeterlinck and Balázs (an aesthetic with which "The Bloody Chamber" is suffused); and Joris-Karl Huysmans's *Là-Bas* (1891), itself luridly and autobiographically based around a character's research into Gilles de Rais, a possible model for the Bluebeard legend. Hence the characterization of the bride in "The Bloody Chamber" is spotted with allusions to the Balázs and Maeterlinck opera libretti, specifically her desire to light the dingy castle in the search "for evidence of [her] husband's true nature" (24).

Yet these texts are not provocatively nihilist in the same manner, say, as Donald Barthelme's equally densely coded version. There, the excess of reference works against any attempt to interpret the symbols by parodying the device of the symbol itself.[56] Allusions obviously aid in the compilation of a textual atmosphere, references to Bluebeard's castle in *The Magic Toyshop* serving to suggest gothic claustrophobia in the same manner as references to the "deliquescent harmonies of Debussy" adumbrate the decadent, watery mirror-bound world of "The Bloody Chamber"; yet they are not merely or purely atmospheric. Within the framework of generic metafiction, Carter's elaborately allusive texts can be seen to function not as groupings of empty signifiers nor as self-consciously artful postmodernist pastiche, but rather as networks of citation that seek to gather a catalogue of representations that comment both on the representations in the narrative and on the ideological functioning of representation itself. As Hutcheon writes, it is the ironic and parodic use of historical representations "which work[s] to disrupt any passive consumption of such images," and it is in this manner that the fairy tales, enmeshed within—as much as expressions of—a history of literary adaptation and interpretation, are appropriated as particularly potent sources of gender representation (*Politics of Postmodernism* 152).[57]

One of the themes Carter navigates is the manner in which the body, particularly the female body, is caught within networks of discourse that engender desires and expectations: how "[o]ur flesh arrives to us out of history" (Carter, *Sadeian Woman* 9). *The Magic Toyshop* opens with a flourish of references—a fantasia of fantasies—which are developed as the novel unfolds. We meet Melanie as she begins narcissistically to explore, via John Donne, her own body, her "America," her "new found land": "[f]or hours she stared at herself, naked, in the mirror . . . sometimes doing cartwheels and handstands out of sheer exhilaration at the supple surprise of herself now she was no longer a little girl" (1). Just as the intertextual "new found land" was already populated, so Melanie's newly discovered flesh is already encoded by pre-existent representations of femininity, and it is these, rather than an unmediated self, that she sees in the mirror. She fantasizes about herself as a Pre-Raphaelite figure, as a model for Toulouse-Lautrec, dragging her hair "sluttishly" across her face, and as a roughly executed "Cranach Venus"—three of the most potent visual representations of femininity: the other-worldly, withdrawn, and languorous longing of the medievalized Pre-Raphaelite woman (echoed in the pseudo-Pre-Raphaelite illustrations of fairy tale heroines which accompany many nineteenth- and twentieth-century tale collections); the Parisian prostitutes of Toulouse-Lautrec; and the pre-pubescent eroticism of Cranach's female nudes. Melanie falls into the same "delicious ecstasy of excitement" as the newly wedded heroine of "The Bloody Chamber," speeding towards "the unguessable country of marriage"; yet the former can only heartily pray for marriage and construct a "phantom bridegroom" to allay fears of premature spinsterhood which loom large in the figure of

Mrs. Rundle. This longing for, or fantasizing about, marriage is enacted in the opening pages of both texts in the form of symbolic dresses which embody the fetishized innocence of the virginal heroine: in "The Bloody Chamber" the translucently erotic nightdress Bluebeard gives his fourth wife foreshadows, in its exposure of the girl's still young body, the relationship to follow (8), while in *The Magic Toyshop* the ritual of Melanie's fantasized fairy tale marriage finds its synecdoche in the "symbolic and virtuous white" of her mother's wedding dress (13).

Melanie is represented as the archetypal fairy tale heroine, longing for her "phantom bridegroom" to legitimize her newly discovered womanhood, her no-longer-sleeping beauty, and Carter uses this familiar situation as a platform from which to explore desire and sexuality as constructed in, and through, representations of femininity. We discover Melanie already caught within a web of representations and expectations, symbolized in these densely coded opening pages in the mirror, before which she stands like the stepmother in the Grimms' "Little Snow-White," inquiring rhetorically "[a]nd am I as beautiful as that?" (16). The "heightened, excited sense" that the heroine in "The Bloody Chamber" feels as she journeys towards the castle is expanded in Melanie's night-time rite-of-passage trip into the enchanted garden, wearing at first her mother's wedding dress and then naked in the apple tree, a fairy tale Eve foreshadowing her coded role as Bluebeard's curious catch. Earlier we see Melanie momentarily caught in the play of the mirror world, "forgetting the fantasy in sudden absorption in the mirrored play of muscle as she flexed her leg again and again"; and while the "bruised and filthy" Melanie, clothed in the bloodied and tattered wedding dress, symbolically smashes the mirror after learning of her parents' death, this seeming disenchantment—an apparent return to reality—in fact marks a step into another realm of fantasy, one in which the complete absence of mirrors marks the breakdown of putative boundaries between the real and the simulated. The "tender, budding part" of Melanie is left behind with the broken mirror as she steps into the shadowy, malign fairy tale of the toyshop. Here, simulations abound, paradigmatically in the absorption of Uncle Philip in his puppets, and Melanie is forced to see her femininity reflected not in the relatively safe play of culturally constructed narcissistic fantasy but in the more ominous gaze of others.

This allusive world in which representation runs riot is the stage upon which both narratives are set, a self-consciously constructed looking-glass world of male and female images in which the latent sexuality of the traditional fairy tale becomes the manifest ground for debate over the nature of gender representations. Carter is renowned for her depiction of eroticized fairy tale characters and environments, ambiguously demonstrated in the several "witch-queen" obituaries that followed her death in 1992, yet it is the historical and cultural construction of desire and the erotic with which her texts are primarily concerned. Her fiction works against what she refers to as the "mythologizing of sexuality" (*Sadeian Woman* 4), a process which is nowhere more apparent than in the bowdlerized canonical fairy tale described by Zipes (drawing on Barthes's notion of contemporary myth): "the classical fairy tale has undergone a process of mythicization. . . . [T]he myth acts to deny its historical and systematic development . . . for the fairy tale must appear harmless, natural, eternal, ahistorical, therapeutic" (*Brothers Grimm* 148–50). Conversely, Carter's fairy tale environments are harmful, historicized, deliberately unnatural fictional constructions. The grotesque world of the toyshop and the decadent atmosphere of Bluebeard's castle act as the closely related stages upon which are juxtaposed the fantasy world of representation and the surface reality, and representations, of the narrative, the one bleeding into and intermingling with the other in the manner of the toyshop's white bull terrier and his portrait, which seem, to Melanie, to interchange: " 'Which dog is it, the real one or the painted one?' "

Elaine Jordan writes that "Melanie's initial narcissism . . . is ready-made to collude with the scenarios her Uncle Philip, the cultural puppet-master, wants to play," and it is this culturally constructed narcissism which is grotesquely parodied in the narratives simulated by Uncle Philip (28). While in her own room

Melanie is still just about able to imagine herself as the mythicized Sleeping Beauty, opening her eyes to see "thorns among roses, as if she woke from a hundred years' night" (53), it is in the puppet theater that the violent undercurrents of specific culturally canonical narratives are uncovered (just as we can uncover the rape that lies encoded—a layer of narrative—in the kiss in "Sleeping Beauty"[58]). Wagner's *Tristan und Isolde* figures repeatedly in both *The Magic Toyshop* and "The Bloody Chamber" as both an archetypal romance—invoking a mythic realm in which the laws of courtly love symbolize an ordered, hierarchical society—and a tale of obsessive, destructive desire (again, Carter draws on this founding instance of late Romanticism as part of a deliberate textual bias towards the heady and potentially oppressive eroticism frequently evoked in the arts of the late nineteenth and early twentieth century).[59] Carter's Bluebeard takes his new bride to a performance on the night before their wedding, and she watches, convinced by the myth of regal romance: "my heart swelled and ached so during the Liebestod that I thought I must truly love him. Yes. I did" (10); while during Uncle Philip's puppet shows, the Liebestod is played by Francie, along with "the love theme" from Tchaikovsky's "Romeo and Juliet Fantasy Overture." To the accompaniment of this idealized courtly, or fairy tale, romance, a puppet enacts the role of a sylphide—Uncle Philip's "poor little girly" (reminding the reader that on first encountering this puppet world Melanie imagined that "the doll was herself"), the romanticized, innocent sylph who dutifully dies at his behest (127–28).

Yet it is in the popular Pre-Raphaelite subject of "Leda and the Swan" that the myth of female passivity is exposed. This is Uncle Philip's pièce de résistance, for which Melanie must simulate Leda. While earlier she had imagined herself as the young sylph, and back in her parents' home had draped herself in her mother's tulle as yet another Cranach Venus, she is now forced to act out the pubescent eroticism of these roles in the guise of Philip's exaggeratedly adolescent Leda, her new found womanhood mocked in his fantasy-led male gaze: "I wanted my Leda to be a little girl. Your tits are too big." His vision of Leda reflects on the stylized girls depicted by Cranach and on the figure of the young sylph; the mythicized image of Leda, like the familiar image of the equally passive Sleeping Beauty, is stripped away to reveal the eroticized fantasy of domineering male and coyly naive female. This is Leda as depicted by the Surrealist artist Paul Delvaux, in which an oversized swan, plodding in boot-like webbed feet, nuzzles the budding breast of a vacant, classicized female nude.[60] Gone is the chaste initial refusal, replaced by the enacting of what amounts to a rape scene, as illustrated in Melanie and Finn's orchestrated rehearsal and in Philip's spoken commentary: "Leda attempts to flee her heavenly visitant but his beauty and majesty bear her to the ground. . . . Almighty Jove in the form of a swan wreaks his will" (166).[61] The fantasy of a child-like Leda is echoed, in "The Bloody Chamber," in Bluebeard's predilection for having his new wife "perch on his knee in a leather armchair" dressed only in "that chaste little Poiret shift of white muslin" (19). This is part of Bluebeard's fantasy of innocence and corruption, the twin realms—coy knowingness dressed in a veil of angelic naiveté—depicted in a Cranach Venus. His collection of pornography expands on the theme of innocence and corruption, of the gaze of the master connoisseur: Gauguin's idealized, sultry natives, Fragonard's staged erotic encounters, the stress always on the virginal or on the relationship of master and servant that is encoded in the gaze of the knowing pornographer on the constructed innocence of his subject.[62] Bluebeard increasingly treats his wife as if acting in a staged sado-masochistic encounter, relishing her discovery of his library—"[m]y little nun has found the prayerbooks"—just as Uncle Philip relishes the idea of a pre-pubescent Leda: "[h]ave the nasty pictures scared Baby?" (17). Carter uses this adult/child theme as a gloss on the folkloric motif of Bluebeard's sudden and unexplained departure: there is no need to explain, as his wife is "only a little girl" and "would not understand" his forays into the masculine sphere of commerce.

Bluebeard's castle is a hall of mirrors in which are reflected the images of his art and literature, just as in *The Magic Toyshop* the boundary between reality and simulation, between person and

puppet, is blurred. The voyeuristic gaze of the pornographer is
multiplied in the shimmering surfaces of the bedroom, the numerous mirrors "incandescent with the reflections of the sea." Carter
uses this setting both to stage the voyeurism of the traditional
pornographic encounter and to explore the postmodernist realm
of simulation, in which we lose sight of who is watching whom.
Just as Melanie, confined to a parallel world in which there are
absolutely no mirrors, is forced to see herself as others see her,
so Bluebeard's wife begins to see herself through the controlling
gaze of her husband: "I saw him watching me in the gilded mirrors
with the assessing eye of a connoisseur inspecting horseflesh . . .
saw myself, suddenly, as he saw me" (11). She is "reborn in his un-
reflective eyes" and in the "fathomless silverings of his mirrors,"
and begins to think she can detect in herself the same "potentiality
for corruption" that she supposes Bluebeard has been aware of all
along, her "thin white face with its promise of debauchery only
a connoisseur could detect" (20). Carter characteristically uses
this drama to explore contemporary theories of the male gaze and
the construction of female desire. Following and amending Freud,
Luce Irigaray has explored the male gaze—so prevalent in Bluebeard's island castle, indeed in the "Bluebeard" tale type itself—
as the enacting of a desire for mastery, "in which the object of
the gaze is cast as its passive, masochistic, feminine victim" (Moi
180 n.8).[63] With the object constructed in this way, it—or she,
the woman—can either remain completely passive or enact the
role of passive object or "lesser male": "[t]he hysteric mimes her
own sexuality in a masculine mode, since this is the only way in
which she can rescue something of her own desire" (Moi 135). We
are thus back where we began, witnessing the social and cultural
construction of female desire by the male viewer or by patriarchal
discourses. This sado-masochistic chain is depicted in Bluebeard's
wife's slowly shifting image of herself, an image influenced by her
time caught in the mirror: "I hardly recognized myself from his
descriptions of me and yet, and yet—might there not be a grain
of beastly truth in them?" (20).

Carter depicts a vision of male sexuality that is built on a hierar-

chy of object and subject, on the staged encounter between knowing sadist and constructed masochist. With sexuality as a Fou-
cauldian articulation of power, Bluebeard's bloody chamber becomes the logical conclusion of his doomed relationships, "a room
designed for desecration and some dark night of unimaginable
lovers whose embraces were annihilation" (28). After a history of
interpretative sidestepping, the forbidden room is thus reinstated
as the core motif of the source tale type. It is not surprising, given
the nature of sexual relations in this setting, both real and represented, that this potential victim should wonder whether she
has not "stumbled upon a little museum of his perversity . . . in-
stalled . . . only for contemplation" (28). Indeed, the metaphoric
linking of torture and sexual relations is prefigured in the form of a
necklace, "a choker of rubies . . . like an extraordinary slit throat,"
kissed ceremoniously by Bluebeard as a prelude to intercourse and
which he later insists she wear prior to being decapitated. Margaret in *The Magic Toyshop* is given a similar wedding present, a
"vicious collar" which physically constricts her movements. In the
novel this objectifies the oppression suffered by the character as
part of her familial relations and also causes her to lose, or choose
to lose, her voice.

Just as the "patriarchal majesty" of Uncle Philip, the embodiment of the voice of the law who "likes silent women," functions
within the coded narrative as a type of Bluebeard, so Aunt Margaret is an equally allusive character. Ruth Bottigheimer refers to
the medieval tradition in which the silencing of women was advocated as a necessary consequence of Eve's actions, a particularly
salient fact given the status of Eve as the archetype of the curious
woman. Bottigheimer detects the continuation of this tradition
in the theme of silencing as punishment or threat in the Grimms'
tales, noting that "the quality, extent, and viciousness of silence
and its associated images clearly breaks down along gender lines."
Finding a particular stress on silent women in these narratives (as
opposed to those of Perrault, for example) and attributing part of
this to specific editorial amendments, she goes on to comment on
the Grimms' version of AT 710:

> It becomes clear through a detailed examination of the
> editorial history of one tale, "Our Lady's Child," that
> depriving a girl of speech is particularly effective in breaking
> her will. This completes the equation of speech with
> individual power that seems to motivate the shifts evident
> in the transformation of individual folk and fairy tale
> heroines during the Early Modern period in European history.
> (*Grimms' Bad Girls* 71–80)[64]

The choice of this particular tale, upon which I have already remarked, once again offers telling narrative parallels. The child
in this story, taken up to heaven by the Virgin Mary to allevi-
ate the sufferings of a poor peasant couple, is entrusted with the
keys to the doors of heaven, all but the last of which she may
open. As punishment for contravening the law she is sent back
to earth without the use of her voice, which is only returned
when she publicly confesses to her deed. The tale is obviously
a Christianized version of the "Bluebeard"/"Fitcher's Fowl" tale
types, one in which the character of Eve is more prominent, and
such folkloric figures are encoded within the character of Margaret, dumb as a puppet in the presence of her Old Testament
patriarch and symbolic of the microcosm of familial relations that
is the toyshop. However, it is possible to read this silent/silenced
female character—and, by extension, her partners-in-tradition—
from a different standpoint, one which serves as an example of
the strategies of refusal and critique at work within Carter's narratives. At the end of *The Magic Toyshop* Margaret regains the power
of speech, hence suggesting the possibility of active withdrawal,
beginning on the day of her marriage and ending on the day of
her escape (another fairy tale echo). Her refusal to speak becomes
what Marina Warner, commenting on the layers of silenced heroines that are "contained" within the character of Shakespeare's
Cordelia, refers to as "a stratagem for survival": "silence isn't entirely absence, but another kind of presence" ("The Silence of
Cordelia" 75). Placed as it is alongside the revelation of Margaret's
incestuous relationship with her brother, which overtly flaunts

societal taboos, silence functions as a subtle act of resistance, one which appropriates a conventional patriarchal image as an active strategy.

This reversal parallels Carter's demystification of her chosen store of representations, as well as her additions to the "Bluebeard" tale type. In her version, the wife is not rescued by her brothers but by her mother, through a process of "maternal telepathy," an event sanctioned by the dominant tradition of female rescue in this tale type. Carter wittily encodes this moment of narrative reversal by referring to the norms of romantic plotting to which she has previously alluded: it is as if, during the close of *Tristan und Isolde*, "Tristan stirred, then leapt from his bier . . . announced in a jaunty aria interposed from Verdi that bygones were bygones . . . [and] proposed to live happily ever after" (39). It is also as if the puppet master "saw his dolls break free," which is precisely what happens in *The Magic Toyshop*, a novel littered with reversals and demystifications. Indeed, as well as being the site of boundary crossing between the real and the simulated, the toyshop also represents the soiled reality of adult relations, set against the fantasy never-never land of Melanie's "previous" life and demonstrating the intertwining of fantasy and reality that occurs in many of Carter's fictions. Demystification is evident in the depiction of the swan in Uncle Philip's drama. While it acts as a symbol of the Oedipal struggle between Philip and Finn, it is also treated as a parody of extreme masculinity, the literalization of a symbol, embodying as it does the figure of Jupiter/Zeus (compare the teasingly parodic representation of Bluebeard's masculinity in "The Bloody Chamber"). In the play, Melanie encounters "a grotesque parody of a swan. . . . It was nothing like the wild, phallic bird of her imaginings. It was dumpy and homely and eccentric. She nearly laughed again to see its lumbering progress" (165), and the account of its burial is a final diminishment of traditionally phallic imagery.[65] This parallels Melanie's gradual shift away from the romantic myth of fairy tale prince and fairy tale marriage. Her imagined "phantom bridegroom" cannot stand up to the all-too-real presence of Finn: "[s]he remembered the lover made up out of books and poems she had dreamed of all summer; he crumpled like the paper he was made of before this insolent, off-hand, terrifying maleness" (45). Carter stresses the unromantic reality, his "extraordinary, extravagant, almost passionate dirtiness," which reaches its peak in the sordid episode in the pleasure garden, and Melanie's closing vision of the drab reality of married life with Finn signals another final deflation. That Melanie sees this image of the future as in some way inevitable, together with the fact that the novel closes as they stand on the precipice of an unknown future, signals the transitional nature of this text within Carter's oeuvre: her unwillingness to provide tidy solutions to a portrayal of the disturbing undercurrents of patriarchal culture and family structures and her as yet still tethered use of fantasy to imagine and explore alternatives.

The recasting of the "Bluebeard" tale type in "The Bloody Chamber" is similarly ambiguous concerning the nature of female desire. I referred earlier to the social and cultural construction of putatively female desire in the sado-masochistic relationship, and while this is certainly evident in the story, Carter, in line with the inquisitive and active heroine that is her model, depicts an at least partially colluding wife who has inherited the strengths of her mother. This is signaled at the start of the narrative when she admits the active role she plays in the game of surprise ostensibly directed by the controlling aristocrat: "[h]e had loved to surprise me in my abstracted solitude at the piano. . . . But . . . after my first shock, I was forced always to mimic surprise, so that he would not be disappointed" (8). The dialectic of innocence and corruption that she imagines to be an intrinsic part of her nature is certainly constructed by her role in the imposed drama, engendering as it does a narcissistic awareness of being desired which establishes a closed circle of arousal. Yet the heroine's "dark, newborn curiosity"—both cognitive and sexual, a legitimate rather than imposed connection in Carter's reading—is an energy that lies at least partly outside of the drama, uncontained by the narrative, in the sense that she is manifestly unsatisfied by the "one-sided struggle" that characterizes their sexual relations. With reference to The Bloody Chamber as a whole, Patricia Duncker has commented that Carter "has no conception of women's sexuality as autonomous desire," yet this seems to be exactly what she is arguing against here and in her contemporaneous study of pornography, *The Sadeian Woman* (Duncker, "Re-imagining the Fairy Tales" 8). In attempting to depict sexual and familial relations as caught within the historical discourses of culture and society, Carter writes against the positing of some unmediated and universalizing model of female desire, exploring rather the construction and manipulation of such desire through the history of gender representations. As in the appropriation of the image of the mute woman and Melanie's discovery and voyeuristic exploration of Finn's peep-hole, the narratives work with the idea of multiple identities and roles which manipulate and comment upon discourses of gender and sexuality.

Indeed, if these texts do have a utopian aspect it is in their representation of folk culture, as an extension of the use of folk narratives and motifs. The two heroes in these tales—heroes of a suitably deflated and self-conscious kind—come from folk communities: Finn, along with Francie and Margaret, represent Irish folk culture, while Jean-Yves, the piano-tuner in "The Bloody Chamber," is "a blacksmith's son from the village across the causeway" whose speech has "the rhythms of the countryside, the rhythms of the tides" (32). Both also have sight defects: Jean-Yves is blind, while Finn, who appears to Melanie as "simple Ivan in a folktale," has "a slight cast in his right eye" which causes his gaze to be "disturbing and oblique" (33). If the former functions in the text as an ironic comment on the dominating nature of male desire and the manner in which it constructs female collusion through its controlling gaze (and is itself caught within this dialectic of reflected narcissism), the status of the latter is less clear. Towards the end of the novel, Melanie sees herself "in the black pupils of his squint" and remembers Donne's image of intermingling souls, "tangling like the puppet strings on the night of the fall." Whether this suggests that Finn's gaze represents the male subject to whom she is now passed on—as commodity, between Philip and Finn—as in many folk narratives, or whether Finn's obliquity is a precursor of Jean-Yves's coded blindness and a part of his unorthodox folk lineage, remains open to question. However, Carter does seem to evoke folk culture as the locus of some form of alternative voice, in relation to which the dominant, orthodox history of Western culture is relativized. The classical themes that Francie plays as accompaniment to Philip's culturally canonical dramas are described as a "tea-room kind of music," while the jigs, reels, and airs played at the Jowles' covert gatherings are sung in all their "wailing glory," culminating in the delirious communal concert that celebrates Philip's final absence. The music is indicative of the portrayal of "the circle of the red people" in the narrative, a leprechaun-like group whose invigorating traditions are set against the worn, leaden heritage of orthodox culture, and where the "hieratic and ancient presence" of incest challenges the violent oppressions of the family unit.[66] While I do not wish to over-emphasize this aspect, particularly in the light of Carter's refusal of primitive utopias in novels such as *Heroes and Villains* (1969) and *The Passion of New Eve* (1977), it bears consideration given her comment on orthodox literary culture as a kind of "folklore for the intelligentsia" (Interview 82). Her use of folk narratives and motifs has certainly produced some of the most innovative examples of recent "survival forms" of the folk and fairy tale, in which the exploration and manipulation of the source material demonstrates a pervasive awareness of its provenance and tradition. Carter's structural, thematic, and stylistic use of this folk material is an example of what Hutcheon refers to as "the feminist re-evaluation of non-canonical forms of discourse," and allies the critique of modes of representation and their implication in the construction of gender roles with a form and tradition that has historically stood outside mainstream culture, literally and symbolically representing the marginalized (*Politics of Postmodernism* 23).

Just as Carter's treatment of the "Bluebeard" tale type in the two narratives under discussion is multi-faceted, so the multiple versions of other fairy tales that she wrote throughout her career reflect her awareness of the open-ended nature of the folk narrative tradition, with its implicit intertextuality, and enact the espousal of the plural and the provisional in a formal parallel to the politics of her texts. Her use of the dark aesthetic of the folktale, as well as its ideological implications as a literary form, echoes the work of early nineteenth-century Romantics such as Hoffman, Tieck, and Novalis, in the manipulation of the subversive potential of a non-canonical narrative tradition. Nevertheless, Carter's interest in the sensual world of the folk and fairy tale—its coded and vivid colors, archetypal settings, earthy simplicity, and, above all, its transformational aesthetic—is rooted in its time: in its explicit focus on issues of gender and as an example of feminist postmodernist fiction that is "both deconstructively critical and constructively creative, paradoxically making us aware of both the limits and the powers of representation" (*Politics of Postmodernism* 98). In other words, Carter's idiosyncratic adaptation of the stylistic potential of the folktale tradition means her texts can be both aesthetically constructive and ideologically deconstructive (well aware of the ties that bind these two), simultaneously located within and reflecting back upon the tradition itself.

To varying degrees, what we find in Carter's work is an interest in the fairy tale that goes beyond the purely critical. This stems from an awareness of the fairy tale as a form encoded with the readings and interpretations of prior generations, along with an awareness of the field of wonder tales that lies beyond the rigidly defined boundaries of the standard canon. Carter edited two volumes of fairy tales which specifically address the position of the folktale heroine, placed "center stage, as large as life," tendentiously seeking to demonstrate "the richness and diversity with which femininity, in practice, is represented in 'unofficial' culture: its strategies, its plot, its hard work," with the broader aim of "a wish to validate my claim to a fair share of the future by staking my claim to my share of the past" (*Virago Book of Fairy Tales* xiii; xiv; xvi).

A similar attitude to folktale traditions is evident in the work of Margaret Atwood. She has commented that "*Grimms' Fairy Tales* was the most influential book I ever read," identifying reasons

that echo views expressed by Carter: "[t]he unexpurgated *Grimms'*
Fairy Tales contains a number of fairy tales in which women are
not only the central characters but win by using their own intel-
ligence. . . . [I]n many of them, women rather than men have the
magic powers" (*Conversations* 46; 115).[67] What is most telling in
this context is that Atwood singles out "Fitcher's Fowl" as one of
her favorite Grimms' tales, one of the stories in which the heroines "show considerable wit and resourcefulness" (*Conversations*
71–72). As the latter is a constituent part of the knot of narratives under scrutiny in this chapter, it is not surprising to find
a large number of allusions to, or readings of, the three related
tale types in Atwood's work: in the novels *Lady Oracle* (1976)
and *The Robber Bride* (1993), in short stories such as "Bluebeard's
Egg" (1983) and "Alien Territory" (1992), and in poems such as
"Hesitations outside the door" (1971). While Carter expands on
the stylistic idiosyncrasies of the fairy tale, Atwood is primarily
concerned with the bare bones of the narratives. At the opening
of "Bluebeard's Egg" we meet Sally "waiting for the sauce she's
reducing to come to a simmer," and it is this act of reducing that
encapsulates Atwood's approach, focusing on the sexual politics
in the tales (131).[68]

Nevertheless, Atwood's adaptations are equally, if less exuber-
antly, allusive. In Carter's two treatments, "Bluebeard" is cast as
a prototypically gothic romance, with "The Bloody Chamber" in
particular modeled on a familiar gothic environment: the fore-
boding labyrinthine setting, within which are placed the central
characters, sharply delineated along gender lines: the young, isolated heroine and the dark, seemingly cruel hero, both indicative
of Carter's manipulation of the conventional narrative shorthand
of popular generic fiction. In the gothic romance—what Joan in
Lady Oracle refers to as the "costume gothic"—the two central
protagonists are broadly characterized according to gender: the
heroine tends to be younger, insecure, emotional, frequently "separated by death or geography from home and parents"; the hero
is older, arrogant, socially superior, and dominant. The heroine is
linked to the domestic, private realm while the hero functions

in, or is linked to, the public sphere.[69] Obviously, "Bluebeard" and its related tale types broadly correspond with this "generic traiting," suggesting the presence of these fairy tales as both antecedents of, and intertextual presences within, the genre of the gothic romance; other characteristics confirm this suggestion: for example, writing about the gothic in particular, Eve Kosofsky Sedgwick notes how "[c]ertain features of the Oedipal family are insistently foregrounded there: the absolutes of license and prohibition," both of which figure in the "Bluebeard" tale type as the twin pillars of patriarchal relations (91). Writing about the romance, Mandy Merck notes how "[m]uch of these stories' narratives are occupied with the man as enigma and the heroine's attempt to figure him out," a theme given paradigmatic expression in the "Beauty and the Beast" tale type (AT 425C), which is based on the transformation of the male protagonist through the patient action of the heroine (50). In comparison, the "Bluebeard" tale type represents the dark reverse: the transformation is metaphorical rather than literal—from man to murderous beast— and the end result is death rather than continuing marriage. This is a failed romance, in which the overpowering curiosity of the heroine, her desire to know Bluebeard's secret, is the cause of the failure of the narrative to bring together, or at least keep together, the two protagonists.[70]

"Bluebeard" is thus evident in the darker textures of the generic norms of the gothic romance, alongside the paradigmatic narrative structure of "Beauty and the Beast." These two contrasting intertextual strands demonstrate the presence of the fairy tale in popular fiction, and it is in this more distant "survival form" that Atwood is particularly interested. Bridget Fowler, introducing her study of popular romantic literature, confirms this influence— "[m]odern romances are fairy tales sieved through a net of realism" (12)—as does Carter: "[t]he fairy tale, as narrative, has far less in common with the modern bourgeois forms of the novel and the feature film than it does with contemporary demotic forms, especially those 'female' forms of romance" (*Virago Book of Fairy Tales* xx). It is thus not surprising to find the director of publishing at

Harlequin, one of the most successful publishers of romance fiction, advising aspiring writers that "[t]he fantasy must have the
same appeal that all of us discovered when we were first exposed to
fairy tales as children" (quoted in Barr Snitow 138). In one sense,
the feminist critique of the fairy tale is borne out by the perpetu-
ation of fairy tale structures and characterizations in romance fiction. The depiction of passive, homely heroines, bound for a role
as object of desire and object of purchase by the active, worldly
hero in the name of stability and tradition, is a standard, if somewhat crude, summary of the general feminist critique, and it is one
which is also laid at the feet of the romance genre: Fowler refers to
the "tranquilizing dreams" of the romance novel, which she sees
as embodying a "regressive utopian consciousness" which "speaks
of a patriarchal order that is natural and necessary"; the notion
of a "regressive utopian consciousness" certainly fits with Zipes's
characterization of the mythical, canonical, bourgeois fairy tale
(Fowler 1–4). In literary terms, the most successful and popular
fairy tales have been "Cinderella," "Sleeping Beauty," and "Beauty
and the Beast," tales in which the behaviour of the heroine can
be appropriated easily as a model for proper female behaviour, a
readily identifiable and socially successful sign of femininity. As
I have shown with reference to "Beauty and the Beast," it is the
model that these tales provide that has been secreted into the
popular romance, where, as Joanna Russ comments, "the feminine mystique is defended and women are promised all sorts of
psychological rewards for remaining loyal to it" (quoted in Barr
Snitow 139; this is a view given historical credence by Fowler's
nomination of "the patriarchal mode of domestic production" as
one of the "decisive material conditions for the romance" [19]).

Yet the gothic romance in particular also figures as an umbrella
term for an alternative tradition of women's writing, first identified by Ellen Moers in *Literary Women* and Dale Spender in *Mothers of the Novel*. Historically tied to a newly emerging body of female readers and writers, it began towards the close of the eighteenth century with figures such as Clara Reeve and Ann Radcliffe, and found early expression in the writings of the Brontës

and Mary Shelley. *Jane Eyre* (1847) in particular is a paradigmatic fusion of the gothic romance and the fairy tale. In these texts, genres are already being quite self-consciously dissected and critiqued. As Karen Rowe comments, "what is on trial in *Jane Eyre* is . . . the validity of an entire concept of romance derived from fairy tale" (" 'Fairy-born and human-bred' " 78). As I have suggested, the fairy tales in question form a very particular group, in which the heroine exhibits varying degrees of submissiveness in relation to the male protagonist. However, I also suggested the presence of the "Bluebeard" tale type as a more subdued, more problematic intertextual strand within the popular romance, and it is thus revealing to find prominent allusion to this particular fairy tale in the female gothic romance tradition. Although ultimately a successful romance in the mold of "Beauty and the Beast," *Jane Eyre* makes frequent allusion to "Bluebeard," particularly in terms of the forbidden attic—situated at the end of "a corridor in some Bluebeard's castle" (108)—which casts a shadow across the entire narrative (a shadow whose presence has returned to haunt this novel in feminist and postcolonial criticism). Jane is a forthright heroine who uncovers Rochester's true nature (his blinding is obliquely alluded to in the figure of the blind piano-tuner in Carter's "The Bloody Chamber"), and her staunch individuality is descended more from the "Bluebeard" heroine than the patient submissiveness of Beauty.[71] Brontë's *Villette* (1853) also makes passing reference to the fairy tale and includes a less ominous attic room. In more comical mode, curious Catherine Morland's anxious desire to open the door of the deceased Mrs. Tilney in Jane Austen's *Northanger Abbey* (1818) is another "Bluebeard" parallel, although one intended gently to mock a heated imagination fired by too many gothic romances. However different in style and intention, the dominant motif in each of these versions is the forbidden room and its possible connection with the past of the male protagonist. We can compare this with the more didactic, orthodox interpretation, in which the motif of putatively dangerous female curiosity takes precedence.[72]

In the narrative structure of novels such as *Jane Eyre* and *Villette*

there is a palpable tension between the traditional, socially ac-
ceptable move towards marriage and domesticity, and the search
for self-definition and autonomy upon which the heroines em-
bark. As Rachel Blau DuPlessis demonstrates in *Writing Beyond the
Ending* (1985), the romance plot has figured as the paradigmatic
narrative structure for women in fiction in the novel, a plot clearly
descended from the "Beauty and the Beast" tale type. It is reveal-
.ing that in novels in which this structure is, if not ignored, then
at least troubled, "Bluebeard" is variously evoked.[73] None of the
three interrelated tales I have been exploring in this chapter have
marriage as their endpoint (except as a very briefly mentioned
occurrence in the future life of the heroine), which is one of the
reasons why they have not achieved canonical status. Marriage,
in these stories, occurs early and must be escaped from once the
narrative secret is revealed to be far from benign. Neither do the
heroines of these tales have to die, that other orthodox option
available for the nineteenth-century female protagonist.

Both Atwood and Carter draw on *Jane Eyre* in particular as a
source text for its "Bluebeard"-inflected suggestion of the darker
undercurrents of the utopian romance narrative. As Rosemary
Jackson indicates, it is useful to position such writers within the
frame of this female tradition, in which the fairy tale genres of
the gothic and the romance, with their finely placed female characters, are explored and critiqued as indicative of the roles assigned to women, throughout the last two centuries, by the dominant social order (103). Following Blau DuPlessis, we can see how
Atwood and Carter write beyond the ending of the traditional
romance narrative—using what Blau DuPlessis, referring to her
own fictional examples, calls "postromantic strategies"—simultaneously evoking the folkloric roots of the orthodox plot and
undercutting it with material from the same narrative source.[74]
Within this expanded tradition we can locate a double process of
revision: of the fairy tale, and of the fairy tale as it figures in popular
adult literature, a process particularly evident in the "Bluebeard"-
influenced *Lady Oracle*, which utilizes the added layer of a more
overt self-referentiality to install a series of interconnected textual
levels.

Nineteenth-century heroines such as those referred to above are frequently represented in the act of reading—Catherine Morland conspicuously consumes gothic romances while the young Jane Eyre reads English fairy tales and the *Arabian Nights*—and I have thus approached the two Atwood texts—"Bluebeard's Egg" and *Lady Oracle*—via the act of reading and rereading. The figure of the "reading protagonist"—the character witnessed reading or referring to a specified text—is present in Carter's "Bluebeard" adaptations: in "The Bloody Chamber," the heroine tells us that she desires to "lose [herself] in a cheap novel," while Melanie in *The Magic Toyshop* reads *Lorna Doone* and, in the light of references to herself as "Jane Eyre" and Victoria as "Mrs. Rochester," has read Brontë's novel. Just as the original Jane Eyre's early reading colors her reaction to Thornfield Hall, so Melanie's view of the dingy toyshop is filtered through the fairy tale. This childhood reading thus figures not merely as incidental detail but as evidence of the process by which specific narrative structures and images are imbibed by the young reader: for example, a number of interpretations of *Jane Eyre* focus on the manner in which Jane, in her autobiographical narrative, both retrospectively reads her life according to fairy tale structures and also charts her growing realization of the limits, boundaries, and pitfalls of this mode of thinking.[75] It is this notion of the inculcation of restrictive expectations and submissive attitudes that has come to figure as one of the standard feminist critiques of the fairy tale, based on the historical shift towards more overtly didactic literary adaptations intended specifically for children. Thus what is at stake here is "the specific implications of internalized romantic patterns" (Rowe, " 'Fairy-born and human-bred' " 69), "the possible political effects of reading romances" (Light 140), and, to modify the title of one such study, the implications of female acculturation through the fairy tale (Lieberman)—themes that can be elucidated by following the figure of the reader, as it functions on various levels, in the two texts I have chosen.[76]

 Lady Oracle is a text in which reading and writing take place on a sometimes dizzying number of levels, yet behind them all is the character of Joan and her liking for the certainties of formulaic

fiction. She comments that she "always found other people's versions of reality very influential," but it is the "trashy books" which
she reads while living with her parents that structure her expectations, for herself and of others (160; 150). Late on in the narrative we witness her in the bathroom, "my refuge," where she
submerges herself in one of Mavis Quilp's "Nurse novels" (a subgenre of the popular romance): "I longed for the simplicity of that
world, where happiness was possible and wounds were only ritual
ones. Why had I been closed out from that impossible white par-
adise where love was as final as death" (284). This mode of reading is characteristic of Joan, a self-confessed "sentimentalist . . .
of the sloppiest kind" (15); "a sucker for ads, especially those that
promised happiness" (29); "an optimist, with a lust for happy endings" (210). On arriving in London she reveals the influence of a
childhood reading of Tennyson's "The Lady of Shalott": "I wanted
castles and princesses, the Lady of Shalott floating down a winding river in a boat. . . . I was a romantic despite myself" (143). We
are back in the realm of the romanticized, doomed maiden evoked
earlier with reference to the Pre-Raphaelites, which reminds us of
Tennyson's Lady as represented by Holman Hunt. Joan's summary
of the poem's conclusion, with the character now "a corpse in a
barge-bottom," echoes the figure of her equally romanticized fairy
tale predecessor, Snow White.

As is the case in *Northanger Abbey*, this reading matter causes
Joan to read her life through the norms of the genre, attempting to
transfer elements of the fictional narratives into the story of her
life which constitutes the novel—a Bildungsroman which, like
Jane Eyre, brings into question the genre of the fairy tale romance
as a suitable structuring narrative for women's lives. Joan is particularly susceptible to viewing or approaching an actual situation
or character according to generic norms and expectations, usually
resulting in disappointment and disillusionment. Suitably enough
for this inveterate Juliet, we first encounter her on a balcony—"I
felt that if I could only manage to stand on one long enough . . .
something would happen: music would sound, a shape would appear below, sinuous and dark, and climb towards me" (7–8)—and

she initially catalogues her men according to the norms of the fictional romantic hero: Arthur, for example, is filtered through the lines of her current reading, "[a] melancholy fighter for almost-lost causes, idealistic and doomed, sort of like Lord Byron, whose biography I had just been skimming" (165), and she soon develops a disturbing resemblance to the passive heroine of the mythicized fairy tale: "I myself was bliss-filled and limpid-eyed: the right man had come along, complete with a cause I could devote myself to. My life had significance" (171).

Of course, as the ironic authorial undercutting repeatedly indicates, Joan is perpetually falling short of her fictional ideal, with the resultant need to escape from herself and her life. She longs for the "magic transformations" of the fairy tale, summed up in the caterpillar allegory of the suitably charlatanesque Spiritualist, Mr. Stewart: " '[t]hat dark place is only a cocoon; we will rest for a time, and after that we will emerge with beautiful wings; we will be butterflies, and fly up toward the sun' " (107). When this fails to occur and her life refuses to follow the neat lines of the literary romance, she creates herself as a fiction for others, along the lines of the fictional ideal. For Arthur she constructs an entire previous life, worried that her "early life and innermost self would have appalled him" (215). Rather than confess to her unromantic first sexual encounter, she conjures an elaborate drama "under a pine tree at the age of sixteen," borrowing details from the "trashy books" she was reading at the time, and for her friends she becomes the "kindly aunt and wisewoman" in order to mask her adolescent isolation (150). As Elisabeth Bronfen comments, Joan's existence "encompasses a slippage between materiality and textuality," with Joan filtering her view of the world through the norms of romantic fiction, at the same time as she attempts, unsuccessfully, to present herself as of the same type as her heroines (415). This slippage between types of narrative and between levels of fiction—what Bronfen refers to as "liminality"—is further complicated when Joan begins to write and publish her own "costume gothics," through which she constructs a world for others. We have witnessed her as reader of texts, as "reader" of her life,

as writer of an imagined life; now she takes on the role of writer
of fiction, published under a pseudonym and projecting an image
of herself as a fairy godmother with the power to turn her readers
"from pumpkins to pure gold" (35); as Gayle Greene remarks, Joan
writes "to avoid knowing herself or the past" (167). Considering
the influence of fairy tale romances on her own life it is predictable
that the fictions she constructs adhere devoutly to the generic
formula, in a way that her life refuses to. Thus the narrative is interspersed with eight extracts from her work in progress, "Stalked
by Love," an archetypal and deliciously realized gothic romance,
complete with aristocratic hero, seemingly less wealthy but nevertheless strident heroine, sardonic rival hero and rival heroine,
and softly pornographic references to heaving breasts barely con-
cealed by the always correct period dress. This is the reader as the
creator of orthodox interpretations in the form of perfect copies,
seeking to enact in fiction what can only be simulated in the real;
life as poorly realized genre fiction, escaped and denied through
the construction of perfect copies—a vicious cycle which is acted
out through the course of the novel.

Sally, in "Bluebeard's Egg," is seemingly a far less idealistic
reader, as demonstrated by her adolescent reading of Agatha
Christie novels, "the kind in which the clever and witty heroine passes over the equally clever and witty first-lead male . . . in
order to marry the second-lead male, the stupid one" (133). As
the allusion to this less prescriptive, less romantically oriented
popular literary genre suggests, Sally's reading of her marriage is
not generically orthodox in the manner of Joan's reading of her
life. Ed is the hero in the same way as "dumb blondes" are heroines, loved because of his transparent stupidity, so monumental
that it makes Sally feel "humble" (132). Read as a fairy tale, as
Sally does, their relationship is far from orthodox: Ed is the less
common figure of the "third son who, armed with nothing but a
certain feeble-minded amiability, manages to make it through the
forest with all its witches and traps and pitfalls and end up with
the princess, who is Sally, of course" (133).[77] It was Sally who
played the traditionally male role of "hunt[ing] him down," as Ed,

a heart surgeon, is seemingly oblivious to "the workings of hearts, real hearts, the kind symbolized by red satin surrounded by lace and trapped by pink bows" (137).

Yet it is Sally's desire to please that results in her reading the marriage in benign terms, terms which are ultimately as restrictively generic as Joan's. The first part of the story pivots around Sally's recollection of a trip to view Ed's new heart machine. Here she witnesses a different Ed, one who functions "in a cramped, darkened room with an examining table in it . . . a dangerous place" in which she feels "exposed and under his control" (142–44). Following the interpretive frame offered by the title, this figures as an allusion to the forbidden room in "Bluebeard" and the Grimms' "Fitcher's Fowl," the latter mentioned by Atwood as a favorite tale and in which the girls are specifically given an egg to test their resolve in avoiding temptation. This also allows for the reading of other elements via these fairy tale intertexts: Ed has had two previous marriages, whose "actual fates have always been vague to Sally," and the fact that "the gap between them is considerably more than five years" leads Sally on a train of thought which culminates in the possibility that "she isn't the true bride after all . . . but the false one," a scenario which she imagines would result in a suitably folkloric ending, with her "put into a barrel stuck full of nails and rolled down hill" (134). Ed becomes that which she desires to know, to penetrate beneath the surface of, moving beyond and disrupting her liking for neatness and tidy organization: she sees him as "constantly developing like a Polaroid print. . . . Ed is a surface, one she has trouble getting beneath" (149); she "examines his face closely, like a geologist . . . looking for telltale signs of mineral treasure: markings, bumps, hollows" (145). Within the intertextual fabric of the story we can read her desire to know Ed, to read past the surface interpretation, in terms of the motif of curiosity in the "Bluebeard" tale type, a reading additionally sanctioned by Sally's enrolment on a course entitled "Forms of Narrative Fiction," during which she is given the task of rewriting the "Fitcher's Fowl" tale type. Her attempt to read around this tale is set against her attempt to read around Ed, and the narrative thus enacts the process of revision on the level of fictional narrative—both Sally's slowly evolving interpretation of "Fitcher's Fowl" and the rereading of "Bluebeard" and its related types that constitutes "Bluebeard's Egg" itself—as well as on the level of actual human relations. This version of gender relations is repeated in another of Atwood's "Bluebeard" adaptations: in part six of "Alien Territory" the marital relationship is again cast in terms of "Bluebeard," with the female character's curiosity stemming from a desire "to understand" her partner. Similarly, in "Bluebeard's Egg" "the puzzle is Ed," significantly evoking the generic formula of the romance, a genre that Sally has supposedly avoided. To quote again Mandy Merck, the romance "transfers that traditional attribute of our gender, mystery, to the opposite sex. Much of these stories' narratives are [sic] occupied with the man as enigma and the heroine's attempt to figure him out" (50). This is "Bluebeard" as detective fiction, complete with a suitably curious female detective and intertextually explained by Sally's childhood reading of Agatha Christie.

Curiosity thus practiced marks the second act of reading in the story, building as it does on an initially benign, well-ordered interpretation, and a similar development in the creative act of reading can be seen in Lady Oracle. As the feminist revision of the fairy tale demonstrates, a new reading stems from a dissatisfaction with the story as it stands or with the story as it has traditionally been read. While on one level Joan is caught within a vicious cycle that perpetuates the search for the perfect simulation, in life, of the generic certainties of the fairy tale romance—a romance reader who projects her reading onto her life, which never lives up to the ideal and thus has to be escaped via both more reading and the construction of real life and fictional scenarios that achieve the simulation of the ideal—it is possible to detect hints of a critique. As a child her mother tells her that men are either nice or bad: "nice men did things for you, bad men did things to you" (69). The world of the fairy tale romance is structured around such binaries, stemming from the unquestionable duality of male and female, a biological essentialism that is carried over into social structures: as Ann Barr Snitow comments, romance fiction has its own ultimate "dream-like truth," embodied in the "pathological experience of sex difference" (134). However, Joan's experience of the "bad man," in the shape of the daffodil flasher, turns out to be more complex and hence to problematize the defined duality: "[w]as the man who untied me a rescuer or a villain? Or, an even more baffling thought: was it possible for a man to be both at once" (64). Similarly, Joan recalls a visit to the fair, including the "Harem" tent and the "Freak Show" with its "Fat Lady." In her dualistic world, Joan identifies with the Fat Lady, ostensibly devoid of a sexualized body and thus invisible as an object of desire, yet in reality the situation is more complex and her memory of the event is confused: "were there two tents or was there only one? The man with the megaphone sounded the same for freaks and dancing girls alike. They were both spectacular, something that had to be seen to be believed" (90).

It is the writing of the poem "Lady Oracle" that proves to be the pivotal shift in the process of reformulating the standard plot. On one level this functions as a crude rewriting of "The Lady of Shalott," with the "bow" of Joan's first real foray into automatic writing becoming the "prow" of Tennyson's poem. Yet for all its melodrama and clanging Jungian imagery, Joan begins to read the text as a transformed gothic:

> On rereading, the book seemed quite peculiar. In fact, except
> for the diction, it seemed a lot like one of my standard
> Costume Gothics, but a Gothic gone wrong. It was upside-
> down somehow. There were the sufferings, the hero in the
> mask of a villain, the villain in the mask of a hero, the flights,
> the looming death, the sense of being imprisoned, but there
> was no happy ending, no true love. The recognition of this
> half-likeness made me uncomfortable. (232)

The story's unorthodox gothic plot is mirrored again in the public interpretation of Joan's fictional death, read generically in the press as the suicide of a disturbed woman: "There I was, on the bottom of the death barge where I'd once longed to be. . . . Several of the articles drew morals: you could sing and dance or you could be happy, but not both" (313). These alternative interpretations of the founding texts of Joan's life presage a gradual shift in her own reading of that life. She admits to being "not serene, not really. I wanted things, for myself" (253), and ultimately carries over the discoveries of the fictional alternative plot into her own outlook: "[l]ove was merely a tool . . . for accomplishing certain ends. No magic, merely chemistry. . . . I'd polished them [her partners] with my love and expected them to shine, brightly enough to return my own reflection, enhanced and sparkling" (282). What emerges, albeit tentatively, is the manipulative, scheming side of her character, previously in the service of an orthodox plot which she was attempting to simulate and which she passed off as necessity, as the writing of herself into a pre-ordained societal pattern. As Gayle Greene points out, this highlights the intertextual figure of "Snow White," with its dichotomy of orthodox passivity and devious tale-telling: "Joan tries to 'pass' for Snow White, to make herself the 'heroine of a life that has no story' . . . while within her, the wicked Queen rages" (178).[78]

Throughout the course of the novel the fictional text under construction becomes gradually more intertwined with the present situation of the exiled Joan, thus repeating the interplay between text as life and life as text that figures throughout Joan's generic autobiography. The generic dualities embodied in the fictional Charlotte and Felicia—latter-day persecuted heroine and flagrant witch—begin to blur, with the fifth extract straining "against the rules" by suggesting sympathy for an increasingly Joan-esque Felicia. Joan grows "tired of Charlotte, with her intact virtue and her tidy ways," and begins to revel in the idea of alternative plots, of herself as "an escape artist," straining against the fairy tale boundaries in which "[y]ou could dance or you could have the love of a good man" (335). Finally, Joan becomes the witch that fairy tale convention dictates, symbolic of a refusal to adhere to the rules: she imagines herself as "a female monster, larger than life . . . hair standing on end with electrical force, volts of malevolent energy shooting from her fingers" (336). This image is imposed, and culturally sanctioned, and as Greene points out, "replicates the angel-monster dichotomy that pervades fiction and myth." Nonetheless, it liberates Joan as storyteller. Cast in an alternative fictional role, she is able to rewrite and to reinterpret the dénouement of her novel and her life in a final conflation of narrative levels.

Fittingly, with Joan cast as the newly liberated storyteller, she follows the example of the heroine of rewriting in "The Robber Bridegroom," drawing out the "Bluebeard" parallels in "Stalked by Love" to provide an alternative reading that no longer casts her in the role she previously imagined. "In a fairy tale I would be one of the two stupid sisters who open the forbidden door and are shocked by the murdered wives, not the third, clever one who keeps to the essentials" (152). The maze in the garden of Redmond Grange becomes the forbidden door of the narrative— "did the maze mean certain death, or did it contain the answer to a riddle, an answer she must learn in order to live?" (331)— and Joan rewrites what had been the penultimate extract in the form of a modified "Bluebeard." In the maze, Felicia (who has become the object of the narrative) discovers four women, each seemingly professing to be Lady Redmond—and thus Joan—and representing aspects of the repressed lives of the writer; through the symbolic door, "the only way out," Redmond is revealed as Bluebeard, and his various guises are read as the various men that have figured in Joan's life, each peddling the standard generic line: " '[l]et me take you away . . . let me rescue you. We will dance together forever, always' " (341–43). Felicia/Joan recognizes herself as "the next one, thin and flawless," the new victim of the prescribed plot. These revelations occur in "the central plot," and what Joan as author and character achieves is an uncovering of the intertextually embedded narrative of "Bluebeard" within the lines of the gothic romance. However, this is a "Bluebeard" that is read not as a cautionary tale of female culpability but as a narrative embodiment of the secret lies of patriarchal relations. In Bruno Bettelheim's reading, a paradigm of the orthodox interpretation, the female character's desire for knowledge is a sign of sexual curiosity and, by extension, of adulterous sexual relations, and the tale is thus cast as a cautionary aid to socialization: "[w]omen, don't give in to your sexual curiosity," don't open the door (302). Conversely, in Joan's reading the tale embodies an equally "central plot" in the narrative of gender relations, "in which girls grow into women to be replaced by 'the next one'" (Greene 187). "Bluebeard" and its related tale types become a paradigm, not of the submissiveness and fidelity necessary for a successful marriage but rather for the fact that they uncover the hidden plot of the fictional ideal of romance. The motif of the dead wives is reread in terms of the multiple identities that refuse to fit the mold of formulaic roles—not a man with several wives but a woman with several selves, confirming Joan's earlier prediction: "[i]f I brought the separate parts of my life together . . . surely there would be an explosion" (217). In place of the single role—the single story, the generic plot—is the explosion of multiplicity, embodied in the enactment of the alternative reading as escape and as critique. As Barbara Godard comments, the emphasis in *Lady Oracle* is ultimately not on fixed formulas and orthodoxies of interpretation, but rather on "perceptual processes, new versions and revision, based on context, not fixed text": "[t]he hidden story offering the possibility of alternative readings of the tales" ("Tales Within Tales" 70). The heroine of "The Robber Bridegroom" once again surfaces as a model for the revelatory process of rereading, and completes the figure of the reader in the text who has traveled from orthodoxy to alternative, from myth to subversive fiction.

In a similar move, Sally in "Bluebeard's Egg" uncovers the "Fitcher's Fowl" narrative that has been hidden behind her previous readings, the "ancient," "prehistoric" element that she has attempted to eradicate in her bid for tidiness. Like the revelatory final conflation of fictionalized autobiography and autobiographical fiction that proves to be the folkloric key to *Lady Oracle*, the pivotal moment occurs when Sally, albeit equivocally, discovers Ed's adulterous activities by the "keyhole desk": uncovers him as an "as if," a potential fiction that creates the possibility that her marriage, in the form of her reading of it, could be equally fictional; that Ed could be both the wizard in the folktale and the forbidden room, the initial gap in the narrative that slowly uncovers its contents—possibilities that she has previously discarded as not fitting her benign reading of Ed, and that would leave her with literally "no story" in her rewriting assignment. As Patricia Duncker comments, the fairy tale "gives Sally her meanings," not only those in which Ed is the adulterer who refers to women as "interchangeable," but also those in which Sally is the clever, manipulative heroine. Following this model, passing references to Sally's "mischievous" activities at dinner parties, her status as the "star pupil" on her various night courses and her slyly witty jokes at Ed's expense are charged with intertextual resonance.

The final image of the story is the egg, Sally's chosen actant, the ultimate "silent other," the weighty symbolism of which she is well aware, having taken a course in Comparative Folklore (Godard, "Palimpsest" 51). Initially she had imagined Ed as the egg, "blank and pristine and lovely," but this interpretation has been discarded in her new reading. It is no longer "cold and white and inert" but "glowing softly as though there's something red and hot inside it"; a symbol of potentiality, of future fictions—"what will come of it?"—that may uncover dusty meanings (164). "Bluebeard's Egg" thus functions as a reading of "Fitcher's Fowl"/"Bluebeard"—a reading which in turn encases a series of thoughts about the fairy tales themselves—and a spur to other readings. The author's reinterpretation again figures as both creation and critique. The fairy tale is the intertext that provides both a structure of coercion, in its generic, canonical form, and suggests alternative strategies through the interpretation of specific non-canonical tales. Rather than the certain rigidity of the orthodox reading of "Bluebeard," Atwood's story ends with unresolved possibilities, indicative of the supple, gradually evolving nature of Sally's various "readings."

Atwood's poetic exploration of "Bluebeard" as domestic drama, "Hesitations outside the door," echoes this search for possibilities:

> I'm telling the wrong lies,
> they are not even useful.
> The right lies would at least
> be keys, they would open the door. (168)

It is the provisional tale as a "right lie," as exploratory fiction, that both uncovers the multiple secrets of the forbidden room and suggests strategies that move beyond the historical dilemma represented in the room itself—fictions that can uncover both past truths and possible futures. As the Opies write, fairy tales are "the space fiction of the past" (20), and it is the speculation they encourage that can lead to the deconstruction of the culturally and historically potent confinement of the forbidden room. This is to follow the transformational aesthetic of the wonder tale as offering a means of imagining "the world inverted, the other side of the mirror, the opposite" (Butor 214). Perhaps it is only in what Duncker characterizes as the "multiplying ambiguities of an extended narrative" ("Re-imagining the Fairy Tales" 12) that the notion of conflicting, contesting stories can be properly explored. (Witness the multiple versions suggested in the fictions discussed in this chapter.) I take Duncker to mean here the levels of reading and writing that weave back and forth in speculative metafictions such as those I have considered, within which the recontextualized fairy tales function intertextually as embedded readings of the palimpsestic narrative and are themselves read, enacting the perpetual state of variation that characterizes the history of the folktale itself and its continuation in multiple "survival forms."

Conclusion

I began this cyclical survey of influence by suggesting its essentially open-ended nature, in the manner of the folkloric story cycle which has served as my makeshift model. To keep faith with this suggestion I would like to conclude by mentioning two representative avenues of enquiry I have not discussed. They are representative to the extent that they suggest the rich seam of material still to be mined.

In attempting to delineate the range of the folktale's influence in recent years and to justify my introductory adoption of Donald Mitchell's suggestion regarding the folksong and twentieth-century European music, I have, in the preceding chapters, tendentiously chosen material which can be slotted relatively neatly into a thematic group, whether a shared conception of a particular aspect of the folktale, or, as in the case of Calvino, the oeuvre of a single author. This has meant the exclusion of isolated literary works, in which the singular relation to the folktale requires attention on its own terms rather than as part of a trend or within the context of other works by the same author. These include two contrasting contemporary story cycles: Gianni Celati's *Voices from the Plains* (Narratori delle pianure, 1985), which returns to a communal storytelling rooted in the landscape of its multiple narrators; and Michel Tournier's *The Midnight Love Feast* (Le Médianoche amoureux, 1989), which adopts the conventions of medieval story cycles as well as various folkloric motifs. Broadly related to the fusion of formalism and the folktale practiced by Calvino, there is fellow Oulipian Jacques Roubaud's *The Princess Hoppy or The Tale of Labrador* (Le Princesse Hoppy ou le conte du Labrador, 1990), Milorad Pavic's *Dictionary of the Khazars* (Hazarski recnik, 1985) and Karen Elizabeth Gordon's fairy tale dictionary *The Red Shoes*

and Other Tattered Tales (1996). Apart from the last of this far
from exhaustive list, each of these works is less concerned with
the rewriting of extant folktales or the use of easily identifiable
motifs, than with what I have been referring to as the "idea" of the
folktale: with styles and structures, historically rooted narrative
traditions, and with the literary representation of oral storytelling
and the concomitant notion of a communality of narration. Thus
the American author Paul Auster, whose novels ostensibly bear
no relation to the folktale, refers to the Grimm brothers' tales and
the *Arabian Nights*—"the oral tradition of storytelling"—as those
narratives that have had "the greatest influence on my work." He
explains further that this is so, not because of the store of motifs
they offer but, evoking Calvino, for the fact that stylistically they
are "bare-bones narratives, narratives largely devoid of details," in
addition to the model of "open-ended structures" offered by cycles
such as the *Arabian Nights* (140–41). Despite my reluctance to
compartmentalize, it is the question of how an influence such as
that described by Auster can be traced through singular literary
texts that unites those texts I name above, each of which is variously expressive of an engagement with—and particular conception of—non-canonical narrative models and traditions of narration. To trace this influence, equipped with a properly informed,
if critical, knowledge of the folktale and folkloristics, would, I
believe, yield genuine insights.[1] As Charles Rosen writes, "[t]he
solidity of the study of sources begins to dissolve as the subject
becomes more significant" (132).

   A second area for future enquiry is more speculative, and concerns the continuing influence of the idea of the orality of the folktale. One thread linking Calvino, Barth, and particularly Coover,
is an interest in hypertext—"the writing done in the nonlin-
ear or nonsequential space made possible by the computer"—and
computer-based interactive narrative fiction.[2] This is one striking extension of a range of topics touched on in the preceding
chapters, including the variously implicit interactivity of metafiction, the plurality and open-endedness extolled in much postmodernist theory, and the shift away from the metanarratives of

narratology towards, on the one hand, an interest in local, discrete tales, such as characterizes Lyotard's discussion of untethered serial chains of *petits récits*, and concomitantly, a spatial or figural conception of narrative.[3] Hypertextual narrative does not offer a formal model, but rather a space around which a user can "navigate"; an open space that can be crossed via potentially limitless routes and which can, if so designed, be supplemented.[4] In conclusion, I would like to suggest that the notion and practice of hypertext, and of narrative fiction written in hypertext, bears fertile comparison with—indeed has been conceived in terms of—ideas of the oral folktale tradition such as have been discussed here: the idea of unfixed, theoretically authorless narratives, including potential narratives, connected via multiple routes, occurring in multiple versions of which none can be granted precedent; of narratives connecting anonymous users in chains of narration, each user generating a story through their manipulation of pre-existent material, or adding to this material to continue the life of a particular narrative strand. No doubt this is a utopian view of hypertextual activity, as well as a markedly idealized and romanticized (literary) view of folktale traditions; yet, again, a connection can be made—"[t]here is continuity, after all, across the ages riven by shifting technologies" (Coover, "The End of Books" 25). Of course, as the author himself acknowledged, the schema laid out in Propp's *Morphology* proposes a nascent form of open, readerly text, providing instructions on how to "create a tale artificially" (111). To date, one of the most widely used software programs for creating hypertext has been Michael Joyce and Jay David Bolter's aptly named *Storyspace*, which the former suggests may be used "to create a novel as supple and multiple as oral narratives" (quoted in Woolley 157).[5] The two-way influence of these developments can already be witnessed in such folktale-related print texts as Coover's *Briar Rose*, in which the simultaneity of story space is enacted in the multiple, non-hierarchical versions which drift through "the eternal city of the tale"; and in Namjoshi's *Building Babel*, in which the rewriting of traditional narrative material serves as a paradigm for interactivity, and as a goad in the building of "The Reader's Text" (182), to be compiled from solicited read-erly interventions.

The shift from narrative grammar to a pragmatics of narrative—a shift charted over the course of the preceding chapters and involving a cyclical interactivity of theory and fictional practice—can be summarized in terms of an increasing concern for the ethics of narration. Some of the constituent questions implicated in such an ethics have been cited above, including the possibility of re-trieving and listening to particular voices; singularity and the ir-reducibility of context; and the relative status of participants in the narrative contract. If, as Rosen says, the study of influence increases in importance as the influence itself becomes more dif-fuse, then the future of the influence of the folktale on litera-ture might lie precisely in the idea of an orality (with all that implies) within the written text. Highlighting an "oral residue" in "the dominant modern novelistic tradition," Peter Brooks has suggested that it is precisely those elements of storytelling fore-grounded in the oral narration of tales that are now, "in the era of textuality," most requiring of our attention: in particular, the lived interaction against and within which the giving and receiv-ing of narrative takes place, and the sense that "[t]he transmission of narrative has cognitive value," that the act of narration is "not inconsequential."[6] Brooks is fully aware of the dangers of nostalgia and mystification, but as we have seen, literature and its attendant disciplines have had repeated and productive recourse to a range of ideas of the folktale and oral narrative. As such, it is fitting that my account of the on-going story cycle of influence should come to rest with reference to ideas of narrative and narration which have found their most resonant (written) expression in the folkloric story cycle itself.

Introduction

1. "The possibilities opened up by the rediscovery of folksong . . . must stand alongside neo-classicism and serial technique as the third and last of the 'answers' to the question: 'How to go on?'" (Donald Mitchell 108–9).
2. Bruce A. Rosenberg's *Folklore and Literature* is the book which comes closest in orientation to the current volume. Rosenberg is, however, more concerned with the literature of the Middle Ages and with the exposition of folkloristics for the student of literature.
3. For the key texts in the debate concerning the relationship between folklore and literature, see Dorson; and Dundes, "The Study of Folklore in Literature and Culture." To borrow the terminology used by Dundes, Dorson's article represents the more traditional, "identification" school, while Dundes himself acknowledges the need for the "interpretation" of any findings as a means of more fully comprehending the literary text and the nature of its relationship with its folkloric intertexts. As such, Dundes's 1965 article set the tone for subsequent contributions to the debate, which have sought to categorize more fully the potential variety of interaction between folklore and literature. The more comprehensive of these include Lewis; Lindahl; and Grobman.
4. In those cases where a non-English text is best known by its original title, I have retained this title throughout.
5. On the question of influence as a critical category, see Renza.

Chapter 1

1. As the only type of folk narrative I discuss is the folktale I have used "folk narrative" and "folktale" as synonyms throughout.
2. For a critique of the widely held view regarding the oral origins of the folktale, see Schenda, for whom "the very basis of the Romantic theories of an oral tradition unbroken since pagan times and of a lower-class origin of so-called folk narrative" is open to question (79).

3. The text by Jakobson and Bogatyrëv is an edited version of an essay which first appeared in 1929 (Bogatyrëv and Jakobson). The latter, together with the essay by Propp, highlights the need for an understanding of the interaction between oral and written narratives, particularly the process by which an oral tale can pass into a literary collection, undergo alteration, and then, in this new version, become part of the oral tale pool once again (a process I consider in my final chapter with reference to the fairy tale). For specific studies of this two-way process, see, for example, Prizel; and Dégh, "What did the Grimm Brothers Give to and Take from the Folk?"

4. Calvino offers here a familiar theoretical idealization of oral narrative traditions, one which we might counter with reference to the very definite hierarchy of versions of canonical fairy tales, for example. Nevertheless, it is precisely the *idea* of the folktale as it appears in theory and fiction with which I am concerned. On the question of variability in oral literature, see the many useful essays collected in Görög-Karady.

5. "Preindividualistic" is a term used by Fredric Jameson in his critique of the anachronism of narratological categories (*The Political Unconscious* 124). I return to Jameson's reading below.

6. Just as the ontological characteristics of the folktale are at odds with modern conceptions of the author, so individual tales fail to conform to modern conceptions of the work. The classic exposition of such conceptions is Michel Foucault's "What Is an Author?" (1969).

7. See Kamenetsky 99–113; and Thompson, *The Folktale* 367–90. I return in more detail to the history of the Grimms' collection in my final chapter.

8. It should also be noted that Thompson sought to expand the cataloguing of folktales beyond the largely European boundaries of Aarne's index, to include any traditional narrative: he notes that outside Europe, "the European tale-types are applicable to very few stories. Yet there is much common matter in the folk-literature of the world. The similarities consist not so often in complete tales as in single motifs" (*Motif-Index* 10). As with the Aarne index, Thompson stresses the principle of "practical usefulness" that underlies his project, exhibited in his desire for inclusiveness and expanded applicability. The methodological stress on similarity over difference—historical context or socio-cultural specificity—is an intrinsic part of these seminal folktale catalogues and is carried over into narratology.

9. Thompson's index was of course published after Propp wrote his study. Ideas concerning the relative merits of the motif as a unit of narrative were, however, already being discussed among Russian literary critics in the early twentieth century, following the nomination of the motif as the "simplest narrative unit" and "plot" as a "cluster of motifs" in the unfinished

Poetics of Plots (Poètika sjuzhetov, 1897–1906) in A. N. Veselovskij's *Poetics* (Poètika). On Veselovskij, see Erlich 10–15.

10. Aarne was aware of the possibility of a motif-based index of folktales but rejected it on the grounds that "it would have necessitated such a cutting into pieces of all complete folk-tales that the scholar would be able to make a much more limited use of the classification" (from the original introduction to *The Types of the Folktale*, as quoted in Thompson, *Folktale* 417).

11. Bolte and Polívka's standard reference work was published in five volumes between 1913 and 1932. At the time of the writing of Propp's *Morphology* the first three volumes, which constitute the main body of the work, were available; the subsequent two volumes consist of a range of scholarly opinion on various aspects of the folktale.

12. On the often ignored context of Propp's work—his links with the Formalist group, the very real problems this caused him when challenged by the state, and the pervasive influence of Marxism—see Anatoly Liberman's encyclopedic introduction in Propp, *Theory and History of Folklore*.

13. Folklore is discussed in one of the central texts of the Formalist school, Viktor Shklovskij's *The Theory of Prose* (O teorii prozy, 1925), which, as Propp summarizes in his introductory survey, argues against the ethnographic approach.

14. "Prefaces to the First and Second Editions of the *Nursery and Household Tales*." Trans. Maria Tatar, in Tatar, *The Hard Facts of the Grimms' Fairy Tales* 208; see also Kamenetsky 102–3.

15. For an analogous reading of Propp's use of folk narratives, and of the model offered by the *Morphology* for the analysis of literary texts, see Rosenberg, 91–107 and 117–27.

16. See also Dundes's earlier essay, "From Etic to Emic Units in the Structural Study of Folklore." For more recent examples of folktale studies influenced by or modeled on Propp's *Morphology*, see Jason and Segal.

17. See Liberman, in Propp, *Theory and History of Folklore* xliv–xlvi.

18. The classic exposition of this theory is "The Structural Study of Myth" (1955).

19. "Nothing . . . could have more resembled the thematization of narrative texts than the post-Proppian structuralist and narratological attempt to see character in narrative as reducible to proper names or predicates. Indeed, the initial operation from which much structuralist and narratological analysis proceeds is arguably of a thematizing kind" (Gibson, *Towards a Postmodern Theory of Narrative* 107).

20. The following account of Greimas's work is necessarily highly selective, as his reading of Propp can only be fully understood within the context

of his concept of structural semantics. While I will attempt to suggest this context, the object of my study obviously limits the space available to a comprehensive exposition. I thus take solace in the sanction given by Jameson in his foreword to a selection of Greimas's essays: faced with the complex scientific terms, concepts, and neologisms of Greimas's work, Jameson writes that we, as readers, should "feel free to bricolate all this, that is, in plainer language, simply to steal the pieces that interest or fascinate us, and to carry off our fragmentary booty to our intellectual caves" (Foreword, in Greimas, *On Meaning* viii). The reader is directed in particular to Ronald Schleifer's introduction to *Structural Semantics*, together with his *A. J. Greimas and the Nature of Meaning*, and to the dictionary written by Greimas and J. Courtés (*Semiotics and Language*), which provides a valuable systematic guide to the myriad terms used in *Structural Semantics*.

21. Greimas completes this part of his analysis by covering all of Propp's "spheres of action," illustrating what he terms "syncretism": the manner in which one actant can be manifested in two actors, and vice versa. For example, Propp's "hero" enacts the actantial categories of "subject" and "receiver" (*Structural Semantics* 203–6)). To avoid excessive paraphrase I have limited my discussion to an overview of Greimas's theoretical processes.

22. Again, the necessary limits of this chapter do not allow for a proper elaboration of this concept, one which forms the bedrock of Greimas's work and is perhaps the paradigmatic expression of the structuralist project (Jameson quotes Umberto Eco's reference to this area of enquiry as "ontological structuralism" [*Political Unconscious* 46]). Following his working through of Propp's functions in *Structural Semantics*, Greimas went on explicitly to formulate the semiotic square in "The Interaction of Semiotic Constraints" (co-authored with F. Rastier). For a detailed guide to the intricacies and manifold implications of the model, see Schleifer, 25–33 in particular.

23. On this aspect of the role of the folktale, see Bascom, "Four Functions of Folklore."

24. Subsequent to the initial burst of narratological activity, and unlike Greimas, Bremond has maintained an interest in the study of folk narrative, as demonstrated for example in his essays on French tales ("Morphology of the French Folktale" and "The Morphology of the French Fairy Tale"), drawing on material from two volumes (1957 and 1964) of Paul Delarue and Marie-Louise Tenèze's *Le conte populaire français*.

25. Jonathan Culler criticizes Bremond's project precisely because he seeks in this way to subvert the teleological nature of plot (*Structuralist Poetics* 208–11).

26. In *Grammaire du Décaméron* (1969), Tzvetan Todorov subjects Boccaccio's

text to an extended structural analysis, in which each story is reduced to an algebraic formula (an approach summarized in his "Structural Analysis of Narrative"). However, the gradual shift away from the ostensibly universal, transhistorical objectivity of narratology can be seen in Barthes's structuralist-oriented analyses of nineteenth-century literature, such as *S/Z* (1970) and "Textual Analysis of a Tale by Poe" (1973). As the title of the latter indicates, Barthes distinguishes between "structural analysis" and a more contextually "open" "textual analysis": "structural analysis, strictly speaking, is applied above all to oral narrative. . . . Textual analysis . . . is applied exclusively to written narrative" ("Textual Analysis" 172).

27. For an insightful deconstructive reading of Propp, Lévi-Strauss, and Lüthi, see Menninghaus ch. 6.

CHAPTER 2

1. Penzer comments on Burton's translation of Basile in the preface to his own edition, which I use here (Basile, Vol. I, vi); Penzer, Terminal Essay, in Somadeva, *The Ocean of Story*, vol. IX, 124. This ten-volume opus itself provides the best English-language introduction to the historical and cultural background of Somadeva's work, in the form of the individually written thematic forewords to each volume. Together with Penzer's extended appendices, bibliographies, and indexes, the complete work is a marvellously self-sufficient whole (see also *Tales from the "Kathasaritsagara,"* trans. Arshia Sattar).

2. Ong's comment on medieval literature is quoted in Gittes 146; I have drawn on Gittes's remarks on the oral elements in medieval cycles. "[A]dditive rather than subordinative" is the first of Ong's "characteristics of orally based thought and expression" in *Orality and Literacy* (37); see also Stahl.

3. In a variation on Ong's argument which attempts to understand the role of the framed tale in the context of oral narratives, Stephen Belcher concludes that framing is above all else a "literary device . . . intended to substitute for the very dimension in which it appears superfluous: the oral performance. The frame creates an artificial performance context to compensate for stasis of the written text" (19).

4. With reference to the popularity of the "story-collection" in medieval western Europe, Helen Cooper comments that "some of the collections are of oriental or classical derivation in their entirety, but many borrow their stories from any source available to them and present a complete mixture of eastern and western folk-tale, history and pseudo-history, myth, legend and fable" (9).

5. I have chosen not to concentrate on Straparola's cycle because of its less traditional, more novelistic style, and because the frame tale, modeled on Boccaccio in its use of an exiled group who narrate as evening entertainment, is less revealing, in the context of this chapter, than the folkloric frames of Basile and the *Arabian Nights*.

6. On the specific historic and cultural background to *The Ocean of Streams of Story*, see the forewords by M. Gaster and Atul Chatterjee, in Somadeva, *The Ocean of Story*, Vols. III and IX respectively.

7. As John Barth comments, "[s]everal of the springs that fed *The Ocean of Story* trickled westward also and separately, with the consequence that Somadeva's vast poem strikes one less as a source of Western narrative motifs than as a kind of anthology or compendium of such sources" ("The Ocean of Story," *The Friday Book* 86). For an introduction to the convoluted textual history of the *Panchatantra*, see E. Dennison Ross's foreword and Penzer's appendix (I), in Somadeva, *The Ocean of Story*, Vol. V; and Chandra Rajan's introduction in an edition which continues the tradition of ascribing the text to its own self-nominated composer, Visnu Sarma (xi–lv). For a contemporary translation, see the aforementioned edition of Rajan; Ramsay Wood's retelling of selected fables, *Kalila and Dimna: Selected Fables of Bidpai*; and Thomas Ballantine Irving's edition, which includes some of the additional tales that became attached to the cycle during its various migrations (*Kalilah and Dimnah*).

8. The *Arabian Nights* is hereafter abbreviated to *Nights*.

9. For a particularly convincing argument in favor of viewing the *Nights* as intrinsically and irreducibly "plural and mercurial," "an artistic production of the collective mind," see Ghazoul.

10. See Kabbani 23–36. For an example of the scope of the *Nights'* influence on English literature, see the essays in Caracciolo.

11. On Galland and d'Herbelot, see Said 63–67; and Irwin 14–17. On the history of European translations of the *Nights*, see Irwin ch. 1; and for a more idiosyncratic approach, Borges, *"The Thousand and One Nights."*

12. As Husain Haddawy comments, Galland produced "not a translation, but a French adaptation, or rather a work of his own creation." It was on this version that the large number of anonymous eighteenth-century English translations were based—"hack versions that inflamed the imagination of Europe" (*The Arabian Nights*, trans. Husain Haddawy, xvi). I use Haddawy's translation of Mahdi's edition as my basic text. Mahdi's editorial commentary has been collected and published separately.

13. For an overview of the history of the *Nights* beyond its European translations, see Pinault 1–16; Irwin chs. 2–4; and Gerhardt chs. 2 and 3. Gerhardt identifies the core block of narratives as "Block I" (29–31).

14. In addition to the frame and five internal cycles, to which I return below, the final part of the block is made up of three far more realistic and structurally unified tales which provide a marked change of tone.

15. Straparola's *Piacevoli Notti* is less structurally neat than *Il Pentamerone* or the *Decameron*, comprising thirteen nights of narration, each including five tales told by five of the assembled ladies-in-waiting, chosen by lot. However, the eighth night consists of six tales and the final night of thirteen (on this final night, the last before Lent, both men and women present stories). Another inconsistency is the appearance of a narrator named "Diana" on the ninth and eleventh night, despite her absence from the explicitly named group of ten ladies-in-waiting hired by the Princess in the frame tale.

16. For a detailed discussion of the structure of Basile's cycle, see Canepa, *From Court to Forest* ch. 4.

17. See also Hinckley.

18. See Cooper ch. 1; as she says, the Middle Ages in Europe was "the great age of artistically self-conscious story-collections" (8). On the influence of Arabic culture and narratives in the Middle Ages, see Metlitzki, especially 95–106, in which she discusses the *Disciplina Clericalis*, the tales of which "were drawn from the international folklore of the East Indian, Byzantine, Persian, Arabian, and Hebrew storehouse" (96).

19. As I suggested in relation to Penzer, the formal aesthetic of folktales and folktale-influenced texts is one aspect that is successfully expressed by the more traditional, positivist scholarship of the early twentieth-century (such as Hinckley's 1934 essay), in which, relative to more recent methodological developments, facts, figures, and historical antecedents are unproblematically compiled.

20. The identification of such common material is obviously greatly helped by detailed annotation, such as that supplied by Penzer for this cycle, and bears out the practical usefulness of folktale catalogues, regardless of their theoretical shortcomings.

21. Canepa discusses a range of forms of organization in *Il Pentamerone* (*From Court to Forest* 98–110).

22. Demonstrating how a formalist concern with narrative structure can further the unpicking of contextual meaning, Bottigheimer has written of the editorial manipulation of particular motifs among related tales in *Kinder- und Hausmärchen*: "when motifs are analyzed collectively, they demonstrate properties that differ considerably from those traditionally attributed to them" ("Motif, Meaning, and Editorial Change in *Grimms' Tales*" 551).

23. Propp demonstrates an awareness of the generative aspect of his enquiries, albeit before generative grammar or structuralist poetics as such were con-

ceived: "any tale element . . . can, as it were, accumulate action, can evolve into an independent story, or can cause one. But like any living thing, the tale can generate only forms that resemble itself. If any cell of a tale organism becomes a small tale within a larger one, it is built . . . according to the same rules as any fairy tale" (89); he also speculates that using his formula, "[i]t is possible to artificially create new plots of an unlimited number" (111).

24. David Pinault cites a theory that the first narrative block ends with the king leaving to uncover the mystery of the fish; nevertheless, the basic point remains the same (31–81).

25. Ghazoul's basic method for dealing with the "superb complexity" of the cycle involves "decomposing the work into smaller units, composing and contrasting these units, and then hopefully arriving at a system in which those units function" (23). He refers to this approach as "differential and integral" and it is obviously based on the working methods of structural linguistics. While Ghazoul's study has influenced my readings, my aim is to concentrate on the texts themselves and the manner in which they appear to manipulate these "smaller units."

26. The *Nights* also displays more obvious signs of the influence of oral forms: for example, in its formulaic description of the beauties of male and female characters and in the repeated use of moral tags as punctuation through the text. Pinault's study is particularly useful in supplying the historical and cultural background to this oral heritage.

27. Max Lüthi includes the "depthlessness" of the protagonists as one of his defining characteristics of the European folktale, where character is always subordinate to plot: "the folktale expresses internal feelings through external events, psychological motivations through external impulses" (*European Folktale* 15).

28. See also Bal.

29. As well as the fact that Shahrazad's stories lead to the preservation of her own life, the now traditional conclusion to the cycle refers to three sons that have resulted from the long course of the *Nights*, and much has been written on the link between textual and sexual generation in the frame tale (and, by extension, on narrative as a means of sustaining life): see, for example, Naddaff; Faris; and Barth, "Don't Count on It: A Note on the Number of *The 1001 Nights*," *Friday Book* 258–81.

30. Barth has summarized the metaphysical implications of the Chinese box structure ("Tales Within Tales Within Tales," *Friday Book* 235–38). Approaching the subject of folkloric frame tales within their original context, Belcher comments on the recent shift within academic folklore studies towards a view of "the concept of the frame" as not "primarily a narrative

mechanism for the linkage of possibly related tales, but rather the series of devices by which a narrator signals, and exploits, the disjunctions between the fictive world evoked in the story being performed and the immediate human context of the narration" (1).

31. As Borges goes on to comment, "[i]n the title *The Thousand and One Nights* there is something very important: the suggestion of an infinite book" (50).

32. See Pinault 53. Many of the Indian cycles, including the *Panchatantra*, were intended for moral instruction and this function was continued in Europe in the Middle Ages—influenced by translations of tales from the *Panchatantra*—in Latin texts of "wisdom literature" such as Alfonsi's *Disciplina Clericalis* and, heavily influenced by Alfonsi, the late thirteenth-century *Gesta Romanorum*.

33. Bakhtin traced the roots of polyphony in the modern novel back, in part, to the realm of the folktale and popular culture: for example, commenting on the historical and cultural milieu from which the modern novel grew, he points to "the literature of the *fabliaux* and *Schwänke* of street songs, folksayings, anecdotes . . . where all 'languages' were masks and where no language could claim to be an authentic, incontestable face" ("Discourse in the Novel" 273).

CHAPTER 3

1. For the purposes of this chapter I have used the standard English translations. While I am aware of the dangers of such a practice—including the necessarily cursory reading of Italian criticism—my anxiety is tempered by the fact that a large section of Calvino's oeuvre is translated by William Weaver, with whom Calvino established a close working relationship, checking proofs and suggesting alterations. I have nevertheless avoided detailed textual analysis. In addition, it is worth remarking that while acutely aware of the negotiations of translation (having himself attempted Italian translations of Joseph Conrad and Raymond Queneau), Calvino thought of his work within broader parameters: in an interview-article written by William Weaver, Calvino comments on the importance "of being Italian in the context of an international literature. Always, even in my tastes as a reader, before I became a writer at all, I have been interested in literature on [sic] a world-wide frame" (Weaver 27).

2. For detailed English bibliographies of Calvino's work, and of secondary criticism, see Hume, *Calvino's Fictions*, and Albert Howard Carter III. A general overview of critical approaches is provided in the Calvino number of *Review of Contemporary Fiction* (6, 2 [1986]), and the aforementioned

Calvino Revisited, ed. Ricci. Calvino's writings on the folktale, including essays on the Grimm brothers, Perrault, and Basile, have been collected in an Italian volume (*Sulla fiaba* [Torino: Einaudi, 1988]) and the proceedings of a symposium dedicated to the subject have been published (*Inchiesta sulle fate: Italo Calvino e la fiaba, a cura di Delia Frigessi* [Bergamo: Pierluigi Lubrina Editore, 1988]). In English, several essays by Woodhouse deal with the influence of the tale on early texts: "Italo Calvino and the Rediscovery of a Genre"; "Fantasy, Alienation and the Racconti of Italo Calvino"; and "From Italo Calvino to Tonio Cavilla: The First Twenty Years"; and two further essays focus on this area in particular: Bacchilega, "Calvino's Journey: Modern Transformations of Folktale, Story, and Myth," and Bronzini, "From the Grimms to Calvino: Folktales in the Year Two Thousand."

3. Calvino also wrote the scenario and two song texts for Berio's mime-ballet *Allez-Hop* (1959; revised 1968). For Berio's own comments on his use of folk material (texts and music), see Berio 106–7 and 148–56; and for a comprehensive introduction to Berio's use of folk material, and to his two major collaborations with Calvino, see Osmond-Smith 78–87 and 98–118 respectively.

4. Ozick goes on to comment that "despite the clamor, there are not so many of these [authentic postmodernists]."

5. Calvino, "Cybernetics and Ghosts," *The Literature Machine* 2–27; the other (translated) versions of this essay are "Notes Towards a Definition of the Narrative Form as a Combinative Process," and "Myth in the Narrative."

6. For an overview of these developments, see Lüthi, *European Folktale* 118–25. With regard to Calvino's volume, Bronzini (in an essay that seems to have been poorly translated) comments that the idea for such a project "arose from editorial need of placing side by side a collection of Italian folktales and other collections of national folktales being published in the series *I Millenni* a short time before. The *Millenni* had already included the *Russian Folktales* together with the *African Tales*, the *Norwegian Tales* and so on" (190).

7. From the preface to the first volume of the first edition of *Kinder- und Hausmärchen* (1812), trans. Maria Tatar, Tatar, *The Hard Facts of the Grimms' Fairy Tales* 210.

8. For a brief introduction to the question of Italian Romanticism, see Carsaniga.

9. Arnim and Brentano collected and published the three-volume collection of folksongs, *Des Knaben Wunderhorn: Alte deutsche Lieder* (The Boy's Magic Horn: Old German Songs), between 1806 and 1808. It was in reply to a request for potential material for a prospective third volume dedicated to

the folktale that the Grimm brothers submitted a manuscript of fifty-three tales, and while this third volume never materialized, the Grimms went on to publish the first volume of the first edition of their own collection in 1812.

10. On the Grimms' tales within the context of European Romanticism, see Kamenetsky ch. 8.

11. In the preface to the second edition of *Kinder- und Hausmärchen* (1819), Wilhelm Grimm detailed the editorial process that had been followed in an attempt to present only "authentic" material: "fragments have been completed, many stories have been told more directly and simply and there are very few tales that do not appear in an improved form" (trans. Tatar, in Tatar, *Hard Facts* 220).

12. Indeed, Calvino points out that one of the defining characteristics of genuinely traditional children's folktales, at least in Italy, is not explicit moralizing or tameness of imagery but rather extravagant scatology.

13. Lüthi comments on the "sharply defined and distinct" imagery of the folktale, which he views as characteristic of its "abstract," "diagrammatic" style (*European Folktale* 24–36).

14. Again, in his attempt to distinguish a phenomenology of the European folk narrative, Lüthi includes discussion of "clear, ultrapure colours," formulas ("triads" in particular) and the "single sharply defined plot line" (*European Folktale* 27, 33 and 34).

15. The primary texts of the Oulipo group are the *Bibliothèque Oulipienne*, pamphlets privately published and circulated; four compilation volumes are available in the original French, together with several theoretical texts. The most famous by-products of the association have been Georges Perec's *La Disparition* (1969; translated into English by Gilbert Adair as *A Void*) and Calvino's own *The Castle of Crossed Destinies* (Il castello dei destini incrociati, 1973). Three English introductions to the Oulipo provide a range of theoretical and fictional examples: *Oulipo: A Primer of Potential Literature*, ed. Motte Jr.; Queneau, et al., *Oulipo Laboratory: Texts from the Bibliothèque Oulipienne*; and *Oulipo Compendium*, ed. Harry Matthews and Alastair Brotchie.

16. As to the question of rewrites, it is of course true that each of the entries in *Italian Folktales* is to varying degrees rewritten.

17. A similar passage occurs in an essay from 1960, written in English, which also refers to "the linear treatment of narration" and "rhythm" of the tale as sources of interest ("Main Currents in Italian Fiction Today" 13).

18. For a comparable view of this aspect of Calvino and the folktale, see Bacchilega, "Calvino's Journey" 86, and Bronzini 195. Ozick writes specifically that "Calvino re-addresses . . . the idea of myth, of 'the tale' " (351).

19. The musicologist Carl Dahlhaus writes of "The Idea of Folk Song" in *Nineteenth-Century Music* 105–11.

20. See also the other essays on "The Relation Between Folk Music and Art Music" in ch. 6 of *Béla Bartók Essays*.

21. Along with his compatriot Zoltán Kodály, Bartók's interest in folk music was stimulated to a large degree by the nationalist movement in early twentieth-century Hungary. Like the Grimms in the early nineteenth century, both composers were interested in discovering authentic folk traditions beyond the diluted *faux-naïf* folkishness of popular song (for a summary of this aspect of Bartók's career, see Kovács).

22. These (translated) adjectives are taken from the various references to Bartók in the essays of Pierre Boulez (*Orientations*), and from Griffiths.

23. Compare Dahlhaus on Chopin, another composer on whom folk music had a pervasive influence: "Virtually the whole of Chopin's oeuvre thrives unmistakably on his practice of 'interiorizing' the essential features of literary genres or functional music. . . . As a result, his music exists in its own right as autonomous art, preserving the moods of the original literary or musical genres as reminiscences" (*Nineteenth-Century Music* 149).

24. The complicated publishing history of the various tales that came to make up *I racconti*—which will be returned to below—is explained in Ricci, *Difficult Games* ch. 1.

25. As Teresa De Lauretis comments, "it is the conceptual basis of structuralism and semiotics that intrigues and affects Calvino the writer" (415). As with the idea of the folktale, it is the *idea* of the methodology.

26. In the brief account of the cultural climate of postwar Italy which follows, it is important to bear in mind that the South was gradually liberated by the Allied forces following the invasion of Sicily in 1943, and thus did not experience, at least not to the same degree, the unifying impetus of a Resistance movement such as occurred in the North. This split was of course merely one instance in the long history of antagonism between North and South, but it was particularly pertinent to the problems facing the attempts at unity which followed liberation.

27. On the role of the Communist party in postwar Italy and "the watershed of 1956"—essential contexts for Calvino's early work—see Ginsborg 204–9; and Duggan, *A Concise History of Italy* ch. 9.

28. On the postwar economic boom, the negative aspects of which are explored by Calvino in this series of fictions (and in *Marcovaldo* (1963)), see Ginsborg ch. 7

29. The central essays of this period (which remain untranslated) are included in the collection *Una pietra sopra: Discorsi de letteratura e società* (1980); see, in particular, "Il midollo del leone" (1955), and the three articles Calvino

wrote for *Il menabò*: "Il mare dell' oggettività" (1960), "La sfida al labirinto" (1962), and "L'antitesi operaia" (1964).

30. The text of a radio broadcast from 1974—"The Structure of *Orlando Furioso*"—delivered on the occasion of the fifth centenary of the birth of Ariosto, is included in *The Literature Machine* (162–74); this selection also includes "Why Read the Classics?" (1981), "The Odysseys Within *The Odyssey*" (1981), and "Ovid and Universal Contiguity" (1979), all of which demonstrate Calvino's continued advocacy of classical literature. These essays form the basis of the posthumous anthology *Perché legger i classici* (Milan: Mondadori, 1991), recently translated as *Why Read the Classics?* (a collection which includes new translations, by Martin McLaughlin, of the aforementioned essays).

31. Gore Vidal's extended report on attending Calvino's funeral, originally written for the *New York Review of Books* in 1985, appears as "Calvino's Death" in *United States: Essays 1952–1992*, together with his influential 1974 piece surveying Calvino's fiction for an American readership ("Calvino's Novels").

32. As this important essay has not been translated into English, passages are taken from the partial translation in Adler (122).

33. For a more precise discussion of the differences in the use of folk music by these three composers, see Donald Mitchell, 109 n. 2. The classic exposition of the unbridgeable gap separating folk music from European art music—"they mix as poorly as oil and water" (162)—is Schönberg's "Folkloristic Symphonies" (1947).

34. For a detailed study of the influence of Collodi's *Le avventure di Pinocchio* (1881–1883) on another Calvino text—*Marcovaldo*—see Jeannet. I discuss Robert Coover's rewriting of Collodi's text in ch. 4.

35. Marcovaldo is representative of the underside of the "economic miracle" of the postwar years in Italy (specifically 1958–1963), which was fueled in part by the cheap labor provided, especially but not exclusively, by the poor and unemployed of the South. As Duggan comments, migration led to "profound dislocation, real and psychological. During the 1950s and 1960s over 9 million Italians migrated to a new region of the country. Men and women, often illiterate, whose families had rarely stirred beyond their rural communities for centuries, and who spoke dialect only, suddenly found themselves amid the neon lights, the hoardings, and the traffic of a huge bustling city" (264–65); this is undoubtedly the world of Marcovaldo (see also Ginsborg 217–29).

36. I refer to the critical consensus here in order slightly to distance myself from a constricted view of what are formally ingenious fusions: of the rural and the urban, the critique and the celebratory, the elegiac and the humorous.

To focus merely on Marcovaldo's anachronistic imagination is to miss these dimensions.

37. Ricci picks out another early hint of textual self-consciousness in "The Enchanted Garden," where the line between the world outside and inside the garden is marked by a fence that twists "like the corner of a sheet of paper" (in *Adam, One Afternoon and Other Stories* (1949), 20; Ricci, *Difficult Games* 22).

38. See also Gillies, "Bartók and his Music in the 1990s," 13; and Griffiths 51. Similarly, Osmond-Smith comments that Berio found his favored technique of "gradually extending a fixed repertoire of focal notes" reflected in various folk musics, "where a small selection of pitches are so often permutated to yield extraordinary melodic riches" (79–80).

39. Following Parry's death, his collaborator Albert B. Lord continued work begun on the recording and analyzing of Serbo-Croatian epic singers, viewed as a unique link with the culture of Homeric performance. Towards the end of his life, Bartók worked at transcribing material in the Parry collection and the result was the posthumous *Serbo-Croatian Folk Songs*, co-authored with Lord himself. For a summary of the context of Parry's work, see Ong ch. 2. Albert B. Lord's classic work, *The Singer of Tales*, provides an overview and extension of Parry's work, and serves as an essential introduction. For a summary of Bartók's extensive work on Eastern European folk musics, see Kovács.

40. On the use of formulae in the folktale, see Lüthi, *European Folktale*, 32–34.

41. The best exposition of this complex mathematical structure is given in Marello. Interestingly, given the theme of music in this chapter, Springer attempts a representation of the structure of *Invisible Cities* in musical notation, as a form of plain chant with an introduction, seven verses, and a coda (app. II). For an overview of the various descriptions and readings of the model, see Albert Howard Carter III 164 n. 2.

42. Calvino's comments on the restrictive units used in the extracts occur in "Se una notte d'inverno un narratore," *Alfabeta* 8 (December 1979): 4. For a translation of Calvino's Oulipian booklet—which has also appeared, in the original French, with an introduction by Greimas himself (*Nuova Corrente*, 34 (1987): 9–28)—see "How I Wrote One of My Books." The tongue-in-cheek nature of such texts is worth bearing in mind.

43. Pier Paolo Pasolini contemporaneously turned to the story cycle in a trilogy of films made in the 1970s (*Il Decamerone* [1970], *I racconti de Canterbury* [1971], and *Il fiore delle Mille e una notte* [1974]). While they make use of the embedded-tale structure, the films are more concerned with the carnivalesque aspect of traditional popular culture. Ten years earlier, in a portmanteau film entitled *Boccaccio '70*, leading figures of the neorealist

cinema (Fellini, Monicelli, de Sica, and Visconti) had similarly turned to the *Decameron*, in an attempt to update elements of the medieval Italian story cycle.

44. Compare the various other descriptions 123, 187, 211, 237.

45. This theme forms the central focus of Hume, *Calvino's Fictions*.

46. See, for example, Bacchilega, "Calvino's Journey," 92–94, and De Lauretis 423.

CHAPTER 4

1. One ramification of a thematic reading of post-1950s literature via the folktale is that it potentially creates a space in which the relationship of European literature with the folktale can be compared with a range of post-colonial literatures, specifically those in which traditional material is used as a means of exploring indigenous narrative traditions and forms of story-telling. Such a dialogue would be particularly useful as a means of charting the course of cultural decolonization, including questions regarding the status of traditional material and the manner in which it is presented in new literatures. Similarly, the potentially antagonistic inclusion of the postcolonial within or alongside the postmodern would relativize the status of the latter as a general sign of contemporaneity, suggesting limits to its applicability (for example, see Mukherjee). In order to avoid generalizations, particularly regarding the "form and nature" of non-European traditional material, I have felt it necessary to focus here on European folktales and European and American literature, aware of the necessary limitations of such a survey. As mentioned before, the *Arabian Nights* is included in this group because of its widespread influence, via oral dissemination and translation, on European literature.

2. "Spiraling" is a term used by Gabriel Josipovici (128).

3. As Fredric Jameson has written, "radical breaks between periods do not generally involve complete changes of content but rather the restructuring of a certain number of elements already given: features that in an earlier period or system were subordinate now become dominant, and features that had been dominant again become secondary" ("Postmodernism and Consumer Society" 177).

4. For a critique of what he refers to as "the modernist paradigm"—the selective, critical use (as here) of Eliot's comments on Joyce as the paradigmatic expression of the relationship between myth and modernism—see Eysteinsson 11, 15, and 123–24.

5. The first chapter of *The Secular Scripture*, "The Word and World of Man,"

provides a rich and suggestive overview of the shifting cultural status of myth and folktale, eminently applicable to discussions of the narrative models which figure most prominently in modernist and postmodernist literature.

6. This is not to say that postmodernist literature has ignored the mythic; rather, in the wake of structuralist myth criticism, it has sought to treat it more directly: as story rather than symbol or ideology, in the form of literal retellings rather than through allusion and archetypal resonance. In "Bellerophoniad," John Barth comments that "since myths themselves are among other things poetic distillations of our ordinary psychic experience and therefore point always to daily reality, to write realistic fictions which point to mythic archetypes is in my opinion to take the wrong end of the mythopoeic stick" (*Chimera* 207–8). Thus we have the historical discontinuities of John Barth's "Perseid" and "Bellerophoniad" (*Chimera*), which elaborately and parodically play with myth as written text, a potentially endless chain of versions which disavow any notion of hierarchy or authenticity. Likewise, Calvino's *The Castle of Crossed Destinies* directly retells mythic narratives in the form of the chance encounters of an interconnected chain of story patterns.

7. See Hutcheon, *A Poetics of Postmodernism* 124–40 and *The Politics of Postmodernism* 47–92; compare Christine Brooke-Rose's markedly similar notion of "palimpsest history," formulated in *Stories, Theories, and Things* 181–90.

8. For a similar treatment of narratology, see Culler, "Story and Discourse in the Analysis of Narrative."

9. See also Bruner, "The Narrative Construction of Reality."

10. For Ricoeur's reading of narratology, in particular Propp and Greimas, see "The Semiotic Constraints on Narrativity," in *Time and Narrative* vol. II.

11. Those works of Lyotard that deal specifically with the question of narrative include *The Postmodern Condition*; *Instructions païennes* (1977), part of which is translated by David Macey as "Lessons in Paganism"; and "Presentations." For an introduction to the role of narrative in Lyotard's work, see *Readings* ch. 2, and Bennington 106–17.

12. This is a translated extract from *Le Postmoderne expliqué aux enfants* (1986).

13. Bennington argues that the charge that Lyotard advocates a narrative-based relativism "relies on a misreading of *The Postmodern Condition*." Although he admits that "the importance accorded to narrative by the book perhaps makes such a misreading inevitable," he contextualizes and thus seeks more fully to understand the frequent reference to narrative within the broader context of Lyotard's concern with the essentially rhetorical nature of language.

14. Lyotard uses the example of storytelling among the Cashinahua Indians in a number of texts, including *The Differend: Phrases in Dispute* (1983), 152–61 (see also "Universal History and Cultural Differences" 320–21).

15. Compare Lyotard's discussion of "the sentence" ("Presentations" 129–33).

16. "Myths are prose narratives which, in the society in which they are told, are considered to be truthful accounts of what happened in the remote past" (Bascom, "The Forms of Folklore: Prose Narratives" 9).

17. Homi K. Bhabha has raised questions regarding the use of such an "Other text," situated to function as "the exegetical horizon of difference, never the active agent of articulation" (31).

18. On Potocki, see Irwin 255–60.

19. Barth discusses this aspect of the *Arabian Nights* in *The Friday Book* x, and *Chimera* 63–64.

20. For an insightful historicist reading of narratology from the standpoint of its reliance on specific narrative models, see Jameson, *The Political Unconscious* ch. 2; and for a brief account of the changing fortunes of narratology, see "Whatever Happened to Narratology?," Brooke-Rose 16–27.

21. Barth's nonfiction, collected in *The Friday Book* and *Further Fridays: Essays, Lectures, and Other Nonfiction, 1984–1994*, is essential for charting the course of a particular mode of extremely self-referential postmodernist American literature.

22. Klinkowitz's objections are essentially the same as those made in his earlier *Literary Disruptions* (1975); as such, he forms a prime target in Tobin's critique of the continued privileging of an historically specific conception of literary originality (Tobin 2).

23. Several of the Dorchester tales are recycled in *The Sot-Weed Factor* (see "It's a Short Story," *Further Fridays* 99).

24. See, for example, *The Friday Book* 9, 85, 158, 224; *Chimera* 20; *Once Upon a Time* 47, 251, 256; *Further Fridays* 228, 238, 252; most revealingly, perhaps, it is included in the brief "About the Author" page included in later editions of *Lost in the Funhouse*.

25. This ostensibly experimental fusion of the performative and the self-referential was very much rooted in tradition, as demonstrated by Barth in a contemporaneous reference to premodern narrative: "[t]he oral and folk tradition in narrative made use of verse or live-voice dynamics, embellished by gesture and expression. . . . Early written fiction . . . reflects this; while it typically and sometimes elaborately acknowledges its condition as writing . . . such fiction is usually about people telling one another stories" ("The Role of the Prosaic in Fiction," *Friday Book* 82).

26. In what follows, I have again abbreviated *Arabian Nights* to *Nights*.

27. As this use of the female/fertility trope demonstrates, Barth's disarmingly

unsophisticated symbolism permeates the novel: the boat in which the couple travel is named "Story," after a boat in one of Peter's earlier novels (to his understandable embarrassment), and, in keeping with the return to tradition, it is "an engineless, unamenitied little sloop." Such seemingly deliberately hackenyed symbols have been a feature of Barth's writing since the early novels, although they are far more common in the later novelistic story cycles. The author himself has commented on a specific example of this feature of his work ("The Prose and Poetry of It All, or, Dippy Verses," *Friday Book* 239–55), but it would seem to be of a piece with Barth's veneration of tradition and his oft-repeated desire to conjure dramatic situations or images as full of archetypal resonance as his favorite models: the *Odyssey*, the *Nights*, *Don Quixote*, and *Huckleberry Finn* (Barth has commented extensively on these "profound, multifaceted, transcendentally appealing narrative icons": see, for example, "The Limits of Imagination" 284–86).

28. Barth also incorporates other elements of the *Nights*: for example, the embedded interludal narrations of Jayda to Somebody and Yasmin, which also gradually fuse with their frame, take place postcoitally, as do all of Shahrazad's, with Jayda thus functioning in part as a fusion of Shahrazad and her ever-present sister; and the end of the novel uses the common *Nights'* convention of the appearance of the disguised caliph, Haroun al-Rashid, and his vizier.

29. Concerning the representation of the Near East in *The Last Voyage of Somebody the Sailor*, Birns cogently defends Barth against potential charges of Orientalism (133–35). For an informed reading of the *Arabian Nights* as one of Europe's "myths of the Orient," see Kabbani 23–36.

30. I am thinking here of *Midnight's Children* (1981), which uses the *Nights* as a paradigm of oppositional narration—"1001, the number of night, of magic, of alternative realities—a number beloved of poets and detested by politicians, for whom all alternative versions of the world are threats" (217); and *Haroun and the Sea of Stories* (1990), in which the *Nights* and *The Ocean of Streams of Story* are literalized as part of a fable against closure: "He looked into the water and saw that it was made up of a thousand thousand thousand and one different currents . . . and Iff explained that these were the Streams of Story, that each colored strand represented and contained a single tale . . . and because the stories were held here in fluid form, they retained the ability to change, to becomes new versions of themselves. . . . It was not dead but alive (72).

31. Making a similar point in more general terms, Hilfer characterizes *The Tidewater Tales* (and *Letters*) as suffering from "an insufficient resistance to the sweep of fantasy" (133). It is the absence of such a potentially generative

resistance to the incorporation and flattening out of his narrative model that I am attempting to articulate.

32. For readings of Coover from the perspective of the folk/fairy tale, see Bacchilega, "Folktales and Meta-Fictions: Their Interaction in Robert Coover's Pricksongs and Descants," and "Cracking the Mirror: Three Re-Visions of 'Snow White.'"

33. Pizer; Morace; Bacchilega, "Cracking the Mirror." For a selected list of the many essays on *Snow White*, see the Barthelme number of *Review of Contemporary Fiction* 11, 2 (1991).

34. Written by Frank Churchill and Larry Morey for Disney's 1937 film *Snow White and the Seven Dwarfs*, "Some Day My Prince Will Come" entered the jazz canon not long before Barthelme's novel was published, as a piece recorded by pianist Bill Evans in 1959 and, in 1961, as the title piece of an album by Miles Davis. The contemporary pervasiveness of the tale is clearly demonstrated by the manifest gap in style and intent that separates the original manifestation of song or tale and their use by Evans/Davis and Barthelme.

35. I have found the most convincing readings of Barthelme to be either those that read the fictions largely on their own terms—such as Klinkowitz in *Donald Barthelme: An Exhibition*—or that make use of the disorientation they engender in the reader, such as McHale and Ron. Again, this is absolutely not to suggest that interpretations of *Snow White* in terms of "Snow White" are quantifiably incorrect, but rather too restricting.

36. Despite my earlier remarks concerning the extent to which it is possible to read Barthelme's *Snow White* in terms of its eponymous intertext, it does make similar reference to its Queen-figure, Jane: her malice, "that artful, richly formed and softly poisonous network of growths," and her "abundant imagination and talent for concoction" (*Snow White* 40, 158).

37. It should be stressed that while the chapter referred to argues for the necessity of individual readings of folkloric intertexts, such an approach is less applicable to Coover to the extent that he appears less interested in the pre-literary or pre-popular history of his chosen material, which is not the case in the texts of Angela Carter and Margaret Atwood. This does not preclude a reading of Coover which would focus specifically on the fairy tales *as* fairy tales, such as that undertaken by Bacchilega ("Folktales and Meta-Fictions" and "Cracking the Mirror").

38. On the subject of the growth of children's literature, see for example the essays in Avery and Briggs, in particular Zipes, "The Origins of the Fairy Tale for Children" and Briggs; see also Rose.

39. Carlo Collodi was the pseudonym of Carlo Lorenzini (1826–1890). *Le avventure di Pinocchio* first appeared in serial form in the *Giornale per i bam-*

bini, one of the first Italian periodicals intended specifically for children. For the following account of Collodi's text, I have drawn on the wonderful introductory essay in Nicholas J. Perella's bilingual edition of the complete original story (Perella).

40. Perella notes that Collodi translated the French texts into "a colorful Tuscan-flavored prose that anticipates the style of *Pinocchio*" (6).

41. In Steven Swann Jones's study of the fairy tale, he places *Pinocchio* firmly within the category of literary fairy tales. While this helps to identify the continuity in Coover's choice of material, Collodi's text is in fact as much an interpretation of the fairy tale, albeit in the generic sense, as Coover's own "The Magic Poker," for example, and to read it as unproblematically continuing in the fairy tale genre is to miss its tendentiousness (33).

42. As suggested by this summary, *Pinocchio in Venice* can also be read as an extended parodic engagement with Thomas Mann's *Death in Venice* (Der Tod in Venedig, 1912), an engagement which Coover signals with exactitude via a number of intertextual references. The parody is in part of result of the bringing together of children's literature and literary artwork, on a stage which resonates with the myth of European high culture (a myth which is itself the subject of Mann's story). While the possibilities for a reading in tandem of the two most significant source texts for *Pinocchio in Venice* is tantalizing, I have of necessity limited myself to tracing Coover's relationship with Collodi.

43. In addition, Coover suggests an ethical dimension to anti-mimetic fiction, in that the fantastical elements (if we can define them as such within a text as multivalent as *Pinocchio in Venice*) are not subject to sublation in the interests of meaning and morality. I am grateful to the second (anonymous) reader of my manuscript for this suggestion.

CHAPTER 5

1. There is some confusion as to the precise definition of this type of tale, stemming from the intrinsically artificial nature of generic groupings. In the Aarne-Thompson index, types 300–749 are tales which include some form of magic, otherwise known as "wonder tales" or *Zaubermärchen;* following the Grimms, *Märchen* has come to signify the genre of the wonder tale, although, like *conte,* it strictly denotes any type of tale, and the Grimms' canon certainly includes tales which fall outside of the AT group devoted to the "wonder tale"; "fairy tale" is a translation of the French *conte de fée,* the literary genre whose history I sketch in this chapter (see Seifert, *Fairy Tales, Sexuality, and Gender* 224 n.1). All of these terms are simply attempts

to classify a certain type of folktale, including its literary descendants, and as they are all necessarily flawed to some degree I have chosen to use the most commonly recognized: "fairy tale." However, the tales I concentrate on are still also folktales in the general sense and I have not stuck rigidly to a differentiation between the folk and the fairies.

2. Representative examples of such critiques include Rowe, "Feminism and Fairy Tales"; Lieberman; Duncker; and Dégh, "Career Choices for Women." For a comprehensive survey of feminist criticism on the fairy tale, see Haase, "Feminist Fairy-Tale Scholarship," included in a special issue of *Marvels and Tales* devoted to taking stock of work in this field. Elizabeth Harries's *Twice Upon a Time*, devoted to fairy tales and women's writing, appeared in the final stages of the editing of the present work.

3. See also Stone. For a summary of the reactions against Lurie's views, see Lieberman, the premise of which is that it is precisely the most widely read tales that have the most widespread effects, regardless of whether or not they misrepresent the source traditions.

4. A prominent attempt at reinstating parallel folk traditions, particularly as illustrative of a wide range of representations of female behavior, can be found in the two collections of world fairy tales edited for Virago by Angela Carter.

5. Despite the fact that she acknowledges the historical primacy of Straparola's collection, Canepa is just as keen as Butor and Brooks to nominate her chosen progenitor: "Basile reivents the fairy tale in literary form"; "[Basile's] collection heralds the entrance of the fairy tale into the authored canon of Western literature" (*From Court to Forest* 11, 81).

6. Firmly to establish the relation between the literary and oral versions of a particular folktale is a virtual impossibility, due to the numerous potential stages involved in the process. A study of this process has referred to these stages—"the tortuous ways by which so-called folktales wind their way from their original narration to a modern reader"—as "filters," a basic list of which would include: the process and means of recording; the change in context that results from the recording and/or transcription; the editing process, including the background of the editor(s) and his/her purpose with regard to the material; linguistic problems involved in recreating and fully comprehending the original tale, resulting from the different ontological status of oral and written narrative; orientation of the potential audience; and, of course, translation (Dollerup et al, "The Ontological Status"). An acknowledgment of this process is essential in any attempt to read modern folktale retellings from a folkloristically informed perspective, and I have borrow the term "filters" when making subsequent reference to this area.

7. See also Thelander. For a concise overview of the rise of the French literary

fairy tale, and of the "[t]he prominence of women as initiators and writers of fairy tales" during the period, see Seifert, *Fairy Tales, Sexuality, and Gender* 5–12.

8. This is not to suggest that all tales written during this period were of this type, nor that the tales were overtly oppositional. Recent accounts of the period, such as that by Joan DeJean, have stressed the critical aspects of the texts produced, but these aspects require a properly historicist frame: as Thelander notes, the tales are "impeccably aristocratic" (493). On the question of the "ideological ambiguities" raised by seventeenth-century French fairy tales written by women, see Seifert, "On Fairy Tales, Subversion, and Ambiguity" (93).

9. For an historically informed reading which seeks to tease out the stylistic heterogeneity of Perrault's volume, see Malarte-Feldman.

10. The recent reformulation of the history of the literary fairy tale can be seen in the shift of focus away from Perrault in the publication of collections which place his tales alongside those of various other writers, predominantly women, without seeking to create a hierarchy. Of those translated collections in English, see Zipes, *Beauties, Beasts and Enchantment* and *The Great Fairy Tale Tradition*; Warner, *Wonder Tales*; and Tatar, *The Classic Fairy Tales*. In a similar vein, Harries offers a polemical account of the workings of "canon formation" in the narrative construction of the received canon of the fairy tale ("Fairy Tales about Fairy Tales"). See also Seifert, "On Fairy Tales, Subversion, and Ambiguity."

11. On this subject—and for a comprehensive reading of Perrault's volume— see Velay-Vallantin.

12. An overview of developments in Grimmian studies is given in McGlathery, *Grimms' Fairy Tales* 29–58. Manfred Grätz has charted the course of German translations of French fairy tales, in line with the belief that it was these translations that introduced the fairy tale into the German tale pool (*Das Märchen in der deutschen Aufklärung. Vom Feenmärchen zum Volksmärchen* [1988]). The passage of literary tales into the oral tradition, as opposed to the more commonly remarked upon reverse process, is the subject of Prizel; again, the passage between the twin realms problematizes any attempt to establish distinct boundaries.

13. Quoted in Tatar, *Hard Facts* 215. The various prefaces to *Kinder- und Hausmärchen* are invaluable for the insights they provide into the Grimms' project and the shift in their attitude to the tales that occurred subsequent to the publication of the two volumes of the first edition. The only complete English translation I have found is that by Tatar in Appendix B of the above text, which includes the prefaces to both volumes of the first edition (1812 and 1814) and the subsequent amalgamation which formed

the preface to the 1819 edition. Further reference to these prefaces is to this translation, and are included in the text.

14. Warner, *From the Beast to the Blonde* 190.

15. For a definitive dismantling of the myth of "Old Marie," see Rölleke. Accounting for the oral passage of Perrault's tales into the German narrative pool, Velten comments that "throughout the eighteenth century the upper classes in Germany were accustomed to have their children educated by French governesses or tutors, who doubtless told the stories to their pupils. The children, in turn, may have told them to the German servants in their household" (5).

16. As Dégh comments, "the Grimms created the artistic form of the *Märchen* by gradual improvement of their text, until it reached perfection in the 1857 version. During the process of variation, a distinctive short narrative genre emerged which contained a characteristic episodic structure, style, and tone" ("What Did the Grimm Brothers Give to and Take from the Folk?" 69); this hybrid form is also sometimes referred to as the *Buchmärchen* (book tale).

17. For a detailed study of the Grimms' treatment of specific tales, see Dollerup et al, "A Case Study of Editorial Filters in Folktales"; and Bottigheimer, " 'Marienkind.' "

18. For an account of these "filters," see Dollerup, et al, "Ontological Status."

19. On the influence of the Grimms' collection on oral traditions, see Dégh, "What Did the Grimm Brothers Give to and Take from the Folk?"

20. As Zipes comments, during the Nazi era the Grimms' tales "had become identical with a German national tradition and character, as if all the Grimms' tales were 'purely' German and belonged to the German cultural tradition"; coupled with a belief in a correlation between violent tales and violent actions, this led to the confiscation and banning of fairy tales by the occupying forces for a brief period following the end of the war ("The Struggle for the Grimms' Throne," 167–68).

21. With reference to Darnton, Bottigheimer has raised important questions regarding the trend among social historians towards the use of folk and fairy tales as historical documents ("Fairy Tales, Folk Narrative Research and History"). As well as the confusions that arise when "historically determined" fictions (343) are used to account for the conditions of history—"in fact, they [the tales] simply offer a parallel source" (346)—there are also the problems attendant on interdisciplinary enquiry: "from the point of view of a folk narrative scholar, many historical studies accept propositions about folk and fairy tales no longer held by mainstream folk narrative scholars, propositions which both date the scholarship and limit the effectiveness of the enquiries" (343).

22. Dégh argues for a similar approach in "What Did the Grimm Brothers Give to and Take from the Folk?"

23. I will be following the Aarne-Thompson classification system (discussed in detail in my first chapter), it being the most comprehensive and widely used catalogue. Originally compiled by Antti Aarne and published in German in 1910, the index of over two thousand basic plots from Europe and the Near East was enlarged and translated into English by Stith Thompson, first in 1928 and subsequently in 1961, as *The Types of the Folktale: A Classification and Bibliography*; the AT numbers in my text refer to this catalogue. For my purposes I have used a more recent slimmed-down version, the numbering of which follows exactly that of Aarne-Thompson (Ashliman). In all references to the Grimms' tales, I follow the standard procedure of including the number given in the final edition (1857), signaled by the abbreviation KHM.

24. A translation of the Grimms' "Blaubart" is included in Zipes's edition of the tales (*The Complete Fairy Tales of the Brothers Grimm* 660–63). This edition includes a translation of all the tales that were omitted from the six editions of *Kinder- und Hausmärchen* prior to the final edition of 1857.

25. A major study of "Bluebeard" appeared during the final stages of the editing of the present work: Mererid Puw Davies, *The Tale of Bluebeard in German Literature: From the Eighteenth Century to the Present*. As indicated by its title, however, Davies's survey does not include the English-language literature I consider in the latter stages of the present chapter.

26. I am basing my reading on two translations of Perrault's tale: the first English translation, by Robert Samber, from his seminal 1729 edition of the tales, reprinted in the Opies' collection (137–41), and a more recent translation by Zipes (*Beauties, Beasts and Enchantment* 31–35), the latter of which is particularly faithful to the original. The survival and dispersal of folktales is considerably dependent upon the "filter" of translation.

27. Béla Balázs's libretto was influenced by Maurice Maeterlinck's 1902 play *Ariane et Barbe-bleue* (Ariadne and Bluebeard), which was itself set as an opera by Paul Dukas in 1907; on the background to Bartók's opera, see Kroó, "*Duke Bluebeard's Castle*," and the essays in John.

28. Compare the manipulative use of traditional female activities by the wicked Queen in the Grimms' "Snow White" ("Schneewittchen," KHM 53), as interpreted by Sandra M. Gilbert and Susan Gubar in *The Madwoman in the Attic*. They read each of the Queen's three murderous plots as revolving around "a poisonous or parodic use of a distinctly female device as a murder weapon," strategies which, in the "patriarchal kingdom of the text," only serve to confer more culturally sanctioned power on "patriarchy's angelic daughter," Snow White (36–44). Similar allusion to the

figure of the wicked Queen is made by both Coover in "The Dead Queen" and Barthelme in *Snow White*.

29. Quotations from the Grimms' tales are from the translation by David Luke (Grimm, *Selected Tales*), although I have opted not to use his translation of the title of "Fitchers Vogel" ("Fetcher's Fowl"). For translated editions of the complete collection I have used those by Margaret Hunt (Grimm, *The Complete Grimm's Fairy Tales*) and Zipes (*The Complete Fairy Tales of the Brothers Grimm*), the latter of which includes a translation of "Das Mordschloss" ("The Castle of Murder" 670–71).

30. This explicit reference in "Fitcher's Fowl" to the "room of blood" not only strengthens the characterization of the generic forbidden room but also directly echoes "The Cellar of Blood," an English variant of tale type AT 955, the third piece in this always incomplete narrative jigsaw (summarized in Briggs 390).

31. However, this reading is also open to question: in the conclusions of the "Bluebeard" and "Castle of Murder" narratives included in the 1812 volume of the first edition of the Grimms' tales, the women are placed in charge of their now deceased partner's wealth (as in the French versions), while in the two variants that replaced these tales in later editions, "Fitcher's Fowl" and "The Robber Bridegroom," no mention is made of this potentially liberating inheritance. At least one commentator has taken this as evidence of the subtle ways in which later editions of these stories were edited in order both to isolate women and reflect or illustrate contemporaneous bourgeois mores (Bottigheimer, *Grimms' Bad Girls and Bold Boys* 130 n. 14).

32. Stith Thompson comments that "the 'Bluebeard' tale with the brother as rescuer has had no wide distribution and does not seem ever to have gained popularity" (*Folktale* 35–36).

33. In the following account of this tale type, "The Robber Bridegroom" is taken from the aforementioned edition of the Grimms' tales translated by David Luke (366–69); "Mr. Fox" is in Katherine M. Briggs, pt. A, vol. II: *Folk Narratives*.

34. In addition, telling a tale to reveal a crime is a relatively common fairy tale motif.

35. Compare Shahrazad in the *Arabian Nights*, whose tales often obliquely reflect and comment upon both her predicament and the actions of Shahrayar. Jerome Clinton argues for a reading of the cycle according to the "thematic and psychological" elements which serve to link the narrative frame with the tales enclosed (48).

36. This possible antecedent or source is given in a more convincing form in Opie (136). They also mention, and dismiss, the more popular belief that the "Bluebeard" story is based on the fifteenth-century pedophile and

compatriot of Joan of Arc, Gilles de Rais (a subject of various studies, including a novel, *Gilles et Jeanne* [1983], by Michel Tournier, a writer much influenced by the folktale). While this issue is unlikely to be resolved, it is enough to suggest the possibility of an earlier historical villain inscribed somewhere within the story, stressing as it does the theme of sexual politics.

37. For a parallel enquiry into the "Bluebeard" tale type, see Bacchilega, *Postmodern Fairy Tales* ch. 5.

38. Within the context of a sustained deconstruction of Perrault's text—another strategy for undermining the weight of interpretative tradition—Menninghaus unpicks the ostensible immanence of the appended morality: "In the supplementary *moralités*—and hence from a standpoint exterior to the fairy tale itself—Perrault's *Barbe-Bleue* is subjected to a double reading that promises to establish the tale's (missing) sense. However, because these *moralités* contradict the foregoing text, and even each other, they ironically undermine any plausible meaning and thus become treacherous supplements that, in the very form of adding it, withdraw the missing sense all the more completely" (92).

39. My reading of this dominant interpretative bias is based on that given by Tatar in "Beauties vs. Beasts" and *The Hard Facts of the Grimms' Fairy Tales* (156–79) in particular.

40. Read in terms of "Bluebeard," "Our Lady's Child" offers the startling possibility of the Virgin Mary as herself a type of Bluebeard. I am grateful to the first (anonymous) reader of my manuscript for this suggestion.

41. Bettelheim introduces his reading of this tale by stating that "'Bluebeard' is a story invented by Perrault for which there are no direct antecedents in folktales as far as we know." Such a view provides an example of exactly the sort of putative authenticity upon which the dominant interpretation is based, ignoring as it does the status of the tale *as* tale, part of a genre whose specific form and history call for inclusion in any interpretation.

42. In a wide-ranging survey of the depiction of cannibalism in illustrations of Grimms' tales, Bottigheimer found that whereas the depiction of female cannibalism is relatively common, the same is not true in the case of male villains. Although the robber bridegroom, in the eponymous tale, "is the only figure in *Grimms' Tales* who actually eats a person on the pages we read," Bottigheimer found only a single, relatively innocuous depiction of this figure in the history of the collection's illustration, leading her to conclude that "[t]here is simply no tradition for illustrating male cannibalism in Grimms' tales," a finding that relates to the dominant interpretation of the knot of tales of which "The Robber Bridegroom" is a part ("The Face of Evil"). Another strand in the interpretation of these tales is represented

by Bartók's aforementioned *Duke Bluebeard's Castle*, which is indicative of the early twentieth-century reading of "Bluebeard" as a representation of the essential impossibility of human relationships, and of man's isolated soul. This view of the tale, in which the female character's insistence on "knowing" her new husband is depicted as potentially positive, if ultimately doomed, could be said to represent a midway point between the dominant interpretation of the culpability of the female character and recent feminist readings. On the subject of fin-de-siècle Bluebeards and their influence on more recent versions, see Benson, " 'History's bearer.' "

43. Benjamin's comment on the fairy tale is particularly apposite here: "The wisest thing—so the fairy tale taught mankind in olden times, and teaches children to this day—is to meet the mythical world with cunning and high spirits" (102).

44. The deaths in these tales are an extreme example of the silencing of women that figures in tales throughout folk narrative history: for example, in the aforementioned AT 710 and in AT 451 (a particularly widespread tale type), in which a young girl must remain silent for a number of years in order to save her brothers. Bottigheimer has shown how the Grimms were increasingly drawn to the depiction of apparently necessarily silenced female characters, citing their versions of, for example, "Our Lady's Child" ("Marienkind," KHM 3), "The Twelve Brothers" ("Die zwölf Brüder," KHM 9) and "The Iron Stove" ("Der Eisenofen," KHM 127). This obviously makes the compulsion to tell in the "Robber Bridegroom" tale type especially significant, both as a provocative confrontational voice and a suitable model for feminist revisions (*Grimms' Bad Girls* 71–80).

45. Nabokov 47

46. "Bluebeard" appears relatively frequently in the literature of Victorian England. For example, Dickens alludes to the tale in several novels and writes his own version in "Nurse's Stories": the story of Captain Murderer, "an offshoot of the Blue Beard family" bearing marked similarities to the "Robber Bridegroom" tale type and, as has been well documented, the gothic novels of Austen and the Brontës adapt the tale to various effect. Nevertheless, as Juliet McMaster has demonstrated, "Thackeray's interest in the tale was extensive and peculiar" (199). As well as passing allusions in the novels, Thackeray retold the story several times, in prose, in his own illustrated versions, and in an uncompleted play written in blank verse. On the presence of Bluebeard in Victorian fiction, see McMaster 199–206; and Todd (70–71; 98–99; 100–101; 124–29), who offers a broader reading of the role of "the Bluebeard scenario."

47. Fish's phrase occurs in *Is There a Text in This Class? The Authority of Interpretive Communities*; it is taken here from Suleiman 192. It is the latter's

stress on this particular branch of "reader-oriented criticism" that informs my use of the concept (see also 142–45).

48. Attic Press have published several volumes of "Fairy Tales for Feminists," including *Cinderella on the Ball* and *Sweeping Beauties*, as well as an anthology (Binchy); the Merseyside Fairy Story Collective worked in the 1970s, producing versions of "Snow White" and "Red Riding Hood."

49. Oates's tale is constructed in six short sections, suggesting that the narrator is the symbolic seventh wife of literary tradition. In a similar vein, the American poet Daryl Hine's "Bluebeard's Wife" comprises six stanzas, ending with the doomed eponymous heroine stepping into the forbidden room—containing "the past/Putrid and crowned"—to join her predecessors, in the belief that " '[l]ove survives/The grave' " (Hine). Cindy Sherman's photographs for an edition of "Fitcher's Fowl" suggest an analogous atmosphere of gothic claustrophobia (Sherman).

50. Warner's tale continues the nineteenth-century vogue for overtly Eastern settings of "Bluebeard," originally influenced by the *Arabian Nights*; as in Thackeray's "Bluebeard's Ghost," the third wife is thus identified as "Fatima."

51. I have not provided folkloristic details for those contemporary adaptations which engage with tale types other than the three on which I have concentrated. All the texts chosen use canonical fairy tale narratives, either from Perrault or the Grimms.

52. See also Anne Sexton's *Transformations* (1971), wry poetic commentaries on a selection of the Grimms' tales.

53. In *The Madwoman in the Attic*, Gilbert and Gubar adopt the wicked Queen of "Snow White" as their representative female plotter, a reading referred to above with reference to the analogous "parodic use of a distinctly female device" by the heroine of the "Bluebeard" tale type. My choice of the heroine of "The Robber Bridegroom"—a variant of the "Bluebeard" heroine—is influenced by Gilbert and Gubar's reading, particularly their characterization of the wicked Queen as a devious storyteller. However, as I am reading feminist fairy tales as "survival forms" which act as double-voiced commentaries from both within and outside the tradition, the choice of a folkloric character who both appropriates the role of actual narrator and narrates successfully seems more resonant.

54. The first chapter of Lanser's book, together with her related essay "Toward a Feminist Narratology," provide a good introduction to this area. The original publication of the latter led to an exchange between Lanser and Nilli Diengott over the relative compatibility of feminism and narratology (*Style* 22 (1988): 42–60). See also Warhol 3–24.

55. The relationship of Carter's work with the fairy tale has been the subject

of much debate. The key critical text is *Angela Carter and the Fairy Tale*, edited by Roemer and Bacchilega, which includes a survey of criticism on the relationship (Benson, "Angela Carter" and "Addendum") and several essays on particular aspects of "The Bloody Chamber."

56. Nevertheless, one thread linking the adaptations of Carter and Barthelme is the influence of a Bluebeard filtered through the decadent fin de siècle aesthetic of the symbolists—hence Barthelme's tale is set in Paris in 1910 and, like Carter's, alludes to representative figures. In Carter's version in particular, this is a melodramatic Bluebeard who is, if not an artist himself, then at least a connoisseur: a lonely soul surrounded by the bizarre and the perverse, necessarily detached from mainstream society because of his essential difference (for a related reading of the figure of the Marquis in "The Bloody Chamber," see Roemer). This is, broadly speaking, the Bluebeard of Balázs and Maeterlinck, who wrote during a period when the potentially erotic mix of sex and death in "Bluebeard" was artistically fashionable. For another carefully coded exploration of this knot of themes, see John Updike's two-part story "George and Vivian," the second part of which is titled "Bluebeard in Ireland."

57. My models for this approach are Hutcheon's reading of Carter's "Black Venus" (*The Politics of Postmodernism* 145–50), and Robert Rawdon Wilson's reading of "The Lady of the House of Love." Both commentaries demonstrate how the layers of allusion are indicative not of a forgetting or refusal of context and history but rather of a detailed concern for historical intersections of (con)texts.

58. This variant of AT 410 is Basile's "Sun, Moon and Talia," told as the fifth tale on the fifth day of *Il Pentamerone*.

59. In Carter's novel *The Passion of New Eve* (1977), Zero, a grotesque parody of masculinity, plays Wagner when alone in his study and has his drugged female worshippers perform dance routines to extracts from the operas (86 and 103).

60. Paul Delvaux's *Leda* (1948) is in the collection of Tate Modern, London.

61. Carter is possibly drawing on Yeats's "Leda and the Swan" (1923), in which the encounter is explicitly represented as a violation.

62. For a comprehensive contextualization of "The Bloody Chamber" within the pornography debates of the late 1970s and 1980s, see Sheets.

63. The following summary draws on Moi's reading of Freud's "On Femininity" (1933) and Irigaray's *Spéculum de l'autre femme* (1974).

64. Shahrukh Husain notes that in medieval European narratives women "lost their voices during the period between betrothal and marriage" (Carter, *The Second Book of Virago Fairy Tales* 227).

65. As Hutcheon has noted, the winged character of Fevvers in Carter's *Nights*

at the Circus (1984) is a more developed parody of the Leda narrative and illustrates the shift in Carter's writing from deflating critique to a wilder disruption and reclamation of imagery (*Politics of Postmodernism* 98).

66. Compare Carter's "The Executioner's Beautiful Daughter" (1974), which also explores the folkloric theme of incest.

67. See also Atwood, "Grimms' Remembered."

68. Interestingly, in light of Atwood's opening phrase, Warner quotes from the correspondence of an aristocratic woman in late seventeenth-century France, who refers to the fashion for communal tale-telling as "simmering": "so she simmered for us, and talked to us about a green isle where a princess grew up who was more beautiful than the day" (*From the Beast to the Blonde* 18).

69. This summary of the genre draws on that given in Cohan and Shires 77–82; Merck; and Robinson; along with those other critical sources cited in the notes which follow.

70. For a reading of these two tale types in relation to the gothic romance (and with reference to Atwood and Carter), see Benson, "Stories of Love and Death." On the general subject of the relation between fairy tales and the norms of the literary romance, see McGlathery, *Fairy Tale Romance*.

71. On *Jane Eyre* as "the first adult, non-burlesque treatment of the Bluebeard theme in English literature," see Sutherland.

72. On the presence of "Bluebeard" in female gothic romance, see McMaster 200–203.

73. Blau DuPlessis's study of the means by which twentieth-century women writers have challenged the role of the heroine in the orthodox narrative structure of the nineteenth-century novel parallels the aforementioned feminist revision of narratology, in that it argues for a recognition of the central role of gender in the archetypal narrative structures of quest and romance—structures essential to the deep structural analyses of narratology.

74. Again, the heroine of "The Robber Bridegroom," who tells her past to change her future, provides a model of narration seeking to subvert the traditional ending.

75. For example, see Rowe, "'Fairy-born and human-bred,'" which includes reference to a number of studies of the structure of *Jane Eyre* as it mirrors and deliberately manipulates generic conventions.

76. The notion of the inculcation of restrictive life-story models can be linked with the narrative-based psychology of Jerome Bruner referred to in the previous chapter, providing one specific instance of "the narrative construction of reality."

77. The traditional folkloric figure of the benignly dumb hero is, to an extent,

the reverse of the crafty heroine, perhaps a reflection of the historical necessity for active female strategies, as opposed to passive luck, in the face of social inequality.

78. Greene is quoting here from Gilbert and Gubar's reading of "Snow White" in the introduction to *The Madwoman in the Attic*, in which the wicked Queen figures as a model for their conception of the nineteenth-century female literary tradition.

Conclusion

1. For two systematic theoretical accounts of the possible interactions between the folktale and literature, beyond the rewriting or borrowing of tales or motifs, see Lewis and Grobman.

2. See Coover, "The End of Books" and "Hyperfiction: Novels for the Computer." Calvino considered the related idea of computer-generated narratives as early as 1973 when, at the behest of IBM, he wrote "The Burning of the Abominable House" (*Numbers in the Dark* 156–69), and later, in his Oulipian text "Prose and Anticombinatorics" (1981). The idea also figures in *If on a Winter's Night a Traveller*. Barth discusses hypertext in his 1992 essay "Browsing" (*Further Fridays* 222–37) and, more tangentially, as part of his most recent story cycle, *On With the Story*.

3. For a comprehensive introduction to this area, see Landow. On hypertext, interactive fiction, and narratology, see Andrew Gibson, "Interactive Fiction and Narrative Space."

4. Hypertext relies on what Coover calls "linking mechanisms": "in place of print's linear, page-turning route, it offers a network of alternate paths through a set of text spaces by way of designated links" ("Hyperfiction" 8).

5. For a questioning account of *Storyspace*, and of one of the founding hypertexts composed using the system (Michael Joyce's *Afternoon: A Story* [1990]), see Aarseth 76–96.

6. "The Tale vs. The Novel" 303, 310, 309, 304. Brooks structures his argument around a reading of Benjamin's "The Storyteller," an essay which seems increasingly prescient in relation to recent developments in narrative theory. An expanded version of "The Tale vs. The Novel" appears as "The Storyteller" in Brooks's *Psychoanalysis and Storytelling* (1994).

Bibliography

In those cases where I have not used the first edition of a text, the initial date given in the citation indicates the year of first publication. Where the text is a translation, the initial date indicates the year of first publication in the original language.

Aarne, Antti, and Stith Thompson. *The Types of the Folktale: A Classification and Bibliography*. FF Communications, no. 184; Helsinki: Suomalainen Tiedeakatemia, 1961.

Aarseth, Espen J. *Cybertext: Perspectives on Ergodic Literature*. Baltimore: Johns Hopkins University Press, 1997.

Adler, Sara Maria. *Calvino: The Writer as Fablemaker*. Maryland, U.S.A.: Ediciones José Porrúa Turanzas, S.A., 1979.

Almansi, Guido. *The Writer as Liar: Narrative Technique in the "Decameron."* London: Routledge and Kegan Paul, 1973.

Anderson, Richard. *Robert Coover*. Boston: Twayne Publishers, 1981.

The Arabian Nights. Trans. Husain Haddawy, based on the text of the fourteenth-century Syrian manuscript edited by Muhsin Mahdi. London: Everyman's Library, 1992.

Ashliman, D. L. *A Guide to Folktales in the English Language*. New York: Greenwood Press, 1987.

Atwood, Margaret. *Lady Oracle*. 1976. London: Virago, 1984.

———. "Hesitations outside the Door." *Poems: 1965–1975*. 1987. London: Virago, 1991. 168–72.

———. "Bluebeard's Egg." *Bluebeard's Egg and Other Stories*. 1983. London: Virago, 1989. 131–64.

———. "Alien Territory." *Good Bones*. London: Bloomsbury, 1992. 75–88.

———. *Conversations*. Ed. Earl G. Ingersoll. London: Virago, 1992.

———. *The Robber Bride*. London: Bloomsbury, 1993.

———. "Grimms' Remembered." Haase 290–92.

Austen, Jane. *Northanger Abbey*. 1818. Oxford: Oxford University Press, 1990.

Auster, Paul. *The Red Notebook and Other Writings*. London: Faber and Faber, 1995.

Avery, Gillian, and Julia Briggs, eds. *Children and Their Books: A Celebration of the Work of Iona and Peter Opie*. Oxford: Clarendon Press, 1990.

Bacchilega, Cristina. "Folktales and Meta-Fictions: Their Interaction in Robert Coover's *Pricksongs and Descants*." *New York Folklore* 6.3–4 (1980): 171–84.

———. "Cracking the Mirror: Three Re-Visions of 'Snow White.' " *boundary 2* 15.3 (1988): 1–25.

———. "Folk and Literary Narrative in a Postmodern Context: The Case of the *Märchen*." *Fabula* 26 (1988): 302–16.

———. "Calvino's Journey: Modern Transformations of Folktale, Story, and Myth." *Journal of Folklore Research* 26.2 (1989): 81–98.

———. *Postmodern Fairy Tales: Gender and Narrative Strategies*. Philadelphia: University of Pennsylvania Press, 1997.

Bakhtin, M. M. *The Dialogic Imagination: Four Essays*. Trans. Caryl Emerson and Michael Holquist. Ed. Michael Holquist. Austin: University of Texas Press, 1981.

Bal, Mieke. "Notes on Narrative Embedding." *Poetics Today* 2.1 (1981): 41–59.

Barr Snitow, Ann. "Mass Market Romance: Pornography for Women Is Different." Eagleton 134–40.

Barth, John. *Lost in the Funhouse: Fiction for print, tape, live voice*. 1968. New York: Anchor Books, 1988.

———. *Chimera*. 1972. New York: Fawcett Crest, 1973.

———. *The Friday Book: Essays and Other Nonfiction*. New York: G.P. Putnam's Sons, 1984.

———. *The Tidewater Tales: A Novel*. New York: Fawcett Columbine, 1987.

———. "The Limits of Imagination." 1988. Ziegler 275–86.

———. *The Last Voyage of Somebody the Sailor*. 1991; Kent: Sceptre, 1992.

———. *Once Upon a Time: A Floating Opera*. 1994. London: Sceptre, 1995.

———. *Further Fridays: Essays, Lectures, and Other Nonfiction, 1984–1994*. Boston: Little, Brown and Company, 1995.

———. *On With the Story: Stories*. Boston: Little, Brown and Company, 1996.

Barthelme, Donald. *Snow White*. 1967. New York: Atheneum, 1972.

———. *The Dead Father*. 1975. Harmondsworth: Penguin, 1986.

———. Interview. April 1980. LeClair and McCaffery 32–44.

———. *Sixty Stories*. 1981. London: Minerva, 1991.

———. "Bluebeard." *Forty Stories*. 1987. London: Minerva, 1992. 92–97.

Barthes, Roland. "Textual Analysis: Poe's 'Valdemar.' " 1973. Trans. Geoff Bennington. Lodge 172–95.

———. *Image Music Text*. Trans. and selected Stephen Heath. London: Fontana, 1977.

Bartók, Béla. *Béla Bartók Essays*. Ed. and selected Benjamin Suchoff. London: Faber and Faber, 1975.

Bascom, William. "Four Functions of Folklore." 1954. *The Study of Folklore*. Ed. Alan Dundes. Englewood Cliffs, N.J.: Prentice Hall, 1965. 279–98.

———. "The Forms of Folklore: Prose Narratives." 1965. *Sacred Narrative: Readings in the Theory of Myth*. Ed. Alan Dundes. Berkeley and Los Angeles: University of California Press, 1984. 5–29.

Basile, Giambattista. *The Pentamerone*. 1634–1636. Trans. (from the modern Italian version of Benedetto Croce [1925]), ed., with preface, notes, and appendixes, N. M. Penzer. 2 vols. London: John Lane the Bodley Head Ltd., 1932.

Belcher, Stephen. "Framed Tales in the Oral Tradition: An Exploration." *Fabula* 35 (1994): 1–19.

Bendix, Regina. "Folk Narrative, Opera and the Expression of Cultural Identity." *Fabula* 31 (1990): 297–303.

Benjamin, Walter. "The Storyteller." *Illuminations*. Trans. Harry Zorn. Ed. Hannah Arendt. New York: Schoken Books, 1969. 83–110.

Bennington, Geoffrey. *Lyotard: Writing the Event*. Manchester: Manchester University Press, 1988.

Benson, Stephen. "Stories of Love and Death: Reading and Writing the Fairy Tale Romance." *Image and Power: Women in Fiction in the Twentieth Century*. Ed. Sarah Sceats and Gail Cunningham. London: Longman, 1996. 103–13.

———. "Angela Carter and the Literary *Märchen*: A Review Essay." Roemer and Bacchilega 30–58.

———. "Addendum." Roemer and Bacchilega 59–64.

———. "'History's bearer': The Afterlife of Bluebeard." *Marvels and Tales* 14 (2000): 244–67.

Berio, Luciano. *Luciano Berio: Two Interviews*. With Rossana Dalmonte and Bálint and András Varga. Trans. and ed. David Osmond-Smith. New York: Marion Boyars, 1985.

Betteleim, Bruno. *The Uses of Enchantment: The Meaning and Importance of Fairy Tales*. 1976. Harmondsworth: Penguin, 1991.

Bhabha, Homi K. "The Commitment to Theory." 1989. *The Location of Culture*. London: Routledge, 1994. 19–39.

Binchy, Maeve, et al. *Ride on Rapunzel: Fairytales Feminists*. Dublin: Attic Press, 1992.

Birns, Nicholas. "Beyond Metafiction: Placing John Barth." *Arizona Quarterly* 49.2 (1993): 113–36.

Blau DuPlessis, Rachel. *Writing Beyond the Ending: Narrative Strategies of Twentieth-Century Women Writers*. Bloomington: Indiana University Press, 1985.

Boccaccio, Giovanni. *The Decameron*. ca. 1351. Trans. Guido Waldman. Oxford: Oxford University Press, 1993.

Bødker, Lauritis, Christina Hole and G. D'Aronco, eds. *European Folk Tales*. Copenhagen: Rosenkilde and Bagger, 1963.

Bogatyrëv, Peter, and Roman Jakobson. "Folklore as a Special Form of Creativity." 1929. *The Prague School: Selected Writings 1929–1949*. Trans. Manfred Jacobson. Ed. Peter Steiner. Austin: University of Texas Press, 1982. 32–46.

Borges, Jorge Luis. "Partial Enchantments of the *Quixote*." *Other Inquisitions*. 43–46.

———. "Kafka and His Precursors." *Other Inquisitions*. 106–8.

———. *Other Inquisitions 1937–1952*. Trans. Ruth L.C. Simms. London: Souvenir Press, 1973.

———. "The Thousand and One Nights." *Seven Nights*. 1980. Trans. Eliot Weinberger. New York: New Directions Books, 1984. 42–57.

Bottigheimer, Ruth B. "Tale Spinners: Submerged Voices in Grimms' Fairy Tales." *New German Critique* 27 (1982): 141–50.

———, ed. *Fairy Tales and Society: Illusion, Allusion, and Paradigm*. Philadelphia: University of Pennsylvania Press, 1986.

———. *Grimms' Bad Girls and Bold Boys: The Social and Moral Vision of the Tales*. New Haven: Yale University Press, 1987.

———. "The Face of Evil." *Fabula* 29 (1988): 326–35.

———. "From Gold to Guilt: The Forces Which Reshaped Grimms' *Tales*." McGlathery, *Brothers* 192–204.

———. "Fairy Tales, Folk Narrative Research and History." *Social History* 14 (1989): 343–57.

———. "'Marienkind' (KHM 3): A Computer-Based Study of Editorial Change and Stylistic Development within Grimms' Tales from 1804–1864." *ARV: Scandinavian Yearbook of Folklore* 46 (1990): 7–31.

———. "Motif, Meaning, and Editorial Change in Grimms' *Tales*: One Plot, Three Tales, and Three Different Stories." Görög-Karady 541–53.

———. "The Publishing History of Grimms' Tales: Reception at the Cash Register." Haase 78–101.

Boulez, Pierre. *Orientations: Collected Writings*. Trans. Martin Cooper. Ed. Jean-Jacques Nattiez. London: Faber and Faber, 1986.

Bradbury, Malcolm. *The Modern American Novel*. New ed. Oxford: Oxford University Press, 1992.

Bremond, Claude. "The Logic of Narrative Possibilities." 1966. Trans. Elaine D. Cancalon. *New Literary History* 11.3 (1979–1980): 387–411.

———. "Morphology of the French Folktale." *Semiotica* 2 (1970): 247–76.

———. "The Morphology of the French Fairy Tale: The Ethical Model." Jason and Segal. 49–76.

———. "A Critique of the Motif." *French Literary Theory Today: A Reader*. Ed. Tzvetan Todorov. Cambridge: Cambridge University Press, 1982. 125–46.

Brewer, Derek. *Symbolic Stories: Traditional Narratives of the Family Drama in English Literature*. Cambridge: Cambridge University Press, 1980.

Briggs, Julia. "Women Writers and Writing for Children: From Sarah Fielding to E. Nesbit." Avery and Briggs. 221–50.

Briggs, Katherine M. *Dictionary of British Folk-Tales in the English Language*. 2 pts. Pt. A. Vols. I and II: *Folk Narratives*. London: Routledge and Kegan Paul, 1970.

Bronfen, Elisabeth. *Over Her Dead Body: Death, Femininity and the Aesthetic*. Manchester: Manchester University Press, 1992.

Brontë, Charlotte. *Jane Eyre*. 1847. Oxford: Oxford University Press, 1980.

———. *Villette*. 1853. Harmondsworth: Penguin, 1985.

Bronzini, Giovanni Battista. "From the Grimms to Calvino: Folk Tales in the Year Two Thousand." Trans. Chiara Simeone. *Storytelling in Contemporary Societies*. Ed. Lutz Röhrich and Sabine Wienker-Piepho. Tübingen: Gunter Narr Verlag, 1990. 189–98.

Brooke-Rose, Christine. *Stories, Theories, and Things*. Cambridge: Cambridge University Press, 1991.

Brooks, Peter. "Toward Supreme Fictions." *Yale French Studies* 43 (1969): 5–14.

———. *Reading for the Plot: Design and Intention in Narrative*. 1984. Cambridge, Mass. and London: Harvard University Press, 1992.

———. "The Tale vs. The Novel." *Why the Novel Matters: A Postmodern Perplex*. Ed. Mark Spilka and Caroline McCracken-Flesher. Bloomington: Indiana University Press, 1990. 303–10.

Broumas, Olga. *Beginning With O*. New Haven and London: Yale University Press, 1977.

Bruner, Jerome. *Acts of Meaning*. Cambridge, Mass. and London: Harvard University Press, 1990.

———. "The Narrative Construction of Reality." *Critical Inquiry* 18 (Autumn 1991): 1–21.

Butor, Michel. "On Fairy Tales." 1960. Trans. Remy Hall. *Inventory: Essays by Michel Butor*. Ed. Richard Howard. London: Jonathan Cape, 1970. 211–23.

Byatt, A. S. "The Story of the Eldest Princess." Park and Heaton. 12–28.

Calvino, Italo, *The Path to the Nest of the Spiders*. 1947. Trans. Archibald Colquhoun. Pref. Italo Calvino (1964). Trans. William Weaver. Hopewell, N.J.: The Ecco Press, 1976.

———. *Adam, One Afternoon and Other Stories*. 1949. Trans. Archibald Colquhoun and Peggy Wright. London: Picador, 1984.

———. *The Argentine Ant*. 1952. Trans. Archibald Colquhoun and Peggy Wright. *Adam, One Afternoon*. 155–190.

———. *Italian Folktales*. 1956. trans. George Martin. Harmondsworth: Penguin, 1982.

——. *A Plunge into Real Estate*. 1957. Trans. D. S. Carne-Ross. *Difficult Loves*. 161–250.

——. *Smog*. 1958. Trans. William Weaver. *Difficult Loves*. 109–60.

——. *Difficult Loves*. 1957, 1958, and 1970. Trans. William Weaver. London: Minerva, 1993.

——. *Our Ancestors*. 1960. Includes *The Cloven Viscount*. 1951. *The Baron in the Trees*. 1957. *The Non-Existent Knight*. 1959. Trans. Archibald Colquhoun. Intro. Italo Calvino. Trans. Isabel Quigly. London: Minerva, 1992.

——. "Main Currents in Italian Fiction Today." *Italian Quarterly* 4.13–14 (1960): 3–14.

——. *Marcovaldo or The Seasons in the City*. 1963. Trans. William Weaver. London: Minerva, 1993.

——. *The Watcher*. 1963. Trans. William Weaver. *The Watcher and Other Stories*. New York: Harcourt Brace Jovanovitch, 1971. 1–74.

——. *Cosmicomics*. 1965. Trans. William Weaver. Harmondsworth: Abacus, 1982.

——. *Time and the Hunter*. 1967. Trans. William Weaver. London: Picador, 1993.

——. "Notes Towards a Definition of the Narrative Form as a Combinative Process." Trans. Bruce Merry. *Twentieth Century Studies* 3 (1971): 93–101.

——. *Invisible Cities*. 1972. Trans. William Weaver. London: Picador, 1979.

——. *The Castle of Crossed Destinies*. 1973. Trans. William Weaver. London: Picador, 1978.

——. *If on a Winter's Night a Traveller*. 1979. Trans. William Weaver. London: Everyman's Library, 1993.

——. "Myth in the Narrative." Trans. (from French) Erica Freiburg. *Surfiction: Fiction Now and Tomorrow*. Ed. Raymond Federman. Chicago: Swallow, 1981. 75–81.

——. "Prose and Anticombinatorics." 1981. Trans. Warren F. Motte Jr. Motte, *Oulipo* 143–52.

——. *The Literature Machine: Essays*. 1982. Trans. Patrick Creagh. London: Picador, 1989.

——. *Mr Palomar*. 1983. Trans. William Weaver. London: Minerva, 1994.

——. *Under the Jaguar Sun*. 1986. Trans. William Weaver. London: Vintage, 1993.

——. "How I Wrote One of My Books." 1987. Trans. Iain White. Queneau.

——. *Six Memos for the Next Millenium*. 1988. Trans. Patrick Creagh. London: Jonathan Cape, 1992.

——. *The Road to San Giovanni*. 1990. Trans. Tim Parks. London: Vintage, 1994.

———. *Numbers in the Dark and Other Stories*. 1993. Trans. Tim Parks. London: Jonathan Cape, 1995.

———. *Why Read the Classics?* 1991. Trans. Martin McLaughlin. London: Vintage, 2000.

Canepa, Nancy L. *From Court to Forest: Giambattista Basile's "Lo cunto de li cunti" and the Birth of the Literary Fairy Tale*. Detroit: Wayne State University Press, 1999.

———, ed. *Out of the Woods: The Origins of the Literary Fairy Tale in Italy and France*. Detroit: Wayne State University Press, 1997.

Cannon, JoAnn. *Italo Calvino: Writer and Critic*. Ravenna, Italy: Longo Editore, 1981.

Caracciolo, Peter L., ed. *The "Arabian Nights" in English Literature: Studies in the Reception of "The Thousand and One Nights" into British Culture*. London: Macmillan, 1988.

Carmichael, Thomas. "Postmodernism Reconsidered: The Return of the Real in John Barth's *Sabbatical* and *The Tidewater Tales*." *Revue Française D'Etudes Américaines* 62 (1994): 329–38.

Carr, Helen, ed. *From My Guy to Sci-Fi: Genre and Women's Writing in the Postmodern World*. London: Pandora, 1989.

Carsaniga, Giovanni. "The Romantic Controversy." *The Cambridge Companion to Italian Literature*. Eds. Peter Brand and Lino Pertile. Rev. ed. Cambridge: Cambridge University Press, 1999. 399–405.

Carter, Albert Howard, III. *Italo Calvino: Metamorphoses of Fantasy*. Ann Arbor, Michigan: UMI Research Press, 1987.

Carter, Angela. *The Magic Toyshop*. 1967. London: Virago, 1993.

———. "The Executioner's Beautiful Daughter." *Fireworks*. 1974. London: Virago in association with Chatto and Windus, 1987. 13–22.

———. *The Passion of New Eve*. 1977. London: Virago, 1982.

———. *The Bloody Chamber and Other Stories*. 1979. Harmondsworth: Penguin, 1981.

———. *The Sadeian Woman: An Exercise in Cultural History*. 1979. London: Virago, 1982.

———. Interview. September 1984. Haffenden 76–96.

———, ed. *The Virago Book of Fairy Tales*. London: Virago, 1990.

———, ed. *The Second Virago Book of Fairy Tales*. London: Virago, 1992.

Celati, Gianni. *Voices from the Plains*. 1985. Trans. Robert Lumley. London: Serpent's Tail, 1989.

Chaytor, H. J. *From Script to Print: An Introduction to Medieval Literature*. Cambridge: Cambridge University Press, 1945.

Chénetier, Marc. "Ideas of Order at Delphi." Ziegler 84–109.

Chernaik, Warren, Marilyn Deegan, and Andrew Gibson, eds. *Beyond the Book:*

Theory, Culture and the Politics of Cyberspace. Oxford: Office for Humanities Communication Publications, 1996.

Clinton, Jerome W. "Madness and Cure in the *Thousand and One Nights*." Bottigheimer 35–51.

Cohan, Steven and Linda M. Shires. *Telling Stories: A Theoretical Analysis of Narrative Fiction*. London: Routledge, 1988.

Collodi, Carlo. *Le avventure di Pinocchio/The Adventures of Pinocchio*. 1881–1883. Trans. Nicholas J. Perella. Berkeley and Los Angeles: University of California Press, 1986.

Cooper, Helen. *The Structure of "The Canterbury Tales."* London: Duckworth, 1983.

Coover, Robert. *The Universal Baseball Association, Inc., J. Henry Waugh, PROP*. 1968. London: Minerva, 1992.

——. *Pricksongs and Descants*. 1969. London: Minerva, 1989.

——. "The Dead Queen." *Quarterly Review of Literature* 18.3–4 (1973): 304–13.

——. Interview. March 1973. Gado. 142–59.

——. Interview. November 1979. LeClair and McCaffery. 63–78.

——. *Aesop's Forest*. California: Capra Press, 1986.

——. *Pinocchio in Venice*. 1991. London: Minerva, 1992.

——. "The End of Books." *New York Times Book Review* 21 June 1992, 1: 23–25.

——. "Hyperfiction: Novels for the Computer." *New York Times Book Review* 29 August 1993, 1: 8–12.

——. *Briar Rose*. New York: Grove Press, 1996.

Culler, Jonathan. *Structuralist Poetics: Structuralism, Linguistics and the Study of Literature*. 1975. London: Routledge, 1989.

——. "Defining Narrative Units." *Style and Structure in Literature: Essays in the New Stylistics*. Ed. Roger Fowler, Oxford: Basil Blackwell, 1975. 123–42.

——. "Story and Discourse in the Analysis of Narrative." *The Pursuit of Signs: Semiotics, Literature, Deconstruction*. Ithaca, New York: Cornell University Press, 1981. 169–87.

D'arco, Silvio Avalle. "Systems and Structures in the Folktale." *Twentieth Century Studies* 3 (1971): 67–75.

Dahlhaus, Carl. *Between Romanticism and Modernism: Four Studies in the Music of the Late Nineteenth Century*. 1974. Trans. Mary Whittall. Berkeley: University of California Press, 1989.

——. *Nineteenth-Century Music*. 1980. Trans. J. Bradford Robinson. Berkeley: University of California Press, 1989.

Darnton, Robert. "Peasants Tell Tales: The Meaning of Mother Goose." *The*

Great Cat Massacre and Other Episodes in French Cultural History. London: Allen Lane The Penguin Press, 1984. 9–72.

Davies, Mererid Puw. *The Tale of Bluebeard in German Literature: From the Eighteenth Century to the Present*. Oxford: Clarendon Press, 2001.

Dégh, Linda. "What Did the Grimm Brothers Give to and Take from the Folk?" McGlathery, *Brothers* 66–90.

———. "Career Choices for Women in Folktales, Fairytales and Modern Media." *Fabula* 30 (1989): 43–62.

DeJean, Joan. "The Salons, 'Preciosity,' and the Sphere of Women's Influence." *A New History of French Literature*. Ed. Denis Hollier. Cambridge, Mass.: Harvard University Press, 1989. 297–303.

———. *Tender Geographies: Women and the Origins of the Novel in France*. New York: Columbia University Press, 1991.

De Lauretis, Teresa. "Narrative Discourse in Calvino: Praxis or Poiesis?" *Publications of the Modern Language Association* 90 (1975): 414–25.

Dickens, Charles. "Nurse's Stories." *The Uncommercial Traveller*. 1860. London: Chapman and Hall, Ltd., n.d. 172–84.

Diengott, Nilli. "Narratology and Feminism." *Style* 22.1 (1988): 42–51.

Dollerup, Guy, Bengt Holbek, Iven Reventlow and Carsten Rosenberg Hansen. "The Ontological Status, the Formative Elements, the 'Filters' and Existences of Folktales." *Fabula* 25 (1984): 241–65.

Bollerup, Guy, Ivan Reventlow and Carsten Rosenberg Hansen. "A Case Study of Editorial Filters in Foltales: A Discussion of the 'Allerleirauh' Tales in Grimm." *Fabula* 27 (1987): 12–30.

Dorson, Richard M. "The Identification of Folkore in American Literature." *Journal of American Folklore* 70 (1957): 1–8.

Duggan, Christopher. *A Concise History of Italy*. Cambridge: Cambridge University Press, 1994.

Duncker, Patricia. "Re-imagining the Fairy Tales: Angela Carter's Bloody Chambers." *Literature and History* 10.1 (1984): 3–13.

———. *Sisters and Strangers: An Introduction to Contemporary Feminist Fiction*. Oxford: Blackwell, 1992.

Dundes, Alan. "From Etic to Emic Units in the Structural Study of Folklore." *Journal of American Folklore* 75 (1962): 95–105.

———. "The Study of Folklore in Literature and Culture: Identification and Interpretation." *Journal of American Folklore* 78 (1965): 136–42.

Eagleton, Mary, ed. *Feminist Literary Theory: A Reader*. Oxford: Basil Blackwell, 1986.

Èjxenbaum, Boris M. "The Theory of the Formal Method." 1926. Trans. I. R. Titunik. Matejka and Pomorska. 3–37.

Eliot, T. S. "*Ulysses*, Order, and Myth." 1923. *Selected Prose of T. S. Eliot*. Ed. Frank Kermode. London: Faber and Faber, 1975. 175–78.

Ellis, John. *One Fairy Story Too Many: The Brothers Grimm and Their Tales*. Chicago: University of Chicago Press, 1983.

Erlich, Victor. *Russian Formalism: History-Doctrine*. The Hague: Mouton and Co., 1955.

Eysteinsson, Astrauder. *The Concept of Modernism*. Ithaca and London: Cornell University Press, 1990.

Faris, Wendy B. "1001 Words: Fiction Against Death." *The Georgia Review* 36 (1982): 811–30.

Foucault, Michel, "What Is an Author?" 1969. Trans. Josué V. Harari. *Aesthetics, Method, and Epistemology: Essential Works of Foucault, 1954–1984*. Vol. 2. Ed. James Faubion. Harmondsworth: Penguin, 2000. 205–23.

Fowler, Bridget. *The Alienated Reader: Women and Popular Romantic Literature in the Twentieth Century*. Hertfordshire: Harvester Wheatsheaf, 1991.

Fowler, Roger. *Linguistics and the Novel*. 1977. London and New York: Routledge, 1989.

France, Anatole. "The Seven Wives of Bluebeard." 1909. Trans. D. B. Stewart. Zipes, *Penguin Book* 566–82.

Frye, Northrop. *The Secular Scripture: A Study of the Structure of Romance*. Cambridge, Mass. and London: Harvard University Press, 1976.

Gado, Frank, ed. *First Person: Conversations on Writers and Writing*. New York: Union College Press, 1973.

Genette, Gérard. *Narrative Discourse: An Attempt at a Method*. 1972. Trans. Jane E. Lewin. Oxford: Basil Blackwell, 1980.

———. *Narrative Discourse Revisited*. 1983. Trans. Jane E. Lewin. Ithaca and New York: Cornell University Press, 1988.

Gerhardt, Mia. *The Art of Storytelling: A Literary Study of "The Thousand and One Nights."* Leiden, Holland: E. J. Brill, 1963.

Ghazoul, Ferial Jabouri. *"The Arabian Nights": A Structural Analysis*. Cairo: Cairo Associated Institution, 1980.

Gibson, Andrew. *Reading Narrative Discourse: Studies in the Novel from Cervantes to Beckett*. London: Macmillan, 1990.

———. *Towards a Postmodern Theory of Narrative*. Edinburgh: Edinburgh University Press, 1996.

———. "Interactive Fiction and Narrative Space." Chernaik, Deegan, and Gibson 79–92.

Gilbert, Sandra M. "What Do Feminists Want? A Postcard from the Volcano." 1980. Showalter 29–45.

Gilbert, Sandra M., and Susan Gubar. *The Madwoman in the Attic: The Woman*

Writer and the Nineteenth-Century Literary Imagination. New Haven: Yale University Press, 1979.

Gillies, Malcolm, ed. *The Bartók Companion*. London: Faber and Faber, 1993.

———. "Bartók and His Music in the 1990s." Gillies, *Bartók* 3–19.

Ginsborg, Paul. *A History of Contemporary Italy: Society and Politics 1943–1988*. Harmondsworth: Penguin, 1990.

Gittes, Katherine S. *Framing "The Canterbury Tales": Chaucer and the Medieval Frame Narrative Tradition*. Westport, N.Y.: Greenwood Press, 1991.

Godard, Barbara. "Tales Within Tales: Margaret Atwood's Folk Narratives." *Canadian Literature* 109 (Summer 1986): 57–84.

———. "Palimpsest: Margaret Atwood's 'Bluebeard's Egg.'" *Recherches Anglaises et Nord Americaines* 20 (1987): 51–60.

Gordon, Karen Elizabeth. *The Red Shoes and Other Tattered Tales*. Normal, Illinois: Dalkey Archive, 1996.

Görög-Karady, Veronika, ed. *From One Tale . . . to the Other: Variability in Oral Literature*. Paris: Éditions du centre national de la recherche scientifique, 1990.

Gould, Eric. *Mythical Intentions in Modern Literature*. Princeton: Princeton University Press, 1981.

Grace, Sherrill E. "Courting Bluebeard with Bartók, Atwood, and Fowles: Modern Treatment of the Bluebeard Theme." *Journal of Modern Literature* 11 (1984): 245–62.

Gramsci, Antonio. *Selections From Cultural Writings*. Trans. William Boelhower. Ed. David Forgacs and Geoffrey Nowell-Smith. London: Lawrence and Wishart, 1983.

Greene, Gayle. *Changing the Story: Feminist Fiction and the Tradition*. Bloomington and Indianapolis: Indiana University Press, 1991.

Greimas, Algirdas-Julien. *Structural Semantics: An Attempt at a Method*. 1966. Trans. Daniele McDowell, Ronald Schleifer, and Alan Velie. Intro. Ronald Schleifer. Lincoln and London: University of Nebraska Press, 1983.

———. "Narrative Grammar: Units and Levels." Trans. Phillip Bodrock. *Modern Language Notes* 86 (1971): 793–806.

———. *On Meaning: Selected Writings in Semiotic Theory*. Trans. Paul J. Perron and Frank H. Collins. Fore. Fredric Jameson. London: Frances Pinter, 1987.

Greimas, Algirdas-Julien, and F. Rastier. "The Interaction of Semiotic Constraints." *Yale French Studies* 41 (1968): 86–105.

Greimas, Algirdas-Julien, and J. Courtés. *Semiotics and Language: An Analytical Dictionary*. Trans. Larry Crist et al. Bloomington: Indiana University Press, 1982.

Griffiths, Paul. *Bartók*. London: J. M. Dent & Sons Ltd., 1984.

Grimm, Jacob and Wilhelm. *The Complete Grimm's Fairy Tales*. Trans. Margaret
    Hunt. 1884. Rev. James Stern. 1975. London: Routledge, 1993.
——. *Selected Tales*. Trans. David Luke. Harmondsworth: Penguin, 1982.
——. *The Complete Fairy Tales of the Brothers Grimm*. Trans. Jack Zipes. New
    York: Bantam Books, 1992.
Grobman, Neil R. "A Schema for the Study of the Sources and Literary Sim-
    ulations of Folkloric Phenomena." *Southern Folklore Quarterly* 43 (1979):
    17–37.
Haase, Donald, ed. *The Reception of Grimms' Fairy Tales: Responses, Reactions,
    Revisions*. Detroit: Wayne University Press, 1993.
——. "Feminist Fairy-Tale Scholarship: A Critical Survey and Bibliography."
    Marvels and Tales 14 (2000): 15–63.
Haffenden, John. *Novelists in Interview*. London: Methuen, 1985.
Haraway, Donna. Contribution to "Books for a Desert Island." *Women Studies
    Quarterly* 13.1 (1985): 32.
Harries, Elizabeth Wanning. "Fairy Tales about Fairy Tales: Notes on Canon
    Formation." Canepa 152–75.
——. *Twice Upon a Time: Women Writers and the History of the Fairy Tale*.
    Princeton: Princeton University Press, 2001.
Harris, Charles B. *Passionate Virtuosity: The Fiction of John Barth*. Urbana: Uni-
    versity of Illinois Press, 1983.
Hawkes, Terence. *Structuralism and Semiotics*. London: Methuen, 1977.
Hebel, Udo J., comp. *Intertextuality, Allusion and Quotation: An International
    Bibliography of Critical Studies*. New York: Greenwood Press, 1989.
Herrnstein Smith, Barbara. "Narrative Versions, Narrative Theories." W. J. T.
    Mitchell 209–33.
Hilfer, Tony. *American Fiction Since 1940*. London and New York: Longman,
    1992.
Hinckely, Henry Barrett. "The Framing-Tale." *Modern Language Notes* 49.2
    (1934): 69–80.
Hine, Daryl. "Bluebeard's Wife." *The Wooden Horse*. New York: Atheneum,
    1965. 6–7.
Hobsbawm, Eric. *Age of Extremes: The Short Twentieth Century 1914–1991*.
    London: Abacus, 1995.
Hume, Kathryn. *Fantasy and Mimesis: Responses to Reality in Western Literature*.
    New York and London: Methuen, 1984.
——. "Italo Calvino's Cosmic Comedy: Mythography for the Scientific Age."
    Papers on Language and Literature 20.1 (1984): 80–95.
——. "Calvino's Framed Narrations: Writers, Readers, and Reality." *Review of
    Contemporary Fiction* 6.2 (Summer 1986): 71–80.
——. *Calvino's Fictions: Cogito and Cosmos*. Oxford: Clarendon Press, 1992.

Hutcheon, Linda. *A Poetics of Postmodernism: History, Theory, Fiction*. New York and London: Routledge, 1988.

———. *The Politics of Postmodernism*. London and New York: Routledge, 1989.

Ingram, Forrest L. *Representative Short Story Cycles of the Twentieth Century: Studies in a Literary Genre*. The Hague: Mouton, 1971.

Irwin, Robert. *"The Arabian Nights": A Companion*. Harmondsworth: Penguin, 1995.

Jackson, Rosemary. *Fantasy: The Literature of Subversion*. 1981. London and New York: Routledge, 1991.

Jakobson, Roman. "On Russian Fairy Tales." 1945. *Selected Writings*. Vol. IV: *Slavic Epic Studies*. The Hague: Mouton and Co., 1966. 82–100.

———. "Linguistics and Poetics." 1960. Lodge 32–57.

Jakobson, Roman and Petr Bogatyrëv. "On the Boundary between Studies of Folklore and Literature." 1931. Trans. Herbert Eagle. Matejka and Pomorska. 91–93.

Jameson, Fredric. *The Prison-House of Language: A Critical Account of Structuralism and Russian Formalism*. 1972. Princeton: Princeton University Press, 1974.

———. *The Political Unconscious: Narrative as a Socially Symbolic Act*. 1981. London and New York: Routledge, 1989.

———. "Postmodernism and Consumer Society." 1988. *Modernism/Postmodernism*. Ed. Peter Brooker. London: Longman, 1992. 163–79.

———. *Postmodernism; or, The Cultural Logic of Late Capitalism*. Durham: Duke University Press, 1991.

Jason, Heda, and Dimitri Segal, eds. *Patterns in Oral Literature*. The Hague and Paris: Mouton Publishers, 1977.

Jeannet, Angela M. "Collodi's Grandchildren: Reading *Marcovaldo*." *Italica* 71.1 (1994): 56–77.

John, Nicholas, ed. *The Stage Works of Béla Bartók*. Opera Guide 44. London: John Calder, 1991.

Jordan, Elaine. "Enthralment: Angela Carter's Speculative Fictions." *Plotting Change: Contemporary Women's Fiction*. Ed. Linda Anderson. London: Edward Arnold, 1990. 19–40.

Josipovici, Gabriel. "Linearity and Fragmentation." *The Lessons of Modernism*. 2nd edn. London: Macmillan, 1987. 124–39.

Kabbani, Rana. *Imperial Fictions: Europe's Myths of the Orient*. Rev. ed. London: Pandora, 1994.

Kalilah and Dimnah: An English Version of Bidpai's Fables Based upon Ancient Arabic and Spanish Manuscripts. Ed. Thomas Ballantine Irving. Newark, Delaware: Juan de la Cuesta, 1980.

Kalila and Dimna: Selected Fables of Bidpai. Retold Ramsay Wood. Rochester, Vermont: Inner Traditions International, Ltd., 1986.

Kamenetsky, Christa. *The Brothers Grimm and Their Critics: Folktales and the Quest for Meaning.* Athens: Ohio University Press, 1992.

Kermode, Frank. "Secrets and Narrative Sequence." W. J. T. Mitchell 79–98.

Klinkowitz, Jerome. *Donald Barthelme: An Exhibition.* Durham and London: Duke University Press, 1991.

———. "John Barth: Writing Fiction in an Age of Criticism." *American Writing Today.* Ed. Richard Kostelanetz. Troy, New York: Whitson Publishing Company, 1991. 424–35.

Kovács, Sándor. "The Ethnomusicologist." Gillies 51–63.

Kroó, György. "*Duke Bluebeard's Castle.*" *Studia Musicologica* 1 (1961): 251–340.

———. "Opera: *Duke Bluebeard's Castle.*" Gillies 349–59.

Landow, George P. *Hypertext 2.0: The Convergence of Contemporary Critical Theory and Technology.* Baltimore: Johns Hopkins University Press, 1997.

Lanser, Susan Sniader. "Toward a Feminist Narratology." 1986. *Feminisms: An Anthology of Literary Theory and Criticism.* Ed. Robyn R. Warhol and Diane Price Herndl. New Brunswick, New Jersey: Rutgers University Press, 1991. 610–29.

———. "Shifting the Paradigm: Feminism and Narratology." *Style* 22.1 (1988): 52–60.

———. *Fictions of Authority: Women Writers and Narrative Voice.* Ithaca and London: Cornell University Press, 1992.

La Polla, Franco. "A Note on *Marcovaldo.*" *Review of Contemporary Fiction* 6.2 (1986): 38–41.

LeClair, Tom, and Larry McCaffery, eds. *Anything Can Happen: Interviews with Contemporary Novelists.* Urbana: University of Illinois Press, 1983.

Le Lionnais, François. "Lipo: First Manifesto." 1973. Trans. Warren F. Motte, Jr. Motte 26–28.

Lescure, Jean. "Brief History of the Oulipo." 1973. Trans. Warren F. Motte, Jr. Motte 32–39.

Lévi-Strauss, Claude. *Structural Anthropology.* 1958. Trans. Claire Jacobson and Brooke Grundfest Schoepf. London: Allen Lane The Penguin Press, 1968.

———. "Structural Analysis in Linguistics and Anthropology." 1945. *Structural Anthropology.* 31–54.

———. "The Structural Study of Myth." 1955. *Structural Anthropology.* 206–31.

———. "Structure and Form: Reflections on a Work by Vladimir Propp." 1960. *Structural Anthropology.* Vol. II. 1973. Trans. Monique Layton. Harmondsworth: Penguin, 1978. 115–45.

Lewis, Mary Ellen B. "The Study of Folklore in Literature: An Expanded View." *Southern Folklore Quarterly* 40 (1976): 346–51.

Lieberman, Marcia K. "'Some Day My Prince Will Come': Female Acculturation through the Fairy Tale." *College English* 34 (1972): 383–95.

Light, Alison. "'Returning to Manderley': Romantic Fiction, Female Sexuality
and Class." Eagleton 140–45.

Lindahl, Carl. "On the Borders of Oral and Written Art." *Folklore Forum* 11.2
(1978): 94–124.

Liszka, James Jakób. "A Critique of the Formalist-Structuralist Analysis of Narration." *The Semiotic of Myth: A Critical Study of the Symbol.* Bloomington
and Indianapolis: Indiana University Press, 1989.

Lodge, David, ed. *Modern Criticism and Theory: A Reader.* London: Longman,
1988.

Lord, Albert. *The Singer of Tales.* Cambridge, Mass.: Harvard University Press,
1960.

Lurie, Alison. "Fairy Tale Liberation." *New York Review of Books* 17 December
1970: 42–44.

———. "Witches and Fairies: Fitzgerald to Updike." *New York Review of Books*
2 December 1971: 6–10.

Lüthi, Max. *The European Folktale: Form and Nature.* 1947. Trans. John D. Niles.
Bloomington: Indiana University Press, 1986.

———. *Once Upon a Time: On the Nature of Fairy Tales.* 1970. Trans. Lee
Chadeayne and Paul Gottwald. Bloomington: Indiana University Press,
1976.

Lyotard, Jean-François. *The Postmodern Condition: A Report on Knowledge.*
1979. Trans. Geoff Bennington and Brian Massumi. Fore. Fredric Jameson.
Manchester: Manchester University Press, 1984.

———. "Presentations." Trans. Kathleen McLaughlin. *Philosophy in France
Today.* Ed. Alan Montefiore. Cambridge: Cambridge University Press,
1983.

———. *The Differend: Phrases in Dispute.* 1983. Trans. George Van Den Abbeele.
Minneapolis: University of Minnesota Press, 1988.

———. "Lessons in Paganism." Trans. David Macey. *The Lyotard Reader.* 122–54.

———. "Universal History and Cultural Difference." *The Lyotard Reader.*
314–23.

———. *The Lyotard Reader.* Ed. Andrew Benjamin. Oxford: Blackwell, 1989.

McCaffery, Larry. *The Metafictional Muse: The Works of Robert Coover, Donald
Barthelme, and William H. Gass.* Pittsburgh: University of Pittsburgh Press,
1982.

McGlathery, James M., ed. *The Brothers Grimm and Folktale.* Urbana and Chicago: University of Illinois Press, 1988.

———. *Fairy Tale Romance: The Grimms, Basile, and Perrault.* Urbana and Chicago: University of Illinois Press, 1991.

——. *Grimms' Fairy Tales: A History of Criticism on a Popular Classic.* Columbia: Camden House, 1993.

McHale, Brian, and Moshe Ron. "On Not-Knowing How to Read Barthelme's 'The Indian Uprising.'" *Review of Contemporary Fiction* 11.2 (1991): 50–68.

McMaster, Juliet. "'Bluebeard at Breakfast': An Unpublished Thackeray Manuscript." *Dickens Studies Annual* 8 (1981): 197–230.

Mahdi, Muhsin. *The Thousand and One Nights.* Leiden, Holland: E. J. Brill, 1995.

Mahfouz, Naguib. *Arabian Nights and Days.* 1982. Trans. Denys Johnson-Davies. London: Doubleday, 1995.

Maitland, Sara. "The Wicked Stepmother's Lament." 1987. *A Book of Spells.* 147–54.

——. "Angel Maker." *A Book of Spells.* 1–10.

——. *A Book of Spells.* 1987. London: Minerva, 1991.

——. "Rapunzel Revisited." 185–91. *Women Fly When Men Aren't Watching: Short Stories.* London: Minerva, 1993.

Malarte-Feldman, Claire-Lise. "Perrault's 'Contes': An Irregular Pearl of Classical Literature." Canepa 99–128.

Marello, Laura. "Form and Formula in Calvino's *Invisible Cities.*" *Review of Contemporary Fiction* 6.2 (1986): 95–100.

Marvels and Tales. Spec. issue. *Fairy Tale Liberation: Thirty Years Later.* 14.1 (2000).

Matejka, Ladislav, and Krystyna Pomorska, eds. *Readings in Russian Poetics: Formalist and Structuralist Views.* Cambridge, Mass. and London: The M.I.T. Press, 1971.

Matthews, Harry and Alastair Brotchie, eds. *Oulipo Compendium.* Atlas Arkhive 6. London: Atlas, 1998.

Meletinsky, Eleasar M. "Typological Study of the Folktale." Trans. Robin Dietrich. *Genre* 4 (1971): 249–79.

Menninghaus, Winfried. *In Praise of Nonsense: Kant and Bluebeard.* 1995. Trans. Henry Pickford. Stanford: Stanford University Press, 1999.

Merck, Mandy. "A Case of AIDS." *Perversions.* London: Virago, 1993. 45–58.

Metlitzki, Dorothee. *The Matter of Araby in Medieval England.* New Haven and London: Yale University Press, 1977.

Mieder, Wolfgang. *Tradition and Innovation in Folk Literature.* Hanover and London: University Press of New England, 1987.

Miller, Nancy K. "Parables and Politics: Feminist Criticism in 1986." *Paragraph* 8 (October 1986): 40–54.

Mitchell, Donald. *The Language of Modern Music.* New ed. London: Faber and Faber, 1993.

Mitchell, W. J. T., ed. *On Narrative.* Chicago and London: The University of Chicago Press, 1981.

Moers, Ellen. "Female Gothic." *Literary Women*. New York: Doublday, 1976. 90–110.

Moi, Toril. *Sexual/Textual Politics: Feminist Literary Theory*. 1985. London and New York: Routledge, 1990.

Morace, Robert A. "Donald Barthelme's *Snow White*: The Novel, the Critics, and the Culture." *Critique* 26 (1984): 1–10.

Motte, Warren F., Jr. Trans. and ed. *Oulipo: A Primer of Potential Literature*. Lincoln and London: University of Nebraska Press, 1986.

———. "Calvino's Combinatorics." *Review of Contemporary Fiction* 6.2 (1986): 81–87.

———. "Telling Games." Ricci, *Calvino* 117–30.

Mukherjee, Arun P. "Whose Post-Colonialism and Whose Postmodernism?" *World Literature Written in English* 30.2 (1990): 1–9.

Nabokov, Vladimir. *Bend Sinister*. 1947. Harmondsworth: Penguin, 1974.

Naddaff, Sandra. *Arabesque: Narrative Structure and the Aesthetics of Repetition in "1001 Nights."* Evanstown, Illinois: Northwestern University Press, 1991.

Namjoshi, Suniti. *Feminist Fables*. 1981. London: Virago, 1994.

———. *Building Babel*. North Melbourne, Victoria: Spinifex, 1996.

Nattiez, Jean-Jacques, "On Reading Boulez." Boulez 11–28.

Oates, Joyce Carol. "Blue-Bearded Lover." 1988. Park and Heaton 182–84.

Ong, Walter J. *Orality and Literacy: The Technologizing of the Word*. London and New York: Routledge, 1988.

Onley, Gloria. "Power Politics in Bluebeard's Castle." *Canadian Literature* 60 (Spring 1974): 21–42.

Opie, Iona and Peter. *The Classic Fairy Tales*. 1974. Hertfordshire: Granada, 1980.

Osmond-Smith, David. *Berio*. Oxford: Oxford University Press, 1991.

Ostriker, Alicia. "The Thieves of Language: Women Poets and Revisionist Mythmaking." Showalter 314–38.

Ozick, Cynthia. "Italo Calvino: Bringing Stories to Their Senses." *What Henry James Knew and Other Essays*. London: Vintage, 1994. 350–55.

Pavic, Milorad. *Dictionary of the Khazars: A Lexicon Novel*. 1985. Trans. Christina Pribicevic-Zoric. London: Hamish Hamilton, 1989.

Park, Christine, and Caroline Heaton, eds. *Caught in a Story: Contemporary Fairytales and Fables*. London: Vintage, 1992.

Perella, Nicholas J. "An Essay on *Pinocchio*." Collodi 1–69.

Pinault, David. *Story-Telling Techniques in "The Arabian Nights."* Leiden, Holland: E. J. Brill, 1992.

Pizer, John. "The Disenchantment of Snow White: Robert Walser, Donald Barthelme and the Modern/Postmodern Anti-fairy Tale." *Canadian Review of Comparative Literature* 17 (1990): 330–47.

Plath, Sylvia. "Bluebeard." *Collected Poems*. Ed. Ted Hughes. London: Faber and Faber, 1981. 305.

Prince, Gerald. *A Dictionary of Narratology*. Aldershot: Scolar Press, 1988.

Prizel, Yuri. "Evolution of a Tale: From Literary to Folk." *Southern Folklore Quarterly* 38 (1974): 211–22.

Propp, Vladimir. *Morphology of the Folktale*. 1928. Trans. Laurence Scott. Intro. Svatava Pirkova-Jakobson. 2nd ed. rev. Louis A. Wagner. Intro. Alan Dundes. Austin: University of Texas Press, 1968.

——. "Fairy Tale Transformations." 1928. Trans. C. H. Severens. Matejka and Pomorska. 94–114.

——. *Theory and History of Folklore*. Trans. Ariadna Y. Martin and Richard P. Martin. Ed. Anatoly Liberman. Manchester: Manchester University Press, 1984.

Queneau, Raymond, et al. *Oulipo Laboratory: Texts from the "Bibliothèque Oulipienne."* Trans. Harry Matthews, Iain White and Warren F. Motte, Jr. Intro. Alastair Brotchie. London: Atlas Press, 1995.

Ranke, Kurt, ed. *Folktales of Germany*. Trans. Lotte Baumann Chicago: University of Chicago Press, 1966.

Rawdon Wilson, Robert. "SLIP PAGE: Angela Carter, In/Out/In the Post-Modern Nexus." *Past the Last Post: Theorizing Post-Colonialism and Post-Modernism*. Ed. Ian Adam and Helen Tiffin. Hertfordshire: Harvester Wheatsheaf, 1993. 109–24.

Readings, Bill. *Introducing Lyotard*. London: Routledge, 1991.

Renza, Louis A. "Influence." *Critical Terms for Literary Study*. Ed. Frank Lentricchia and Thomas McLaughlin. Chicago: University of Chicago Press, 1990. 186–202.

Ricci, Franco, ed. *Calvino Revisited*. Ottawa, Canada: Dovehouse Editions Inc., 1989.

——. *Difficult Games: A Reading of "I racconti" by Italo Calvino*. Ontario, Canada: Wilfrid Laurier University Press, 1990.

Ricoeur, Paul. Interview. 1981. *Dialogues with Contemporary Thinkers: The Phenomenological Heritage*. Interview by Richard Kearney. Manchester: Manchester University Press, 1984. 15–46.

——. *Time and Narrative*. Vol. I. 1983. Trans. Kathleen McLaughlin and David Pellauer. Chicago and London: The University of Chicago Press, 1984.

——. *Time and Narrative*. Vol. II. 1984. Trans. Kathleen McLaughlin and David Pellauer. Chicago and London: The University of Chicago Press, 1985.

——. "Life in Quest of Narrative." *On Paul Ricoeur: Narrative and Interpretation*. Ed. David Wood. London: Routledge, 1991. 20–33.

Righter, William. *Myth and Literature*. London: Routledge and Kegan Paul, 1975.

Rimmon-Kenan, Shlomith. *Narrative Fiction: Contemporary Poetics*. London and New York: Routledge, 1989.

Robinson, Lillian S. "On Reading Trash." *Sex, Class, and Culture*. 1978. New York and London: Methuen, 1986. 200–222.

Roemer, Danielle M. "The Contextualization of the Marquis in Angela Carter's 'The Bloody Chamber.'" Roemer and Bacchilega 107–27.

———. and Cristina Bacchilega, eds. *Angela Carter and the Fairy Tale*. Detroit: Wayne State University Press, 2001. Originally published as *Marvels and Tales* 12.1 (1998).

Rölleke, Heinz. "The 'Utterly Hessian' Fairy Tales by 'Old Marie': The End of a Myth." 1975. Trans. Ruth B. Bottigheimer. Bottigheimer 287–300.

Rose, Jacqueline. *The Case of Peter Pan or The Impossibility of Children's Fiction*. London: Macmillan, 1984.

Rosen, Charles. "Brahms: Influence, Plagiarism, and Inspiration." *Critical Entertainments: Music Old and New*. Cambridge, Mass.: Harvard University Press, 2000.

Rosenberg, Bruce A. *Folklore and Literature: Rival Siblings*. Knoxville: University of Tennessee Press, 1991.

Roubaud, Jacques. *The Princess Hoppy; or, The Tale of Labrador*. 1990. Trans. Bernard Hoepffner. Normal, Illinois: Dalkey Archive, 1993.

Rowe, Karen E. "Feminism and Fairy Tales." *Women's Studies* 6 (1979): 237–57.

———. "'Fairy-born and human-bred:' Jane Eyre's Education in Romance." *The Voyage In: Fictions of Female Development*. Ed. Elizabeth Abel, Marianne Hirsch, and Elizabeth Langland. Hanover and London: University Press of New England, 1983.

Rushdie, Salman. *Midnight's Children*. 1981. London: Picador, 1982.

———. *Haroun and the Sea of Stories*. 1990. London: Granta Books, 1991.

Said, Edward. *Orientalism*. 1978. Harmondsworth: Penguin, 1991.

Schafer, Roy. *A New Language for Psychoanlysis*. New Haven: Yale University Press, 1976.

———. "Narration in the Psychoanalytic Dialogue." W. J. T. Mitchell 25–50.

Schenda, Rudolf. "Telling Tales—Spreading Tales: Change in the Communicative Forms of a Popular Genre." Trans. Ruth B. Bottigheimer. Bottigheimer 75–94.

Schleifer, Ronald. *A. J. Greimas and the Nature of Meaning: Linguistics, Semiotics and Discourse Theory*. London and Sydney: Croom Helm, 1987.

Scholes, Robert. *Structuralism in Literature: An Introduction*. New Haven and London: Yale University Press, 1974.

Schönberg, Arnold. "Folkloristic Symphonies." 1947. *Style and Idea: Selected Writings of Arnold Schönberg.* Trans. Leo Black. Ed. Leonard Stein. Berkeley: University of California Press. 161–66.

Schulz, Max F. *The Muses of John Barth: Tradition and Metafiction From "Lost in the Funhouse" to "The Tidewater Tales."* Baltimore and London: The Johns Hopkins University Press, 1990.

Sedgwick, Eve Kosofsky. *Between Men: English Literature and Male Homosocial Desire.* New York: Columbia University Press, 1985.

Seifert, Lewis C. *Fairy Tales, Sexuality, and Gender in France, 1690–1715.* Cambridge: Cambridge University Press, 1996.

———. "On Fairy Tales, Subversion, and Ambiguity: Femininst Approaches to Seventeenth-Century *Contes de fées.*" *Marvels and Tales* 14 (2000): 80–98.

Sexton, Anne. *Transformations.* 1971. London: Oxford University Press, 1972.

Sheets, Robin Ann. "Pornography, Fairy Tales, and Feminism: Angela Carter's 'The Bloody Chamber.'" *Journal of the History of Sexuality* 1 (1991): 633–57.

Sherman, Cindy. *Fitcher's Bird.* New York: Rizzoli, 1992.

Showalter, Elaine, ed. *The New Feminist Criticism: Essays on Women, Literature and Theory.* 1986. London: Virago, 1992.

———. "Feminist Criticism in the Wilderness." 1981. Showalter 243–70.

Somadeva. *The Ocean of Story.* ca. 1070. Trans. C. H. Tawney. Ed. N. M. Penzer. 10 vols. London: Privately Printed, 1924–1928.

———. *Tales from the "Kathasaritsagara."* Trans. Arshia Sattar. Fore. Wendy Doniger. Harmondsworth: Penguin, 1996.

Sontag, Susan. *Against Interpretation and Other Essays.* 1966. New York: Anchor Books, 1990.

Spence, Donald P. *Narrative Truth and Historical Truth: Meaning and Interpretation in Psychoanalysis.* New York: W. W. Norton and Company, 1982.

Spender, Dale. "Ann Radcliffe and the Gothic." *Mothers of the Novel: 100 Good Women Writers Before Jane Austen.* London: Pandora, 1986. 230–45.

Springer, Carolyn. "Textual Geography: The Role of the Reader in *Invisible Cities.*" *Modern Language Notes* 15 (1985): 289–99.

Stahl, Sandra K. D. "Style in Oral and Written Narratives." *Southern Folklore Quarterly* 43 (1979): 39–62.

Stone, Kay. "Things Walt Disney Never Told Us." *Women and Folklore.* Ed. Claire R. Farrer. Austin: University of Texas Press, 1975.

Straparola, Giovanni Francesco. *The Most Delectable Nights of Straparola of Caravaggio.* 1550–1553. Trans. anon. 2 vols. Paris: Charles Carrington, 1906.

Suleiman, Susan Rubin. *Subversive Intent: Gender, Politics, and the Avant-Garde.* Cambridge, Mass.: Harvard University Press, 1990.

Sutherland, John. "Can Jane Eyre Be Happy?" *Can Jane Eyre Be Happy? More Puzzles in Classic Fiction.* Oxford: Oxford University Press, 1997. 68–80.

Swann Jones, Steven. *The Fairy Tale: The Magic Mirror of the Imagination*. New York: Twayne Publishers, 1995.

Szabolsci, Bence. "Bartók's Principles of Composition." *Bartók Studies*. Ed. Todd Crow. Detroit: Information Coordinators, 1976. 19–21.

Tales From the Thousand and One Nights. Trans. N. J. Dawood. Harmondsworth: Penguin, 1973.

Tanner, Tony. *City of Words: American Fiction 1950–1970*. London: Jonathan Cape, 1971.

Tatar, Maria. *The Hard Facts of the Grimms' Fairy Tales*. New Jersey: Princeton University Press, 1987.

———. "Beauties vs. Beasts in the Grimms' *Nursery and Household Tales*." McGlathery 133–45.

———, ed. *The Classic Fairy Tales*. New York: W. W. Norton, 1998.

Thackeray, William Makepeace. "Bluebeard's Ghost." 1843. Zipes, *Penguin Book* 337–56.

Thelander, Dorothy R. "Mother Goose and Her Goslings: The France of Louis XIV as Seen through the Fairy Tale." *Journal of Modern History* 54 (1982): 467–96.

Thompson, Stith. *The Folktale*. New York: Holt, Rinehart and Winston, 1946.

———. *Motif-Index of Folk-Literature: A Classification of Narrative Elements in Folktales, Ballads, Myths, Fables, Mediaeval Romances, Exempla, Fabliaux, Jest-Books, and Local Legends*. Rev. ed. 6 vols. Copenhagen: Rosenkilde and Bagger, 1955–1958.

Tobin, Patricia. *John Barth and the Anxiety of Continuance*. Philadelphia: University of Philadelphia Press, 1992.

Todorov, Tzvetan. "Structural Analysis of Narrative." Trans. Arnold Weinstein. *Novel* 3.1 (1969): 70–76.

———. *The Poetics of Prose*. 1971. Trans. Richard Howard. Oxford: Basil Blackwell, 1977.

Tolkien, J. R. R. "On Fairy-Stories." 1938–1939. *Tree and Leaf*. Boston: Houghton and Mifflin, 1965.

Tournier, Michel. *The Midnight Love Feast*. 1989. Trans. Barbara Wright. London: Minerva, 1992.

Townsend Warner, Sylvia. "Bluebeard's Daughter." *Cat's Cradle-Book*. London: Chatto and Windus, 1960. 160–86.

Trodd, Anthea. *Domestic Crime in the Victorian Novel*. London: Macmillan, 1989.

Trotter, David. *The English Novel in History 1895–1920*. London: Routledge, 1993.

Updike, John. "Metropolises of the Mind." 1974. *Hugging the Shore*. 457–62.

———. "Card Tricks." 1977. *Hugging the Shore*. 463–70.

——. *Hugging the Shore: Essays and Criticism.* London: André Deutsch, 1984.

——. "George and Vivian." *The Afterlife and Other Stories.* London: Hamish Hamilton, 1995. 154–89.

Varsava, Jerry A. "Calvino's Combinative Aesthetics: Theory and Practice." *Review of Contemporary Fiction* 6.2 (1986): 11–18.

Velay-Vallantin, Catherine. "Tales as a Mirror: Perrault in the *Bibliothèque bleue.*" *The Culture of Print: Power and the Uses of Print in Early Modern Europe.* Trans. Lydia G. Cochrane. Ed. Roger Chartier. Princeton, N.J.: Princeton University Press, 1989. 92–135.

Velten, H. V. "The Influence of Charles Perrault's *Contes de ma Mère L'Oie* on German Folklore." *The Germanic Review* 5.1 (1930): 4–18.

Vidal, Gore. "Calvino's Novels." 1974. *United States.* 476–95.

——. "Calvino's Death." 1985. *United States.* 496–507.

——. *United States: Essays 1952–1992.* London: André Deutsch, 1993.

Visnu Sarma. *The Pancatantra.* Trans. Chandra Rajan. Harmondsworth: Penguin, 1995.

Ward Jouve, Nicole. "Too Short for a Book? *The Thousand and One Nights:* The Short Story and the Book." *Re-Reading the Short Story.* Ed. Clare Hanson. London: Macmillan, 1989. 34–44. Rpt. in *White Woman Speaks with Forked Tongue: Criticism as Autobiography.* London: Routledge, 1991. 182–92.

Warhol, Robyn R. *Gendered Interventions: Narrative Discourse in the Victorian Novel.* New Brunswick, N. J.: Rutgers University Press, 1989.

Warner, Marina. "The Silence of Cordelia." *Wordlessness.* Ed. Bart Verschaffel and Mark Verminck. Dublin: The Lilliput Press, 1993. 74–87.

——, ed. *Wonder Tales: Six Stories of Enchantment.* London: Chatto and Windus, 1994.

——. *From the Beast to the Blonde: On Fairy Tales and Their Tellers.* London: Chatto and Windus, 1994.

Weaver, William. "Calvino: An Interview and Its Story." Ricci, *Calvino.* 17–31.

Weber, Eugen. "Fairies and Hard Facts: The Reality of Folktales." *Journal of the History of Ideas* 42 (1981): 93–113.

White, Hayden. *The Content of the Form: Narrative Discourse and Historical Representation.* Baltimore and London: Johns Hopkins University Press, 1987.

White, John J. *Mythology in the Modern Novel: A Study of Prefigurative Techniques.* Princeton: Princeton University Press, 1971.

Woodhouse, J. R. "Italo Calvino and the Rediscovery of a Genre." *Italian Quarterly* 12 (1968): 45–66.

——. *Italo Calvino: A Reappraisal and an Appreciation of the Trilogy.* Hull: University of Hull, 1968.

———. "Fantasy, Alienation and the *Racconti* of Italo Calvino." *Forum for Modern Language Studies* 6 (1970): 399–412.

———. "From Italo Calvino to Tonio Cavilla: The First Twenty Years." Ricci, *Calvino*. 33–50.

Woolley, Benjamin. *Virtual Worlds: A Journey in Hype and Hyperreality*. Harmondsworth: Penguin, 1993.

Ziegler, Heide. "The Tale of the Author, or Scheherazade's Betrayal." *Review of Contemporary Fiction* 8.3 (1988): 82–88.

———, ed. *Facing Texts: Encounters Between Contemporary Writers and Critics*. Durham and London: Duke University Press, 1988.

Zipes, Jack. *Fairy Tales and the Art of Subversion: The Classical Genre for Children and the Process of Civilization*. New York: Wildman, 1983.

———, ed. *Don't Bet on the Prince: Contemporary Feminist Fairy Tales and Their Tellers*. 1986. Hampshire: Scolar Press, 1993.

———. *The Brothers Grimm: From Enchanted Forests to the Modern World*. New York: Routledge, 1988.

———. "The Origins of the Fairy Tale for Children or, How Script Was Used to Tame the Beast in Us." Avery and Briggs. 119–34.

———, trans. *Beauties, Beasts and Enchantment: Classic French Fairy Tales*. New York: Meridian, 1991.

———. "The Struggle for the Grimms' Throne: The Legacy of the Grimms' Tales in the FRG and GDR since 1945." Haase 167–206.

———, ed. *The Penguin Book of Western Fairy Tales*. Harmondsworth: Penguin, 1993.

———, ed. *The Oxford Companion to Fairy Tales*. Oxford: Oxford University Press, 2000.

———, ed. *The Great Fairy Tale Tradition*. New York: W. W. Norton, 2001.

Index

Aarne, Antti: *The Types of the Folktale*, 23–24, 31, 38, 40, 55, 56, 252 n. 8, 253n. 10, 274n. 23
Abish, Walter, 133
Afanas'ev, A. N., 26
Apuleius, Lucius: "Cupid and Psyche," 194
Arabian Nights, The, 13, 44, 45, 46, 47, 53–54, 56, 57, 62–65, 128–29, 131, 134, 258n. 26; John Barth and, 134, 136–47; Robert Coover and, 151; frame tale, 51, 258n. 29; frame tale, compared with "The Robber Bridegroom," 195–96, 275n. 35; history of, 48–50, 107; in *If on a Winter's Night a Traveller* (Calvino), 108–9, 110; "Sindbad the Sailor and Sindbad the Porter," 50, 58, 142–43; "The Story of the Hunchback," 54, 59–62, 142; ur-text, 50, 257n. 14
Ariosto, Lodovico: *Orlando Furioso*, 70, 71, 86, 107
Atwood, Margaret: and the fairy tale, 14, 84, 148, 212, 229–30. Works: "Alien Territory," 230; "Bluebeard's Egg," 230, 238–40, 244–45; "Hesitations outside the Door," 230, 245–46; *Lady Oracle*, 230, 235–38, 240–44; *The Robber Bride*, 230

Austen, Jane: *Northanger Abbey*, 233, 235, 236
Auster, Paul, 248
Austin, J. L., 121
author, concept of, 21, 40, 48, 84, 252n. 6

Bacchilega, Cristina, 216
Bakhtin, Mikhail M., 65, 259n. 33
Bal, Mieke, 120
Balázs, Béla: *Duke Bluebeard's Castle*, 183, 216, 274n. 27, 279n. 56
Barr Snitow, Ann, 241
Barth, John, 14, 130–47, 148, 167, 170; and the *Arabian Nights*, 134, 136–47, 268n. 28; and hypertext, 248, 281n. 2; "late" period of, 131–34; as modernist, 133; and postmodernism, 118, 130–32, 266n. 6; (re)turn to narrative, 134–35, 137, 267n. 25; and story cycles, 128, 131, 132–35, 144, 256n. 7; symbolism in, 267n. 27. Works: *Chimera*, 131, 132, 135; "Dunyazadiad," 136–38, 141, 145; *The Floating Opera*, 132; *The Last Voyage of Somebody the Sailor*, 130, 131, 134, 138, 142–43; *Letters*, 132, 133; *Lost in the Funhouse*, 131, 134, 135; *On With the Story: Stories*, 133, 138, 145; *Once Upon a Time: A Floating Opera*, 134,

www.ingramcontent.com/pod-product-compliance
Lightning Source LLC
Chambersburg PA
CBHW070439100426
42812CB00031B/3334/J